MANAGEMENT OF INTERNAL SECURITY
And Related Issues

Management of Internal Security

And Related Issues

KRISHNA MOHAN MATHUR

GYAN

GYAN PUBLISHING HOUSE

New Delhi 110 002

Management of Internal Security
And Related Issues
(Police, Defence Studies, Management)

ISBN : 81-212-0492-5
Library of Congress Card No. 93-900337

Published 1995 in India by
Gyan Publishing House
5 Ansari Road
New Delhi -110 002

Laser typesetting at Heena Computers, New Delhi
and printed at Mehra Offset Press, New Delhi

Dedicated to the Trainees and Faculty
Members of the
Internal Security Academy, Mount Abu

PREFACE

The present volume, a collection of essays, is an attempt to analyse and discuss the various aspects dealing with management of internal security and its related issues. Each essay in this volume, is more or less discrete and complete by itself. While editing the contents of the present work, it has been noticed that some major concepts have come in for repeated treatment under different chapter themes. This happened unconciously since these essays were written independently of one another over the past few years. Repetition is probably worth its while for highlighting these ideas more clearly. The principal purpose of this collection is to encourage the readers to actively pursue and discuss the various problems related to internal security. The present work directly stems from my present assignment as a trainer at Internal Security Academy Mount Abu. A complex set of communal, social, economic, ecological, moral and political factors has brought issues related to internal security to the centre of national agenda across the globe. Internal security of a nation-state has to possibly cope with a vast range of challenges and threats varying from mere law and order problems to low intensity operations and proxy wars, and evolve responses to deal with complex and diverse phenomena that include handling communal riots, managing natural disasters, fighting terrorism, insurgency and extremist movements. Internal Security in the present day scenario cannot be judged merely by the performance of the police and Central Police Organisations in terms of their success or otherwise but the final criteria of success or failure will remain the political and psychological effects upon the people.

The first chapter, titled "Management of Internal Security—Problems and Prospects" presents a professional police manager's approach in dealing with internal security problems of the Country. There is an urgent need to modernise the police forces and ensure more realistic job-oriented training. There is need for dynamic, dedicated and competent managers of internal security at Central, State and district levels who have realistic awareness of the constraints within which they work and have capability to remain forward-looking, humane and self confident in handling crisis situations. Second chapter deals with "Improving Police Performance through training-Search for thrust areas". Police performance undoubted needs improvement both qualitatively and quantitatively. Given the organisational constraints and political environment, police performance certainly needs thrust in behavioural areas like courtesy, politeness and protection of human rights. Training can definitely help in bringing attitudinal change in police and CPOs and can gradually improve the quality of policing. Third Chapter covers rural unrest and agrarian unrest in India. Fourth Chapter analysis the conflicts of plural society and their impact on internal security. Conflicts in various forms have created serious threat to the internal security of the Country. There is crisis of identity in several states of North Eastern region. Half of the battle can be won if one can foresee the approaching conflict and adequately prepare himself to resolve and sublimate the conflict situation by persuasion and negotiations. Fifth Chapter highlights the various management problems which are faced in handling disasters and crisis situations like earthquakes and cyclones. Sixth Chapter discuss internal security operations and their impact on human rights. This volume also contains four appendices. Universal Declaration of human rights is given in Appendix 'A'. A comparative study of United Nations declarations human rights and the fundamental rights are given in Appendix 'B'. Human Rights contained in various sections of Criminal Procedure Code 1993 are given in Appendix 'C'. Inaugural address delivered by the author on 2nd May 1994 is given in Appendix 'D'.

The present study has made an earnest effort to identify some basic challenges and issues and invite public dialogue on the subject under discussion. There are no ready-made solutions to the complex and multi-dimensional challenges of internal security but an awareness of the complexities will help quest of solutions in the long run. The present study is a very modest attempt to fill the void. I hope this book will initiate some serious research and thinking by social scientists and police officers. This work does not claim to be either exhaustive nor comprehensive. I have only attempted to initiate a national dialogue on the issues and offer my comments and views on vaious issues. My most cherished institutional affiliation with Internal Security Academy, Mount Abu provided me with an excellent setting where I could discuss my ideas with the trainees and participants of various courses and the guest faculty members who visited the Academy. I have great pleaure in expressing my deep felt and profound gratitude to Dr. P.D. Sharma, Professor of Political Science who always encouraged and inspired me in my academic endeavours. My thanks are also due to Director General, CRPF, and Director SVP National Police Academy, Hyderabad. I am deeply thankful to Shri R.S. Mooshahary, IPS Director Internal Security Academy who gave necessary encouragement and opportunity to complete this book. My special thanks are due to Sarvashri K.F. Rustomji, N.S. Saxena, P.R. Rajgopal, K.P.S. Gill, J.F. Ribeiro, G.C. Singhvi, S. Venugopal Rao and many other police officers of India who have deeply influenced my thinking about the internal security and its varied problems. Prof. K.L. Kamal, Prof. Ramesh K. Arora, Prof. Ram Ahuja, Prof. S.R. Maheshwari, Dr. R.N. Singh, Dr. Om Prakash, Prof. S.S. Srivastava and Dr. S. Subramaniam also deserve my special thanks. Conventional acknowledgement are really inadequate to express how much this book owes to all those who gave me their support. I deeply appreciate the confidence shown by M/s Gyan Publishing House, New Delhi-110002 in publishing this book in a record time.

The research and writing for this book took almost four years. My wife Prabha Mathur and my children Shikha, Pragya and Shiv Shubhang gave me the moral support and encouraged me by sparing from all domestic liabilities for devoting full attention to complete the work. I have been able to write this book only with their co-operation and spontaneous help at all stages. I am thankful to my friends and colleagues including trainee officers with whom I have interacted to crystallise my nebulous ideas. My heart-felt thanks are due to Shri T. Velayudhan, Shri K. Santosh Kumar, Shri R.B. Singh who have provided me instant help in preparing this book. Shri V.S. Anandan, Librarian and other staff of ISA Library deserve special mention for making available all references and books which are used by me for reference. This book is an oblation to the Almightly Lord Shiv whose grace and blessings remained the divine force behind my academic endeavours.

KRISHNA MOHAN MATHUR

Mount Abu

Contents

	Preface	(vii)
1.	Problems and Prospects	1
2.	Improving Police Performance	63
3.	Rural Unrest and Agrarian Movement in India	96
4.	Conflicts of Plural Society	116
5.	Management of Disasters and Crisis Situations	155
6.	Internal Security Operations	180
	Appendix A	238
	Appendix B	245
	Appendix C	248
	Appendix D	251
	Bibliography	264
	Index	271

1

MANAGEMENT OF INTERNAL SECURITY : PROBLEMS AND PROSPECTS

Peter F. Drucker, the Father of modern management, has observed; " The word management " is a singularly difficult one........ It not only denotes a function but also the people who discharged it. It denotes a social position and rank but also a discipline and field of study".[1] Management has many connotations; it is a discipline-that is an organised body of knowledge; it is a social function and embedded in a culture of a society a tradition of values, customs and beliefs and in governmental and political systems; management is also people who manage rather than 'forces' or facts and the vision, dedication and integrity of managers determine whether there is management or mismanagement; management is practice, its essence is not knowing but doing. Management is an objective function and ought to be grounded in the responsibility for performance. Management is a generic function of performance, with tasks of leadership, direction and decision-making with its specific managerial skills, its own specific techniques, tools and strategies. Management, in words of Peter Drucker, is the organ, the life-giving, acting, dynamic organ of the institution it manages..... organs however are never defined by what they do, let alone by how they do it. They are defined by their contribution."[2] Beckor (1968) has differentiated four main groups of meanings of management, namely (1) management as an activity, (2) management as a team in the enterprise, (3) management as a social category and (4) management as a body of knowledge Fayol (1916) singles out as functions: planning, organising, commanding, coordinating and controlling, Gulick (1937) sums up the management activities in the acronym "POSDCORB", planning, organising, staffing, directing, coordinating, reporting and budgeting. The functions of management are generally differentiated at three levels: top management, middle and lower management. For purpose of the present paper, author proposes to divide four main functions of the total management process, planning, organising, directing and controlling. Planning includes goals decision-making and making concrete plans. Organising implies static and dynamic aspects of organisation, basic principles of organising and structure of organisations. Directing is motivating and stimulating the members of the organisation to make an effort to attain the organisation's objectives. It includes training and motivational techniques. Controlling covers elements of control systems, and monitoring of all activities and systems. Management of Internal Security can be broadly analysed under the following parts : (1) Management of I.S. at the Central Government level; (2) Management of I.S. at State Government level; (3) Management of I.S. at district and grassroot levels. Management of I.S. will also includes management of all internal security organisations at the Central and State levels. At the operational level management of I.S. implies performance of all managerial functions.

Managerial Approach to Internal Security

Management approach to Internal Security entails having a set of clear objectives, planning and organising for its achievement and formulation of well planned operational strategy to identify, neutralize and cope with newly emerging threats to internal security of the country. One can roughly divide the activities required for management of internal security into following clusters:-

— Identifying and recognising threats to internal security through intelligence agencies including external intelligence agency.

— Communication and decision skills.

— Coordinating skills for coordination of activities of state police organisations with central police organisations.

— Providing funds for modernisation, purchase of communication requirements etc. and monitoring their utilization.

— Providing economic, political and social measures to supplement internal security operations.

— Working out operational strategies and plans for dealing with terrorist activities, insurgency activities communal activities in an effective manner.

— Planning and execution of personnel policies human resource development of police and Central Police Organisations.

— Policy planning and formulation of contingency plans for various internal security problems like terrorism, insurgency, air hijacking, natural calamities, communal riots at state and Central levels.

— Developing and managing effective information system for internal security problems and operations at the Central & State levels.

— Planning, organising, staffing, motivating and monitoring of internal security plans for various states/regions and providing coordinating role to the state agencies.

— Strategic planning of Internal Security Organisations which must be both centralized and decentralized-centralized so that strategies and control systems can be integrated and decentralised so that units in each strategic environment can act and be treated with appropriate differentiation.

In short for effective management of internal security what matters is whether all internal security problems of different states/regions have been properly identified, whether adequate raquired strategic plans to deal with them have been formulated and carried out by internal security organisations; whether required funds, equipment and other operational requirements have been met and whether all operational plans have been properly coordinated together harmoniously and whether regular monitoring and coordination of their activities is being carried out. Training, Development and Research activities are important activities for effective management of internal security of any country. Internal Security Academy Mt. Abu has been entrusted with the task of training officers of the State Police Organisations and Central Police Organisations in all internal security matters. It conducts 6 days seminars for the officers of the rank of Deputy Inspectors General of Police and short duration courses for District Magistrates, Superintendents of Police and Deputy Superintendents of Police.

Some Dimensions of Management of Internal Security

Management of Internal Security can be broadly conceptualized in terms of the following dimensions :-

(i) Management functions of planning, organising, coordinating, controlling directing and staffing of Internal Security operations.

(ii) Management in terms of creation, maintenance and stimulation of internal security organisations with focus on their organisational missions and functions.

(iii) Management of Internal Security in terms of technique and leadership for Internal Security operations.

(iv) Management in terms of responsibility means accountability for others performance and management of change.

(v) Management implies formulation of policies, systems and their execution through various agencies/ organisations with a view to achieve desired results.

(vi) Management in terms of political economic and social measures to be adopted for countering various Internal Security problems or in terms of management of Psychological operations against insurgency and internal security challenges.

(vii) Management of environment social, cultural, economic technological and political which directly or indirectly effect the internal security of the country.

(viii) Management of security of VVIP/VIPs.

(ix) Management of natural and man made disasters like floods, earthquakes, air & rail accidents.

(x) Management of security of Indian missions abroad from terrorist attacks.

(xi) Management of aviation security.

There are many new tools in the areas of management for which we are not yet equipped with tested, proven approaches. Newer areas of challenges and new management problems have arisen, where we have done little work so far and where we have so far only ignorance rather than even a modicum of knowledge. Management of Internal Security is one such areas. In the present paper a very modest attempt has been made to initiate preliminary approach into this area, to think of policies, principles and practices required to meet the new challenges of internal security. The present paper has limited its analysis in the context of India as a study of unit in the context of internal security. The various dimensions of the task of management of internal security can not be easily covered in one paper and therefore only a few important aspects have been covered in the present paper. What we fail to see is, according to K.F. Rustamji, that security is indivisable. It concerns not only the highest in the land, it concerns all others-judges, soldiers, policemen, editors, businessmen, lawyers, right down to the woman who feels insure when she moves in the street and the man who is threatened because he will not pay tribute to the local goonda. Insecurity is a problem which concerns all of us. Insecurity is a threat to free and open way of life which is the essence of a democracy. Thus all of us have to play our part in the management of internal security.[3] Influx of foreign refugees from Bangladesh, Ceylon and Pakistan has created serious internal security problems. Management of Bangladesh refugees is a serious challenge for Mizoram, Tripura and Assam.

"Plural Executives" for Management of Internal Security

Henri Fayol, one of the great pioneers in management theory regarded management as the most critical activity in human affairs. In its very broad sense "management"of internal security is still in its infancy and we are only at the first stages of recognising the vital part it can play in handling various facets of national security. Politicians and Political executives at the central and state levels of administration seldom move beyond setting the directions to be persued, approving action programmes and contingency plans, approving the funds required and monitoring subsequent performance; the actual translating of directions into action is entrusted to public service executives at the highest levels of administration. Prime Ministers Secretariat, Home Minister & State Minister for Internal Security, Home Secretary and heads of the Central Police Organisations in India generally constitute the "Plural Executive" at the centre to manage internal security of the country.[4] At the state level Chief Minister, Home Minister, Chief Secretary, Home Secretary and Directorate General of Police constitute the state "Plural Executive" for managing internal security of the state. However at the district level generally district Commissioner/Collector and Superintendents of Police jointly constitute "Plural Executive" for management of internal security at the district level. In order to oversee intelligence and the security aspects of it, there should be a board with the Cabinet Secretary or Home Secretary as Chairman, which regularly revises the targets and reviews the methods and after each meeting the Home Minister should apprise the President and Prime Minister of the steps being taken. For management of internal security at the centre and in the states there are many formal and informal committees. Most Committees are non-managerial in nature. However some groups are given the powers to make decisions and to undertake one or all of the managerial functions of planning, organising, shifting, leading and controlling. It is this latter type of committee that is referred to as the "plural executive". The plural executives can be established by law or it may result from a managerial decision of the central or state governments. The plural executive is often found in the field of strategy or policy-making but the extent of authority to manage and to make decision held by a plural executive in central or state government bodies is not always easy to ascertain. Shri N. S. Saksena has analysed why there are no security experts in the country and has given the following reasons; (1) security expertise does not pay and one has to work excessively hard to acquire such expertise. (2) successive pay commissions have given no thought to the fact that high grade expertise within a service must have sufficiently attractive remunerations attached to it. (3) very few secretaries and heads of departments in Delhi have any idea of what standard of expertise is possible in this modern world and what needs to be done to produce such first grade extent with their false sense of values the secretaries are not willing to give higher pay and even a higher ranks in the warrant of precedence than secretaries to the Govt. of India.[5] Therefore plural security executives come to the rescue. Minister of State for Home Shri Rajesh Pilot said " the Centre had set up a high-powered group under the Home Secretary to investigate all underworld connections and sources of huge amounts flowing into India, ostensibly aimed at destabilising the country. He said that the group which would include the RAW Chief, had been asked to submit its findings within three months. There is solid proof of the Dubai-based under world don, Dawood Ibrahim's involvement in the Bombay blast case. 142 persons have been arrested so far in connection with the Bombay riots and 23 cases have been registered. The Ministery of Internal Security is the coordinating agency for maintenance of internal security at the central level and it has a high powered Advisory Council consisting of senior officers of MHA, Directors General of Intelligence Bureau, Central Reserve Police, BSF and other Central Police Organisations. At the state level, coordination committees generally consist of Home Secretary, Director General Police & D.G.P. law and order of the state. There are no statutory bodies for management of internal security at the centre and in the states but various such plural executive committees are formed on Adhoc basis on requirement basic.[6]

The Concept of Internal Security in ancient Indian Scriptures

In Vedic period, the community suffered from internal upheavels and pangs of a growing pastoral society. The ancient scriptures like Vedic Samhitas, Kautilyas, Artha Sashtra elaborately illustrate the insecure living conditions of the pastoral vedic community. The townships unearthed in the Indus basin and other sites of the contemporary civilization give a fairly clear picture of the religious, social and political life of the people who had drawn up elaborate arrangements for internal security.[7] Kautilya, Manu and Sukra have conceived the state as an organic unit, constituted of seven parts (angas) viz. the King, Amatya, Kosa, Danda, Maitra, Janapada and lastly Pura.[8] The security of the people was ensured by a well-organised policing system having two distinct lines i.e. Civilian departments entrusted with police powers and a cadre of regular police officers. The hard core of regular police officers was composed of a three tier system constituted by pradesta (for the rural areas) the nagaraka (for the urban areas) at the top, the rural and urban stharikas in the middle and the urban gopas at the bottom. Principles of Internal Security and the system of policing deployment in ancient towns and villages were effectively followed and improved by the successive Hindu Kings as can be gathered from ancient scriptures and the epigraphic inscriptions of this period.[9] Kautilya has analysed the dangers to the security of the society in his Arthasashtra thus : " The various kinds of dangers are: that which is of external origin and of internal abetment; that which is of internal origin and of external abetment, that which is of external origin and of external abetment and that which is of internal origin and of internal abetment".[10] Regarding management of internal security, Kautilya Arthasashtra provides detailed account of espionage and intelligence net work, techniques of criminal investigation, methods of interrogation, and well administered police organisational set up with a Sangrahana for 10 villages, a Kharvatika for 200 villages and a Sthaniya for 800 villages.[11] In Mahabharat in Shanti Parva, the concept of internal security has been conceptualised as under "Internal Security and good law and order implies that a young newly wed beautiful bride laden with ornaments and good clothes may walk across the market place at midnight unescorted without any fear or risk to her". The fundamental principles of our ancient polity required every function of the state to be conditioned to the need to preserve both society and state.[12]

Recent Internal Security Challenges

Ethno-national and religio-political radicalism have been on the rise in democratic societies. The revolution of rising expectations has caused an increasing sense of relative deprivation among people. The revolution in information technology has increased the sense of awareness and invariably the expectations of the people. During last four decades India has made rapid strides towards modernisation and industrialisation to transform an agrarian economy into an industrialised system. The tremendous sale and availability of small arms, lethal weapons and explosives in the international world has added a brutal dimension to social violence and political conflicts by the escalation in lethality. Unbridled pursuit of drug trafficking and narco-terrorism by money landering have posed serious threats to the internal security of the country. The erosion of moral values, the changing social norms, rapid urbanisation, move towards nuclear families, dynamics of unemployment and criminalisation of politics have created serious problems of internal security. The roots of the problems of internal security lie in the rapidly widening gap between expectations and satisfaction in the political economic & socio-cultural system of the country. Ethno-religious nationalism have created a growing resurgence of disruptive forces threatening peace, security and economic well being of the people. Management of above security problems serious challenges to administrators.

Internal Security Threat Analysis and the Securit/ Threat Survey

Internal Security, in its generic form and internal security threat survey, in its specific application are essential elements of the total management function. An internal security threat assessment analysis is a rational and orderly approach to survey the various existing threats and the future anticipated probabilities. Internal Security threats emerge from the internal vulnerability-weaknesses, flaws, or anything that may conceivable be exploited by some elements. Threat occurrence rates/probabilities are best developed from reports of occurrence or incident reports wherever this historical data exist. Threat perceptions to internal security can differ from individuals to individuals, governments to governments. At Central and State levels, both "inner" and outer cabinets need to get involved in internal security threat assessment. Home Secretary, Director Intelligence Bureau & Secretary Director Research and Analysis Wing with the Ministry of internal security are constantly involved in assessment and analysis of threats and management of internal security. Internal security represents the inner strength and the health potential of the nation state to preserve its international personality by its capacity to secure (1) its sovereign power, (2) government (3) defined territory and permanent population, from all internal threats.[13] Security involves the preservation of deeply held, shared values like democracy, secularism, social justice, development etc. The erosion of the ordered state is thus the most serious of the maladies from which our republic body politic is suffering. Threat analysis of internal security can help managers in identifying core areas of internal security of India. A survey of threats to internal security has enabled the author to identify following core areas :-

1. Defence against subversion espionage, and sabotage activities of hostile powers like Pakistan's I.S.I. activities.

2. Defence against internal threats of disintegration-terrorism, insurgency and other extremist & left wing Naxalite activities.

3. Defence against internal disorders and disturbances caused by communal riots, political violence etc; for example a total of 2132 persons were killed in 1149 cases communal riots cases in 13 states between June 1, 1991 to July 31, 1993.

4. Defence to the economic structure from economic offences, Bank scams and white collar crimes.

5. Security against social conflicts arising in plural societies due to ethnic/religious and communal divide.

6. VVIP and VIP security.

7. Security against Nacro-terrorism and drug addiction.

8. Aircraft security and security at airports-security from mid-air hijacking.

9. Security of industrial undertaking and vital installations in India and security of Indian missions abroad.

10. Security from natural and man-made disasters and crises situations like earthquakes, floods, epidemics bomb explosion.

11. Security from political corruption, instability and political violence.

12. Security of economic political and social structures from internal and external threats and destabilisation attempts.

13. Security of the geo-strategic and geo-economic interests and national ecological-environment from internal and external threats.

14. Defence of the country against depredation of organised criminals and lumpen elements including kidnapping, abduction and assaults.

15. Our political system itself is under severe strain due to enlarging controversial areas between the centre and the states. Population explosion, sense of denial of social justice to the poor and the role of money and muscle power has put severe strain on our political system.

16. Problems of communalism and fundamentalism pose a serious threat to the integrity and unity of the country.

17. Erosion in social and moral values, the legal inadequacies, the short-sightedness of politicians, increasing violence in our society, craze for becoming rich overnight, white collar crimes and too much emphasis on personal liberty have resulted in various anti-social activities which cause serious threats to the security of the society.[14]

18. Growing lawlessness in police, organisational deviance, custodian deaths, demoralisation of police, police strickes, illegal detention and torture, rape in police custody harassment of witnesses, wanton misapplication of penal powers against innocent persons, arrogant and brutal handling of law and order situations, fake encounters, active connivance in vice-rackets like gambling, prostitution, smuggling etc. are some of the ugly facts of police indiscipline which seriously pose serious threat to the internal security and social fabric of the Indian polity.[15] Curbing the excesses and atrocities of the security forces is thus necessary not only for the protection of human rights but also for maintaining the territorial integrity of the country.[16]

19. Illegal overstaying of Pakistani Nationals or influx of Bangladeshi refugees or Sri Lankan Tamils also can pose a threat to the internal security of the country. Tensions are running high in Arunachal Pradesh over the presence of about 60,000 Chakma refugees. On July 2, 1993 Chief Minister of Tamil Nadu said that the presence of 80,000 Sri Lankan Tamil Refugees in camps jeopardise the security of the state as potential harbourers of the LTTE. A total of 13,150 Pakistan Nationals have been overstaying in India. Of these 3604 Pakistan Nationals were in Rajasthan, 2556 in Maharashtra, 1663 in Uttar Pradesh, 1473 in Gujarat and 1461 in Madhya Pradesh.

20. Increasing lawlessness and violence in states like Bihar, UP, Maharashtra pose a serious threat to the internal security of the country. According to Indian Express August 1, 1993 the growing terror and lawlessness in Bihar can be estimated from the following figures- (Figures of Crime in Bihar State).

Year	*Murder*	*Dacoity*	*Kidnapping and ransom*
1982	46	71	16
1983	64	107	42

1984	67	105	83
1985	52	56	31
1986	56	59	69
1987	77	44	34
1988	63	29	—
1989	45	29	36
1990	76	56	49
1991	70	60	32
1992	109	116	74
1993 (Up to May)	37	51	50

Above figures adequate indicate how Bihar is seriously threatened by Internal security problems.

Planning for Internal Security

Management, according to Peter F. Drucker, "has no choice but to anticipate the future, to attempt to mould it and to balance short range and long-range goals. Managers, therefore need to be skilled in making decisions with long futurity on a systematic basis".[17] Planning is strategic decision-making or perhaps strategic planning, it is the continuous process of making decisions systematically and with the greatest knowledge of their futurity; organising systematically the efforts needed to carry out these decisions and measuring the results of these long range and short range decisions against the expectations through organised systematic feedback. Peter Drucker has clarified the concept of strategic planning by saying that :-

(1) "It is not a box of tricks, a bundle of techniques. It is analytical thinking and commitment of resources to action;"

(2) "Strategic planning is not forecasting. It is not master-minding the future."

(3) "Strategic planning does not deal with future decisions. It deals with the futurity of present decisions."

(4) Strategic planning is not an attempt to eliminate risks. It is not even an attempt to minimize risk"[18] Strategic planning implies the following four things-(1) Systematic and purposeful work on attaining goals be done; (2) Planning start out with sloughing off yesterday and that abondonment be planned as part of the systematic attempt to attain tomorrow; (3) We look for new and different ways to attain objectives and (4) We think through time dimensions and ask "what do we have to start work to get results when we need them."[19] Planning for internal security is a continuous process of making decisions systematically with the great knowledge of the future challenges to internal security. The need to be prepared for a grave emergency has been highlighted by Bombay bomb blasts.[20] Long range and short range planning at various economic, political and operational levels is required for dealing with challenges of insurgency in north eastern states terrorism in Kashmir, communal violence in Central India and organised crimes in Bihar, Gujarat and Bombay. Security today covers all aspects of life: social, economic, cultural, humanitarian and environmental, which are all pervasive and are essential for an enduring quality of life and continued economic development.[21] All internal security challenges call for preparedness and advance action. At present natural calamities like earthquakes, floods, droughts, cyclones, famine, environmental tragedies as exemplified by the Bhopal gas tragedy and the Chernobyl disaster require "crisis proactive" approach rather than crisis- reactive approach. There is a need for National Emergency Management organisation to coordinate the government and private efforts in tackling emergencies. On July 8, 1993 Mr. N.N. Vohra, Home Secretary asked the seven north-east state administrations to urgently review and revamp existing arrangements for enforcing surveillance along the borders to prevent the induction of sophisticated weapons and smuggling of drugs and underlined proper action-plan for optimum utilization

of police forces available with the centre and the states.[22] There is an urgent need for long term planning and modernisation of Central Police Organisations: to enhance their operational capability.

Organisations for Internal Security Duties

State police is basically responsible for law and order and internal security of the state but there are a number of Central Police Organisations which are providing assistance to the states in this tremendous task. The following Central Police Organisations are providing specialised internal security duties in India as shown against each:-

1. *Central Reserve Police Force* — It is primarily for internal security duties including anti-insurgency duties in north-east states and anti-terrorist operations in Kashmir and Punjab.

2. *Border Security Force* — It is primarily for preventing trans-border crimes and prevent smuggling at the border but it is also being used for internal security duties due to shortage of CRP contingents.

3. *Central Industrial Security Force* — is specialised in providing security to public sector undertakings.

4. *Railways Protection Force* — is primarily for protection of Railway property.

5. *Indo-Tibetan Border Police* — for safeguarding Indo-Tribetian borders but it is providing security to banks in Punjab also.

6. *Assam Rifles* — provide security of international borders besides carrying out internal security duties in insurgency infested areas of north-east states.

7. *National Security Guards* — known as the Black cats is basically anti-terrorist force but it has become known for VIP security duties.

8. *Special Protection Group* — It is responsible for the security of the Prime Minister in India and abroad.

9. *Costal Guards* — have been created to provide protection to the coastal areas from smuggling and other coastal crime.

10. *C.B.I.* — It is basically a central agency investigating corruption cases, economic offences & other important cases.

11. *Army*—Whenever Central Police Organisations are not available, or there is serious urgency, army is frequently being used for internal security duties. It is performing anti-terrorist duties in Kashmir and Punjab and anti-insurgency duties in north eastern states.

Cost effectiveness of the whole system needs to be worked out. Proliferation of police and para-military forces is justified upto a certain extent on the grounds of functional requirements and specialisation. The question is how far proliferation will be useful and viable in the present day context ?[23] Proliferation of internal security organisations can lead to problems of training, equipment, resources and even inter-services rivalries and jealousies which can be counter-productive. The central government has a very important role to play in planning, evaluation and coordination of Central Police Organisations particularly in respect of training, equipment, modernisation and financial resources. The sheer weight of the numerical strength of the Central Police Organisations throw up many critical issues of management and control and problems of over-lapping jurisdications. The cost of internal security is going up every year but actually much more money has to be spent to modernise the police and provide minimum welfare measures including housing facilities for the Central Police Organisations particularly C.R.P.F.[24] Since there are serious internal and external threats to the country, India needs well trained and highly motivated internal security organisations.

Management of Intelligence for Internal Security

JIC (Joint Intelligence Committee) is a standing body consisting of members from various disciplines, like Foreign Affairs, Home, Intelligence, Defence etc. They prepare reports, mostly concerning India's security, for the benefit of the government.[25] The Intelligence set-up of India is given in the following figure —

India's Intelligence Set-up
↓
PM
↓
Cabinet Secretariat
↓
Joint Intelligence Committee

- Secretary External Intelligence
  - RAW
  - ARC
  - SSB
- Secretary Internal Intelligence
  - IB
  - CBI
- Director Military Intelligence
  - DMI
  - DNI
  - DAI

The Intelligence Bureau, patterned on the British M 15, is responsible for domestic intelligence including counter-espionage operations. During the last four decades Intelligence Bureau has grown both in strength and power. It has its offices in every state and is supposed to liais on a regular basis with the state CIDs and special branches. The intelligence is generally divided into three sections political, criminal and economic and daily intelligence reports are prepared for its headquarters at New Delhi.

Research and Analysis Wing (RAW) is patterned after Central Intelligence Agency (CIA) of U.S.A. and M 16 of Britain and is responsible for external intelligence. In 1984 the RAW Administrative service was formed. Although RAW is responsible for external intelligence yet there are allegations that it has at times interfered in domestic affairs. Intelligence agencies all over the world act through four well known methods of covert intelligence namely (1) agent building and cell building, (2) surveillance, (3) censorship and (4) interrogation. Generally all intelligence passes though the well known five stages namely (1) Collection; (2) Collation; (3) Analysis (4) Assessment and (5) Estimation. All intelligence agencies and state special branches gathering intelligence need to be equipped with latest electronic gadgets and computers as a part of modernisation programme.[26] Research and Analysis wing has many sections like AIR monitoring section, the Electronic Technical Section (E.T.S.). The Aviation Research Centre (A.R.C.) and Special Service Bureau (SSB) for carrying out its assigned role of collecting foreign intelligence. The cloak and dagger exploits of secret service agencies make thrilling reading when dramatised by the likes of John Le Carre but their real work is more mundane, less noble and more sinister than the popular genre of espionage, counter-espionage and spy fictions generally portray to the readers. The Illustrated Weekly of India October 14-20, 1990 brought out lot of reading material on our intelligence agencies. In 1977 Justice J.C. Shah expressed shock when former I.B. Chief confessed that it was a routine function of the bureau to keep tabs on political dissidents and the intelligence collected was not always reduced to writing but conveyed to the Prime Minister or Chief Minister in the course of daily briefings. There is a need for rethinking in the intelligence agency's policy of being incommunicado to the press and certain amount of accountability is required.

Staffing and Personnel Policies for Internal Security Organisations

How to go about recruiting, training and motivating internal security managers who are committed to contemporary management concepts and who are able to enhance the possibility of meeting the assigned missions and objective while using the available human resources is a real challenge. In internal security management, the team approach is very important. The basic objectives of each team of internal security managers are to deliver professional concerned services to the community and also ensure good quality work-life for the persons of the team and the organisation. The question of morale goes hand in hand with the important management considerations of motivation and good quality of work life. Motivation to carry out internal security duties for long hours in a hostile environment to the internal security organisational persons is a key factor in management of internal security. The human resource development of internal security organisations is the key to organisational effectiveness. Good leaders can create an atmosphere that encourages self-motivation and internal drive to the participating troops and I.S. contingents. According to Shri N.S. Saksena "the majority of the police chiefs do not command the confidence of their men because they do not have the courage to stand up to their chief ministers".[27] Experience of last twenty years has proved that Central Police Organisations can not entirely depend on I.P.S. Cadre for field postings particularly in difficult insurgency infested or terrorist-effected areas. State Minister for Internal Security Shri Rajesh Pilot said in reply to a Lok Sabha question that the government had decided that the posting and transfer of the officers of the rank of Inspector General and above in the Central Para-military forces would be made with the prior approval of the Government.[28] The major Central Police Organisations are field organisations while IPS officers generally are not willing for deputation if they do not get postings of their choice. Deputationists are naturally not in a position to develop a circumspect interest or demonstrate a genuine concern for the working of the Central Police Organisations because they come to them as birds of passage or as "guest artists". This necessitates separate I.P.S. Cadres for Central Police Organisations. The basic issue also pertains to the career prospects of directly recruited officers of the Central Police Organisations and their promotional prospects as well as a fair share in peace postings. There is hardly any difference between the DAGOs and the IPS officers in respect of education qualifications age and other professional aspects. While the IPS officers becomes a generalist, the DAGOs become specialists in the area of skills and operations of the C.P.O. concerned and therefore CPO personnel policy needs review.[29]

Internal security is the net result of a process in policing in which each policeman has to participate. It is the final outcome of good work in thanas and good work in the field to collect intelligence. Above all, according to KF Rustamji, it is the work of thousands of lower rank police subordinates who walk the streets. For improving the security who really matter in security is the thana staff and the constable in the street. In the police we have not yet learnt how to tap the information which thousands possess but are reluctant to communicate to the police. The sad fact is that in our democracy we seldom think in a democratic way[30] we make no attempt to tap the goodwill of people who want security. For effective internal security management, we have to learn to get intelligence from the common man. Local Police thana staff and the constable on the street need to be provided with adequate training, equipment motivation and sense of commitment. Proper career planning and welfare measures must be ensured for thana level police staff if internal security is to be revamped in true sense.

During the last four decades there is frequent use of Army for internal security duties. There is need for strict limits to army deployment as the nation's ultimate weapon can not be frittered away frequently without dangerous consequences. Army has been deployed in Kashmir and north eastern states on internal security duties and it is bound to affect on the morals and discipline of the army.

Women Police Stations for each District in Tamil Nadu

The Tamil Nadu state government has decided to establish one All Women Police Station in each of the 23 districts in the state[31] Madras would have two such stations apart from the one functioning since April 1992 while Madurai, Coimbatore, and Bargur in Dharampuri district would have one each. Post have been created for appointment of 28 Inspectors, 32 Sub-inspectors, 40 Head Constables and 290

Constables for the new stations which would be provided with telephone facilities at a cost of Rs. 4.48 lakhs and mopeds at a cost of Rs. 3.36 lakh. The two additional all women police stations to come up in Madras would each have one inspector, three sub-inspectors six head constables and 23 constables and those at Madurai and Coimbatore would have each one inspector one sub-inspector, 2 head constables and 14 constables. The station at Bargur would have one inspector one sub inspector one head constable and nine constables. All these all women police stations are expected to augment protection to the women and will handle cases of crime and atrocities against women.

Coordination as a Management Function

Since maintenance of internal security demands utilization of a number of persons of state police and paramilitary forces, coordination in their respective assigned roles become very important. Administrative coordination is first required between the state and the centre if state requires Central Police Organisations contingents to supplement their requirements of manpower. The following are some of the problem areas in coordination:-

(1) Differences in orientation towards particular goals and tasks and methods of operations;

(2) Differences in sorting out deployment pattern and allotment of specific areas & tasks to different contingents;

(3) Differences in culture, norms and interpersonal relations due to similar rank structuring;

(4) Problems of accommodation, water electricity and other basic needs and requirements of paramilitary forces;

(5) Misplaced sense of prestige and superiority complexes;

(6) Differing rules, regulations and departmental instructions in matters of deployment and organisational strategies;

(7) Unilateral withdrawal by CRP/BSF when state governments are reluctant to spare the CRP/BSF contingents;

(8) Problems in sharing rewards, commandation and credits for good work and at times fixing responsibilities for failures during operations;

(9) Problems of coordinating/reports/intelligence reports.

The centre has issued guidelines to all state governments recently with the objective of ensuring regular reviews of the law and order situation at all levels as well as for effective coordination between states and central police agencies. Mr. Pilot the Union Minister of State Internal security has suggested a weekly review of the law and order situation between the district magistrates, Superintendent of Police, the Intelligence Bureau and CID Officials. A fortnightly review at the Inspector General level and a monthly review by the states Director General of Police were also suggested.[32] A three monthly report will be sent to home ministry for better coordination between the state and centre. In the case of states with special problems like the Naxalites in Andhra Pradesh and the LTTE in Tamil Nadu he had suggested that they send detailed time-bound action plans while seeking centre's help. According to him, para-military forces are like fire fighting force and should be used as such instead of being used in states for long periods.

Problem areas of coordination between civil police and Central Police Organisations are manifold and recurring at periodical intervals. State police have to requisite and utilize the services of the CRP, BSF and other Central Police Organisations for tackling various serious internal security problems and there arises the need for coordination. "In the negative sense coordination aims at removing conflicts and over-lapping efforts of different independent units engaged in a common task. In the positive sense, it attempts to bring about voluntary and mutual cooperation and thereby good team work among the employees of various independent organisations resulting in the best possible results."[33] There is abuse of para-military forces by the state police and the explosive expansion of para-military forces is resulting in the blurring of their assigned roles of cope with the mounting threats to internal security."[34] Sixth Report of the National Police Commission has observed : " Not withstanding the fact that there are clear instructions about the role of the army and para-military forces, there are frequent instances of friction between these forces and the district administration."[35] There is need for effective coordination between different intelligence agencies and organisations involved in internal security duties.

Training and Motivation for Management of Internal Security

Internal Security Academy, Mount Abu is the premier national institute for training senior level and middle level managers of internal security.[36] The ISA conducts three different types of internal security courses for the officers of the ranks of (i) Deputy Superintendents of Police (ii) District Magistrates and Superintendents of Police and (iii) Dy. Inspectors General of Police. SVP National Police Academy, Hyderabad and State Police Colleges/Academies are also required to provide required input of internal security aspects in the training syllabus for senior police officers. Similarly for subordinate ranks and other ranks of the police, there is need for more job-oriented internal security training. For effective training in internal security duties, police trainers must utilize training methods such as (a) simulation (b) case study method (c) incident method (d) management and behavioural science games and (e) tactical exercises without troops (TWET). Training in the use of protective clothing like bullet proof jackets, video-camera handling, use of tear gas and other riot-dispersal equipment must form an integral part of training syllabus of police officers who are earmarked for internal security duties. Police tactics and strategies for anti-terrorist operations and anti-insurgency duties like cordon and search, raids, night embushes, mobile and foot patrolling need to be essential inputs for such training.

Motivation is very important for all those who are engaged in internal security duties. Providing adequate and positive motivation to Central Police Organisations and the state police is a big challenge for police leadership. According to K.F. Rustamji failure of the Indian Police Service (IPS) to give correct leadership to the force and the inability to combine a proper espirit-de-corps and service discipline are the foremost causes of the steadily declining efficiency of the police. Exemplary good conduct of leaders, genuine concern for the subordinates, guts to take up deserving cases of promotions, fair play and justice in matters of promotions, transfers postings and other service conditions can go a long way in motivating subordinate and other ranks of the police forces. Motivation to the Central Police Organisation and police forces engaged in internal security duties is necessary for getting positive results and operational success. Gallantry medals for good operational performance, monetary compensation for duties performed on holidays and festivals, extra allowances for work beyond 8 hours, better housing facilities, C.S.D. army canteen facilities and timely redressal of grievances are some of the practical motivational techniques which can bring good results. We can usefully adopt Japanese management approaches which produces a highly efficient, flixible and cost-effective organisation and is characterised by team work, holistic concern for workers, welfare, defined career paths, use of informal control mechanisms and worker input into decision-making.[37] The problem of understanding human motivation is indeed formidable and is not yet completely solved. What a manager of internal security can do in the field to induce motivation towards the accomplishment of objectives is to clearly take into account the differences between, individuals, groups, times and organisational climates and apply with imagination various available strategies for motivating the police force operating in the field.

Control as a Management Tool

According to Management science controls are needed for measurable and non-measurable events since they form the part of goal getting and value setting. For various social interactions controls must be timely, congruent, appropriate meaningful and operational. For getting immediate information of various internal security operations, each state police and Central Police Organisation has; "Control-Room" system which monitors all events, pattern of deployment and keeps track of day to day events. Today very often there are allegations against the police and Central Police Organisations and some of the allegations are not without some substance of gross violations of human rights. In India security forces resort to third degree methods during interrogation and investigation which frequently come to notice. Custodian deaths, custodian rapes and allegations of "Fake encounters" are often made against the police". Those who wonder why our police and para-military have become so corrupt and inhuman, and why the army is now showing symptoms of the same disease need only look at the results of our various inquiry reports to discover the answer".[38] The Supreme Court in State of UP, vs. Raj Narain 1975 (4) SCC 428 has rightly pointed out that "to cover with the veil of secrecy, the common routine business, is not in the interest of the public. "National Police Commission in its eighth report of 1981 states; what we desire is to create the awareness of direct accountability to the people at the various levels in the police hierarchy. For effective management of police and para-military forces, effective controls over their behaviour becomes one of the most important obligations of the senior police leaders. In a recent judgement of the Supreme Court in Saheli vs. Commissioner of Police 1990 (1) SCC 422, the court has held that " compensation can be ordered to be paid by the concerned government when its policemen causes bodily harm including battering assault, false imprisonment, physical injury and death. "A seasoned police officer Shri N.S. Saksena is of the opinion that use of third degree methods and fake encounters are generally counter-productive. In words of Shri N.S.

Saksena "the quest for instant results has led to fake encounters which in turn have made matters worse....... Illegal killings have never led to an improvement in the situation although this is often the short-cut proposed."[39] During internal security operations against insurgents, terrorists and violent communal elements, very effective control over activities of the police and para-military forces need to be exercised by their officers and the governments.

Control of Firearms and Explosives

The recent bomb blasts at Bombay, Calcutta, Delhi and other parts of the country have highlighted the need for effective control of firearms and explosives. A vigorous and sustained drive must be maintained by the state police to an earth all unlicensed firearms and unlicensed storage of explosives. Violations of any connected rules by the licensed firearms holders or explosive shop owners, must also be deterrently dealt with".[40] In Punjab, Kashmir and north-eastern states there is the special problem of smuggling sophisticated weapons and explosives of the most modern type including RDX from Pakistan and other foreign countries from the seventies onwards the use of fire arms by the lawless elements became frequent in UP, Bihar, West Bengal, Delhi and in the Naxalite infested areas all over India inspite of Arms Act of 1959. It is well known that influential politicians help anti-socials and other undesirable persons in getting fire arms licenses and thereby securing their loyality and assistance.[41]

Media Management

In a democratic society, electronic and mass media play an important role in educating the masses and in building up public opinion. Shri K.F. Rustamji has observed; "there are many people in authority who can never understand the need for giving information in a democracy, who take any criticism adversely even if it is correct, never meet the media people frankly and discuss the situation with them."[42] For effective management of media persons, regular meetings and briefings with the media people by the senior managers of internal security are essential. There should be close and mutual understanding of each other's role, dilemma and areas of responsibility. Communication management with the press, mass media, public and the government are also important aspects which managers of internal security can not ignore at any time. Police managers have to keep proper and effective communication with the mass media to build up police image and to contradict rumours and in correct reporting about crimes, incidents and various police operations. There are many persons in the media field who only want to hurt the feelings of those in authority because of some casual slight or because they feel that the normal stance of the media should be one of insulting the administration or of criticising the police actions. They never know what a man who is risking his life feels when he is wrongly accused in print of weakness or negligence or brutality when he was expecting appreciation.[43] Proper and effective media management can easily bring a change in the perceptions of the media persons. One of the reasons for the successful containment of terrorism and better image of leaders of the Punjab Police is good handling and management of media. Punjab Police under the leadership of Shri K.P.S.Gill, have taken media men to the most terrorist affected areas and shown them the difficult and hazardous conditions under which security forces were operating in Punjab. This has brought about a radical change in the media's perception of role of security forces operating in Punjab. Police leaders have to establish a close and personal rapport with the media men if they want media to project internal security operations launched by the internal security organisations in a correct perspective.

Decision-Making for Internal Security

For management of internal security threats like terrorism, insurgency and communal riots, state governments generally request the Centre to send CRPF and other Central Police Organisation contingents to tackle the difficult tasks of preserving internal security. Sometimes even the army is demanded or requisitioned by the state governments. The recent controversy on the deployment of the Army in Kashmir Valley for tackling terrorism highlights the problem of a federal democratic country that has to preserve the political structure and the value system laid down in the constitution. The decision to deploy Army will have to be made within the legal confencs and with regard to maintaining the supremacy of the civilian authority.[44] Before deciding to go in for Central Police Organisation or Army for internal security duties, training, experience, equipment and availability of the contingents for the task will have to be kept in mind. In USA there is a National Security Council consisting of President, Vice-President, the Secretary of state, security for Defence, the National Security Adviser, the joint chiefs of staff and the Director, CIA to take an integrated view of domestic, foreign and military policies concerning national security, with a multi-disciplined and dedicated secretariat to enforce monitor and tackle internal security problems. Our strategic national interests demand the immediate setting up of a National security council. A Former editor of the Statesman Shri Sunanda K. Datta Ray has said: "The north-east in ethnic turmoil is India in microdosm and there is lack of perspective at the central decision making level....Vote banks play a major role in Congress(I) calculations."[45] A very strange constraint and handicap of the Central government has been pointed out by the Kapur Commission thus: "Although the Home Minister is in charge of the police and the police administration and is answerable to Parliament in the matter, still he has no power to direct the police as to how it would exercise its statutory powers, duties or discretion." At many occasions, the Central Government and state governments can have different political parties in power and their political perceptions may differ regarding the threats to the internal security. The case of 6th December 1992 destruction of disputed structure at Ayodhya is a clear pointer to these varying political perceptions. The time has come for introspection. To carry out a holistic analysis of internal security imperatives that show from the prevailing security environment and to effective work out effective strategic decision-making on a large-term nationalistic perspective, unified command and a single point decision-making approach at the apex level is the real need of the country.

A fundamental question is where should rest the main responsibility for maintaining law and order and internal security ? The experience of the past few state, which have direct or indirect bearing on internal security. Some of the important laws are mentioned below:-

(i) Unlawful activities (Pervention) Act 1967.

(ii) Prevention of seditions meetings Act 1911.

(iii) Terrorist and Disruptive activities (Prevention) Act 1987 as amended uptodate.

(iv) Armed Forces (Spl. Forces) Act 1958.

(v) Police Act 1861.

(vi) Indian Penal Code.

(vii) Criminal procedure code.

(viii) Arms Act 1959 as amended uptodate.

(ix) Indian Explosives Act 1978.

(x) The National Security Act 1980 as amended uptodate.

(xi) Prevention to Damage to Public Property Act 1984.

(xii) Suppression of unlawful act against safety of Civil Aviation Act 1982.

(xiii) Anti- Hijacking Act 1982.

(xiv) The terrorist affected area (Spl. courts) Act 1984.

(xv) Essential Service Maintenance Act 1968.

(xvi) The Civil Defence Act 1968.

(xvii) Prevention of corruption Act.

(xviii) Narcotic Drugs and Psychotropic substance Act.

(xix) Protection of Civil Rights Act 1976.

(xx) Environment protection Act 1986.

We have inherited a heavy burden of existing laws relating to internal security and have added a number of new laws to maintain law and order and internal security of the country.[46]

On August 12, 1993 Lok Sabha passed a Bill amending the conservation of Foreign Exchange and prevention of smuggling and preventive detention of a person indulging in smuggling for a period of two years.[47] Unless there was a political will to implement the stringent laws and acts pertaining to internal security, the situation would not improve, years especially just before during and after the Emergency makes it painfully clear that internal security can not continue to be dealt with as at present in a pragmented fashion, divided between a score or more of states. It has to be dealt with as a whole and at the highest political level i.e. through Parliament and by the Central government.[48] Nevertheless it obviously can not be divorced from state control and responsibility. The state governments will have to be the main agencies through which the central govt. should deploy and operate law enforcement agencies including Central Police Organisations. Law and order administration and internal security should be brought on the concurrent list so that decision-making regarding deployment of Army or Central Police Organisations can be made jointly or collectively by the central and state governments. There is need for a strong political will to improve the organisational health of the police.[49] Modernisation of police, improvement in training, better equipment, transport and communications and better motivation are some of the urgent requirements of Central Police Organisations for effectively managing internal security of the country.

Directions Through Law Making for Internal Security

Parliament and state legislatures make laws related to internal security for providing directions to the people and the law enforcing agencies.

India might well top the countries which have framed the largest number of laws. We are proliferating laws yet no one bothers to reflect whether the plethora of laws and regulations already enacted and existing are being effectively administered to serve their purposes. We seen to take the result for granted the moment a law is placed on the statute book. We are anxious not so much to implement a law successfully as to enact it. Often with an eye on securing publicity of certain political ideologies. It is very difficult to prepare a complete and exhaustive list of laws both Central and Minister of State for Finance said on August 12, 1993 that 38 foreign nationals have so for been arrested in connection with smuggling activities and 142 persons have been arrested so far in connection with the Bombay blasts. Our laws relating to internal security though amended in recent years are still not commensurate with the requirements of the situation and their enforcement far from so.

Unfortunately the criminal justice system in India is a complete mess. "It has become the biggest force in the land. Our courts are congested. Anybody can do anything and get away with it; if not for ever, at least for ten years and by that time the deed itself is forgotten. Does this not invite insecurity."[50]

Modernisation of Police and Central Police Organisation

For management of Internal Security modernisation of police and para-military forces like CRP, BSF and other is most indispensable. It is necessary to clearly define the role of each of the Central Police Organisation, spell out their objectives and operational philosophy, fix the areas of responsibility and determine accountability.[51] Better training, better equipment, better communication, better housing facilities, better transport can be ensured by modernisation grants if funds are properly utilized. Modernisation grant scheme caters funds for computers, weapons, transport, housing and other schemes for modernisation of police forces.[52] Housing facilities for Central Reserve Police more need to be augmented as the satisfaction rate of housing is less than even 6 percent. There is need for a crash programme to build more family accommodation and other facilities for CRP personnel. Rationalisation of CRP deployment is needed and the present practice of shifting CRPF personnel from place to place is undesirable and irrational and affects their morale and welfare.

Internal Security Minister Mr. Rajesh Pilot said during question hour in the Lok Sabha on August 5, 1993 that one third of the Rs. 30 crore grant earmarked for the modernisation of the police forces has been given to Tamilnadu government in view of the increasing threats from the Liberation Tigers of Tamil Eleam (LTTE). In addition 500. All 475 have been supplied to Tamil Nadu at nominal prices. Mr. Pilot said special cells consisting of the central and state agencies had been set up at the district level to check the menace of RDX smuggling. Due to this coordination the designs of the extremists to create trouble in many parts of the country had been foiled.[53]

C B I To Modernise Probe Techniques

New Director of CBI, K. Vijaya Rama Rao said as part of its modernisation drive, the CBI would soon build a computer network and reorient the training programmes for its staff and officers.[54]

"The modern techniques of investigation will be useful in serious offences like murders which have no clues, bomb blasts, document examination, ballastics, economic offences and corruption cases, which is a fallout of economic crimes," Rao said.

The computerisation of CBI would help in sifting, analysing and monitoring the information available in various cases.

The Problem Areas the Challenge of Widening Chasms

"While draconian laws were passed against economic offenders these aroused only amusement as smugglers, profiteers, black marketeers and tax evaders not only became the financers of the ruling party but they acquired political clout and quite a few attained high officers.[55] While we talk of rule of law, public morality and high moral values, we find ourselves uncomfortable with violations of human rights, corruption in high places and erosion of moral values, Shri K.F. Rustamji has said; "why is it that we have got use to applying the wrong tests to policing ? If the crime figure increases which it must, if registration is good, we say that the police are incompetent. If a couple of murders occur in the same area due to chance, crime is said to be totally out of control and the police are told to use stern measures to stop it. If an officer wants to use legal methods only, he is said to be weak and inefficient. If he tacitly encourages torture, he is considered firm and practical and he is said to 'understand the realities of the situation."[56] While political leaders talk of democratic police, they ensure that they perpetuate a police force that is dreaded by the people, with officers at the top who have been selected for their ability to wink at brutality and corruption. In conferences and seminars police is exhorted to be responsive to the needs of the people but recommendation for reforms in police are not allowed.

The Crisis of Police Leadership and the Cult of the Super Cop

In management of internal security, the cult of the super-cop is gaining ground. "The super-cop is now an object of adoration even among main-stream media where the police has traditionally provoked a distrust and an unquestionable authority even to sections of the opposition who have been swearing the loudest and longest by democracy."[57] The super-cop is an unprecedented phenomena in India built up by conditions of intense insecurity and defication of some in strategic postings like Shri K.P.S. Gill in Punjab and A.S. Samra in Bombay. The "cult of the super-cop." can provide quick results and counter response to the terrorists and armed Naxalites but it is not a symbol of sound and strong political system of a stable democratic polity. Effective and good police leadership is essential for management of internal security but the cult of the super cop can mean demoralisation in the law-abiding conscientions police officers who get marginalised like Shri Chaman Lal in Punjab. "The more fundamental argument against the cult however is the political mind-set it can create. It will be a sad day for the country when the super-cop begins to appear its saviour and not the system of its proud adoptation and preservation."[58] The police forces in India today are sustained and nurtured by the police professionals who are unpopular with the government, denigrated by the politicians but respected by the people and honoured by the ranks with their evotion to them.[59] Indian police leaders have to be law-abiding, dedicated professional with high moral character.

Problems of Internal Security have not been tackled so far in a satisfactory manner at many fronts due to poor police leadership. Opportunism and Careerism, criminal politician-police leadership nexus and lack of professionalism are some of the depressing facts causing serious crisis of leadership. The Director General of the Bureau of Police Research and Development told the Press in Calcutta at the concluding session of the 20th All India Police Science Congress in November 1986 that the consensus arrived at the Congress was that there has been a failure in the leadership of Indian Police and that something fundamental was wrong with the police system.[60] National Police Commission has recommended separate IPS carde for CPOs on considerations of specialisation, professionalism and sense of belonging to the organisations. Once Indian Police Service Cadre is accepted and implemented for Central Police Organisations, it would open avenues for promotion of officers belonging to these organisations and officers will be involved with that sense of belonging to the organisations which at the moment is rather conspicuous by its absence. The stimulating innovation set out in the preceding paragraphs when implemented will inevitably give rise to a new and meaningful pattern of committed police leadership.[61] Central I.P.S. Cadres should be constituted for the Central Police Organisations and inter-se-seniority of directly recruited cadre officers and IPS should be fixed through amendment in I.P.S. cadre Rules.

Problems of CRPF, and BSF and Other CPOs

CRPF and BSF are generally deployed for internal security duties under the directions of civil police which is itself neither capable nor motivated to handle difficult internal security problems. K.F. Rustamji has rightly said: "There is improper way of using central forces" by putting CRPF and BSF under the operational command of the state forces who see no need for correct policing."[62] Both the BSF and the CRP have been so over stretched that their personnel are not given time for rest and retraining or even home leave.[63] Separation from family, inadequate compensation for work on holidays and Sundays, long and tedius hours of work, non-cooperative state police authorities, unsatisfactory and inadequate living conditions serious effect the operational efficiency of the CRP and BSF. It is not so much the strength of the state police forces but their quality, methods and techniques and their equipment which has fallen below the requisite standard. How can such police force guide and Control Central Police Organisations for Internal security operations. Education of children, separation from family stress due to hostile working environment and inadequate rest are some of the important problems of CRPF and other CPOs. Non-availability of leave when required, tension and stressful barracklife, inadequate housing facilities, long hours of work even on Sundays and other holidays, lack of proper recognition by local police authorities are some of the irritants with CRPF and other police organisations. There is need for proper career planning for all Central Police Organisations so as to motivate them. The principal objectives of career planning can be;

(i) To secure placement of the right man at the right time in the right place.

(ii) To ensure to all employees optimum satisfaction and promotions consistent with their qualifications, competence, experience and capabilities.

(iii) To strength human resource development programmes for effective quality of work life.

(iv) To ensure fair play, justice and equal treatment to all employees in matters of postings, transfer, training opportunities and promotions.

(v) Individual career plans, management development plans and matching of update job-inventories of all posts with organisational needs and developments.

It is of utmost importance for the welfare and morale of the Central Police Organisations, that appropriate career management should be ensured for all ranks including gazetted officers and some reasonable parity of officers should be kept with state forces, separate IPS cadre should be created for officers of Central Police Organisations and they should get regular promotions in parity with state cadre IPS officers. Career planning for SOs & other ranks is also necessary for all Central Police Organisations. Canteen facilities on Army pattern better housing facilities, better equipment and modernisation of outfit and outlook are urgent needs of the Central Police Organisations.[64]

Police and Protection of Human Rights

The Constitution of India has guaranteed fundamental rights to all citizens and has thus assured protection of human rights. Today human rights jurisprudence in India has constitutional status."[65] India as the world's largest democracy can be proud of its being the greatest protector of human rights.

State Police to Look After VVIP Security

State Police Organisations will soon be given exclusive responsibility of providing security to VIPs and VVIPs in their territory. Police of all the State have been asked to raise units of Special Security Force (SSF) to take over the task.[66]

Minister of State for Home Affairs in charge of security, Rajesh Pilot, said that the process was already on and the directors-general of police have been given a deadline of one year hence to get their respective SSFs ready. The step was aimed at relieving the paramilitary personnel from the task which was extraneous to the nature and purpose of their parent outfits.

Entrusting State Police with the exclusive responsibility would also put an end of this practice of VIPs making special requests and asking for men from a particular outfit for their security, as they lacked faith in others.

While the decision to entrust VIP security to State Police might be welcome to paramilitary forces, Delhi Police find themselves in a bind. According to the figures last available, there were about 7,000 of its men deployed for security. There was no dearth of VIPs in Delhi and security was a monumental task, especially if it was to be assigned exclusively to the already stretched police force.

Delhi Police had requested for a sanction of a 300 strong commando force (as against its deployment of 7,000) but even this was pending approval of the Government. Interestingly, DP was directly under the Home Ministry from which the sanction was to come from.

Management of Terrorism

According to available information 19 incidents of terrorist violence took place in the Terai region of Uttar Pradesh during the last four months (upto July 1991) in which eight terrorists were killed and 21 arrested while 15 civilians and three policemen were killed and three civilians were injured. According to Shri Rajesh Pilot, State Minister for Internal Security a special grant of Rs.10 crores was released to the state government to strengthen the police administration in the Terai area and additional para-military forces were also deployed in UP.[67] For effective management of terrorism, following integrated action-plan can be useful—

1. Police force should be revamped by better training, equipment, communication facilities and increasing the strength of police officers in terrorist infested areas.

2. Better coordination of intelligence between the intelligence units of various states and between IB and state intelligence.

3. Seeking people cooperation through village volunteer force.

4. Providing effective and dynamic police leadership.

5. Infiltration routes from across the border should be plugged by additional border deployment.

6. Special anti-terrorist outfits should be formed with better training, motivation, equipment and intelligence input.

7. Misguided youth can be provided employment outside the state and general amnesty programme in an integrated manner.

8. Political economic, social and cultural measures to be taken simultaneously.

Aviation Security

During the last two decades we have seen a substantial rise in the lethality of terrorism directed at world aviation.

Data published by the FAA records 26 explosions abroad airlines in the 19803 with a total of 1207 fatalities, 44 during the 19705 with 650 fatalities and 15 in the 19605 with 286 fatalities three individual years 1985 (390), 1988 (287) and 1989 (278) each had fatalities from explosion abroad aircraft that exceeded all the fatalities for all of the 1960s.[68] The bloody end of the skyjackers of the Lufthansa Jetlines at Somalia's Mogadishu airport has raised hopes everywhere that the menace of aerial terrorism can be contained and managed effectively given the determination not to give in to blackmail and international cooperation in allowing commando raids. The Entabbe Airport rescue act also indicates that management of aviation security is possible if there is a strong political well, well trained commando troops and international cooperation. An encouraging development in the fight against aerial terrorism is that the number of countries offering a haven to skyjackers is gradually strinking. The first of the conventions against aerial terrorism, that of Tokyo in 1963 was designed to punish offences committed aboard aircraft. The Hague convention of 1970 provide adequate measure for aviation security. Aviation security and airport security has to be revamped and contingency plans should be kept ready to meet all unexpected contingencies.

Security at Indian Missions Abroad

In Rajya Sabha the Minister of State for External Affairs said that some attempts were being made abroad to train people in attacking Indian mission and the missions have been cautioned to be careful and review the security arrangements. A study of security measures at Indian Missions abroad has been undertaken by the government and suitable preventive steps taken in the wake of threats from fundamentalists and terrorist groups.[69]

Critical Evaluation of Management of Internal Security

The grave internal security problems that our country is facing can be largely attributed to the lack of proper policy formulation and at times even failure in recognition and identification of the problem.[70] According to K.F.Rustamji, some of the main faults in our policies and action in the management of internal security are as under:-

(1) Panicky and thoughtless decisions.

(2) Defective planning of manpower, weapons and tactics without any long term plans.

(3) Frequent deployment of army over long periods.

(4) Barbarity and banditry by the police forces and reckless searches and insults to citizens.

(5) Improper use of central forces.[71]

24 More RR Battalions to be Raised

A Rs.300 crore Defence Minister proposal to raise an additional 24 Rastriya Rifles (RR) battalions (25000 troops) and related infrastructure is expected to be soon cleared by the Union Cabinet.[72]

Presently the RR has six battalions under two sector headquarters at Anantnag in Kashmir and Amritsar in Punjab. With a meagre 1993-94 maintenance budget of Rs.11.2 crore. RR battalions have been sustained entirely through Army deputations, both for officers and men.

The proposal has simultaneously been sent to the Home Ministry for comments. This has been done as these forces though directly under the control of Army headquarters are meant for internal security duties. Along with other paramilitary forces. RR with an exclusive Army ethos and all India character will be under the command and coordination of security adviser to the concerned state Governor.

The RR raising proposal envisages a total 30 battalions under 6 to 8 sector headquarters. Initially manpower and battalion support weapons will be drawn entirely form the

Army with a provision later to induct certain percentage of fresh recruits and also lateral entrants from Territorial Army (infantry) battalions.

RR will eventually replace all army involved in internal security duties. Their tasks will be rear area security, counter-insurgency operations, maintenance of law and order, aid to civil authorities, including disaster relief and augmentation of the Army during war.

Importantly, the success of the recent move to have a unified command for all forces in J&K under Lt. Gen. M.A. Zaki (Retd), adviser to the Governor depends upon internal security duties presently being done by Army to be transferred to RR.

Recent successes by RR battalions both in Kashmir and Punjab have convinced the authorities on the urgency of their raising schedules. For instance, the dreaded *Panthic* Committee member.

Need for a National Security Council

At present there is a "total absence of a national security doctrine"—a persistent habit of "adhoc decision-making a grossly erroneous identification of security threats. When one turns to the institution created by the United States National Security Act 1947 one finds that the National Security Council (NSC) serves a warning as well as an example. The act imposes on it the duties "to assess and appraise the objectives, commitments and risks of the United states in relation to our actual and potential military power, in the interest of national security, for the purpose of making recommendations to the consider policies on matters of common interest to the departments and agencies of the government concerned with national security and....... make recommendations to the President in connection there with.[73] In India on April 25, 1986, Policy Planning and Review Committee was reconstituted as the Policy Advisory

Committee with enlarged functions covering national security. In India National Security Council can be created by a presidential order and its functions and duties can be set out in the rules of business made under Article 77 (3) of the constitution. India has perhaps the richest fund of experience in law-intensity conflict,namely in tackling tribal and rural insurgencies and urban and rural terrorist movements. An apex body or core group like National Security Council needs to be formed at the Central Government with legal and constitutional authority for making political decisions on security matters. It should evolve conceptual plans, initiate coordination, issue directives to various security agencies and monitor all security operations and should prepare long term strategic security. A similar arrangements, albiet on a smaller scale in essential for each of the states for coordinating and monitoring various internal security operations. A democratic polity, a quasi-federal constitutional system, an ancient people in the process of social transformation, historical *logacies* and diversities, conflict of traditional values with modern one, of secularism with religious fundamentalism, and coexistence of rural with urban culture, make a formidable. Challenge for the managers of internal security and there is no parallel in the world for such a complex situation.[74] For such a situation an indigeneous model of national security strategy and organisational set up are required which should keep national interest above all other considerations while formulating operational polices and decisions.

Diagram Showing National Security Strategy Formulation and Evolution

Community Support Needed for Internal Security

Projection objectives of the police community relations, National Police Commission wrote, "The objective of the police-public relations should be the direct involvement of the people in the prevention and detection of crime and in the maintenance of internal security......they will have to actively cooperate with the police and also participate in organised efforts at self-protection with the support of the police. At the same time, community leaders will have to do everything to promote inter-group unity. "Police and para-military forces can not ensure internal security without the active goodwill and cooperation of the people. The effective control and containment of terrorism in Punjab can be largely attributed to the active involvement and support of the community in fighting the menace.

Role of Electronic and Mass Media

The important role that electronic and mass media plays in influencing and generating responses to and formulating issues of internal security is indispensable in a democratic society. The major issue of correct orientation of the media and its healthy support to the internal security operations need the attention of the authorities as well as the media personnel. The greater involvement of the media personnel with the people handling internal security management and greater contact at an appropriate high level can bring a sea change in development of mutual trust and overall support for the internal security operations.

Management of Law and Order and Riot Situations

Objectives of Law and Order maintenance are always to establish peace in society by seeking people's cooperation and by adhering to the minimum use of force principle. System Approach to deal with such problems can be durded into the following six phases—

Phase 1. Preliminary Preparations.

(a) Collect intelligence and interpret-know sensitive areas.
(b) Establish dialogue between parties.
(c) Involve influential agencies.
(d) Call peace committee meetings-Meet organisers Interview.
(e) Have understanding with the aggrieved-Advise aggrieved to conduct agitation peacefully.
(f) Round up anti-social elements and issue prohibitory orders.
(g) Remove missiles from vulnerable areas and keep vigil on targets.
(h) Get adequate strength in time for deployment near approximations, task forces.
(i) Maintain initiative and maintain tension to put up agitatiors on the defensive.
(j) Preventive measures. Ban on sale of arms/ ammunition/explosives.
(k) Visit routes/spot/place of meeting where you expect trouble. Familiarise troops and men with routes/places.
(l) Know the organiser-personal knowledge of means/ leaders-characters and background of organisers and leaders.
(m) Interviews and personal discussions with leaders are useful-arrange meetings at camp offices-police stations-Circuit House.
(n) Know the Press people and journalists-Personal knowledge of Press correspondents-cultivate good relations with Press.
(o) Keep contingency riot schemes upto date.
(p) Establish Control Rooms in each Distt. Hqrs. and big towns.
(q) Keep army informed of development.

Phase 2. Deployment and Planning Action

(a) Determine Nos. of police men required at each point.
(b) Mass briefing to define general objectives.
(c) Spot briefing at deployment positions.
(d) Have understanding on limits of action & preactions between Police & agitators.
(e) Give troops complete picture of all deployment.
(f) Coordination between troops be estabilished maintain good rapport.
(g) Mobilization of Police/Home Guards and other Para Military forces.
(h) Requisitioning of Magistrate.
(i) Provisioning of P.A. equipment and mobilie sets.
(j) Arrangements for adequate communications (Wireless, Telephone etc.)
(k) Requisitioning of Transport.
(l) Alerting of Army-Coordination with Army for deployment.
(m) Requisitioning services of fire brigade.
(n) Prepare for an eventuality inspite of understanding between police and agitators.
(o) Plan relief and welfare of men-Deployment should be controlled.
(p) Establish contact with spot leaders.
(q) Ambulance-mobilise First-Aid.
(r) Alert Fire Brigade and detail escorts for Fire Brigade.
(s) Control Room functioning be given streamling and it should be manned round the clock.
(t) Brief officers and men about protection of human rights.

Phase 3. Timing of Intervention-Confrontation and Intervention

(a) Catch the mood of the mob to assess situation.
(b) Set objectives to the force confronting the mob.
(c) Determine how much Force to be used and the type of force. Principle of minimum force to be strictly followed.
(d) Select correct time for action-Watch developing situation and ensure human rights are protected.

(e) Plan durations of action-Let out steam from the agitators.
(f) Avoid excesses-Withstand the public fury.
(g) Arrests to made.
(h) Get cases registered/start Registration, investigation, and prosecution of cases.
(i) Take care of dead and injured-arrange Inquests Identification of dead.
(j) Handing over of the dead after inquest.
(k) Guarding against looting of property.
(l) Escorting of ladies and children.
(m) Obtain reports from all sub-units and police forces deployed.
(n) Give specific deployment for Army.

Phase 4. Action on Withdrawal

(a) Allow men to go into specific type of aciton-detail task force.
(b) Make/readjustment after action.
(c) Give precise insturctions for next action.
(d) Stop action when objectives achieved.
(e) Regroup men and deploy in changed situation.
(f) Plan gradual withdrawal to reduce tension from peaceful areas.

Phase 5. Confrontation Action-Post-Riot Action

(a) Inform superior officers about situation Reporting.
(b) Brief press to prevent distortion and for rumour control.
(c) Study the situation & plan further action for restoring normalcy.
(d) Rearrange flow of intelligence.
(e) Plan relief & reduction of officers & men.
(f) Redesign deployment of manpower for relief situations.
(g) Maintain records correct & upto date-Brieng them upto-date.
(h) Register offences & arrest offenders quickly.
(i) Investigation into offences be conducted by experienced officers.

(j) Prevent rumours & take counter actions.
(k) Arrange examination of fire arms and ammunition.
(l) Damage to Police vehicles and other property be assessed.
(m) Special teams for prompt investigation.
(n) Augmenting accommodation in jails and liasion with jail authorities.
(o) Visit hospitals to see police patients and look after their families.
(p) Allow Army to return after action and debriefing.

Phase 6. Restoring Normalcy

(a) Withdrawal of restriction orders. Prohibitory orders.
(b) Progressive withdrawal of policemen from vulnerable points.
(c) Allow business of daily life to run normally to help restore normaley.
(d) Releasing of people who can help restoring normalcy.
(e) Activating peace committees to help normalcy.
(f) Need for frequent review of the Riot Scheme.
(g) Reward suitably those who have done good job.
(h) Allow withdrawal of cases if so considered necessary.
(i) Conduct research on the incident to learn lessons.

Political will is most important in dealing with Law & Order situation.

Various steps suggested above in each phase may not be necessary in every situation but above suggested steps provide us useful guidelines for handling serious law and order situations. Police planning for each law and order situation should be based on sound intellignece and founded on realistic considerations in terms of availability of personnel and equipment. Response time should be minimised as far as possible. Good communication facilities and adequate transport will help prompt handling of law and order situations. Police officers at district and police station problems with the help of systems approach.

Need for Eternal Vigilance and Security Preparedness

Threats to internal security demand eternal vigilance and preparedness on the part of Intelligence agancies, state police organisations and Central Police Organisations. Requirements for modernisation and matching power, training, equipment, communications and all other resources have to be constantly met through adequate allocation of funds. Human Resource development and management of personnel carrying out internal security duties has to be ensured along with adequate welfare, racreational and ameliorative measures to keep pace with the changing time. Pragmatic thinking is called for to accept choices and operation strategies for management of Internal security problems and internal security organisations for which we have adequate examples in other states like USA, Germany, Japan and United Kingdom Mass Media, and intelligence agencies have to keep eternal vigilance. The words "tighten up security" is a misnomer because the security buck stops at the man in the street-the constable". The buck stops at this man who is the most neglected figure in the security apparatus. He seldom knows what is happening, nobody even cares to brief him.[75] If vigilance and preparedness is to be done, constables have to be trained, motivated and given proper briefings.

Break up of Soviet Union Threat to Internal Security

Noted Defence expert and Director of the Institute of Defence Studies and Analysis Air Commodore Jagjit Singh said: "India faces a grave threat to its internal security and stability as huge quantities of clandestine weapons, in the wake of the breakup of the Soviet Union have already reached Pakistan for enduse by terrorists in India"[76] out of 560 missiles missing from the Soviet Union following the break up, 320 were sold to Pakistan arms Bazar in Peshawar in January 1993. 4 to 10 million land mines and two million Russian made Kalashnikov assault rifles were held by Soviet Union but following breakup large amounts have been sold to Pakistan and these arms are likely to create serious internal security problems in India. There is an urgent need for framing a national security policy after getting the inputs from all the security agencies of the country and its proper analysis by security experts.

Recommendations for Effective Management of Internal Security

There are some important recommendation for more effective management of Internal Security operations:—

1. Creation of National and state level Apex bodies for management of internal security and organisation of crisis management groups at both levels.
2. Overhaul of intelligence network and strengthening of Civil Police Organisations at police station level.
3. Conduct of physiological operations for educating masses about internal security problems.
4. Border management to check infiltration and smuggling of arms/ammunition explosives.
5. Unified command for internal security operations.
6. Modification of legal provisions and enactment of laws.
7. Effective management of mass media and electronic media.
8. Effective Civic Action programmes for community support.
9. Effective employment and management of army/airforce for internal security operations.
10. Effective management of Central Police Organisations including their personnel polices and creation of IPS cadres for Central Police Organisations.
11. Political, economic and social measures to remove the causes causing internal security problems.
12. International cooperation and bileteral measures to combat law-intensity operations like terrorism, insurgency and refugee problems.
13. Transnational movement of weapons must be controlled through international measures.
14. There is also paramount need for conducting a coordinated and well targeted psychological warfare for creating security awareness in the masses.

Concluding Remarks

We need dynamic, dedicated and competent managers of internal security at Central, State and district levels who have realistic awareness of the constraints within which they work and have capability to remain forward-looking, human and self confident in handling crisis situations. Both internal Security challenges and internal security organisations are so complex, so constrained and difficult to understand, let alone descipline rigorously that we should keep our managerial approach to them most dynamic, adaptable, effective and result—oriented. In his famous work "The new Realities", Peter Drucker attempted to high-light the importance of national culture for the society. According to him "one of the basic challenges managers in a developing country face is to find and identify those parts of their own tradition, history, and culture than case be used as management building blocks. The difference between Japan's economic success and India's relative backward-ness in largely explained by the fact that Japanese managers were able to plant imported management concepts in their own cultural soil and make them grow." Managers of internal security in India should draw useful lessons from both the western and Japanese experiences." Management of Internal Security of India requires down to earth approach with long term planning and guarding of national interests as supreme priorities.

For management of Internal Security, long term planning and integrated approach involving the concerned states and the Central Government is most essential operational level periodical and need based exchange of intelligence and stratic operational plans can be usefully organised with centre and the concerned states. The need for inter-state and intra-state coordination of intelligence and operations can not be over emphasised. To sustain internal security operations it is necessary that there should be continuity in the policies of the government both at the centre and in the states concerned. For effective management of internal security challenges there should be an Apex Body of professionals including Home Secratary, Director Intelligence Bureau, Director General CRPF, Director General, BSF as permanent members and state Director Generals of Police as coopted members as per requirements. The above mentioned Apex Internal Security Body (AISB) should:

(1) Study the internal security threat perceptions-in all its ramifications in different parts of the country.
(2) Formulate comprehensive operational plans and policies on a long term perspective.
(3) Issue appropriate directions and instructions to the state and the union territories affected.
(4) Ensure effective coordination of intelligence and deployment in various states.
(5) Obtain regular feedback of various on-going operations.

The IB and RAW Chief share a close relationship with the Prime Minister since they are expected to brief him daily. According to Coomi Kapoor, in 1979 L P Singh a former Home Secretary admitted that "It is important to guard against the tendency that equates national interest with the interest of the party in power and with central power politics:"[77] It is not just the intelligence agencies but also security services which need to be scrutinised to decide whether they are fulfilling the objectives for which they were set up. "Deployment of CRPF in Sri Lanka and Maldives, deployment of BSF on riot control, Guard duties in banks by ITBP, Internal security duties for CISF and meddling of RAW in affairs of border states such as encouraging Gorkha land movement and the Bodoland movement, can be viewed as misutilization of security services."[78] Internal Security management demands a good police system, an effective intelligence agency and community awareness of national interests. Internal Security need to be included in the education syllabus of various higher class from VIth standard so that the future citizens are correctly educated about our internal security problems. Seminars, symposiums and workshop on internal security problems should be conducted by various Universities and educational institutions.[79] A continuous research and experimentations to improve the internal security system is a vital part of the dynamic arrangements for management of internal security. Internal security training research and reforms are all continuous processes to be carried out simultaneously by the police and Central Police Organisations of the country to tackle the internal security challenges.

A high powered "Internal Security Think-Tank" should be constituted on a permanent basis with experienced security experts to monitor the problems of internal security and to provide policy guidelines to the police forces operating in the filled[80] Centre must assume direct responsibility for serious internal security should be brought on concurrent list alongwith law and order for this purpose by a constitutional amendment. There is an urgent need to modernise the police forces and ensure more realistic job oriented training. Indian Police Act should be redrafted and Central Police Organisations should be assigned its due role in the management of internal security in the new police Act itself. The subordinate police officers and other ranks deserve more housing facilities, higher salaries, fixed hours of work with holidays & Sundays or compensation thereof and better training for dealing with problems of internal security. Management of internal security faces the greatest dilemma when political authorities want quick results to meet political ends and expect short cuts by the police even if it hurt people intensely and even if it means violations of human rights. The National Police Commission has tried to tackle the anamalies and obstructions to good policing by making several useful recommendations. Once those recommendations are implemented, it is bound of improve the management of internal security of the country. Managers of internal security have to be the greatest protectors of human rights. Great care has to be taken by the police and security forces while launching internal security operations in disturbed areas, in order to protect the human rights of the innocent citizens of the area. Police and Central Police Organisations have recently started in service training courses on human rights in order to sensitize the personnel with the ethos, contents and the philosophy of human rights. "We have a difficult task. But beyond the difficult task I do see the glow of a bright future."[81]

Appendix "A"

Dr. MATHUR'S MATRIX FOR MANAGEMENT OF INTERNAL SECURITY

Factors causing Internal Security Problems	Manifestations of Internal Security Challenges.	Long Term measures for controlling I.S. Problems	Organisations doing Policing for I.S. Threats	Problems in Policing I.S. threat	Role of Other organisations
1. Economic Factors.	1. Agrarian Unrest.	1. Balanced Economic growth of various regions & areas	1. State Civil Police.	1. Training	1. District Administration
2. Political Factors.	2. Economic Offences, bank frauds and smuggling.	2. Character building & re-establishment of value system in society.	2. State Armed Police & Armed Base.	2. Motivation	2. State Govt.
3. Social Factors.	3. Industrial Labour unrest.	3. Social reforms & legislative measures.	3. Central Reserve Police Force.	3. Equipment	3. Central Govt.
4. Religious and Cultural Factors.	4. Regional agitations.	4. Reforms in education system.	4. Border Security Force.	4. Arms/Ammn	4. Political Parties & citizens Forums.
5. International Factors.	5. Linguistic agitaions.	5. Reforms in Police Organisations.	5. Indo-Tibetan Border Police.	5. Transport	5. Education Institutions.
6. Legal Factors.	6. Strikes & Dharnas by essential services.	6. Reforms and restucturing of Criminal Justice System.	6. Central Industrial Security Force.	6. Communication	6. Social control agents & social awakening.
7. Misellaneous Factors.	7. Corruption in services.	7. Spread of Secularism.	7. Intelligence Bureau.	7. Personnel Management	7. Criminal justice System.
	8. Political agitations & Protests.	8. Establishment of Rule of Law.	8. Research & Analysis Wing.	8. Welfare measures	8. Social Movements and spread of nationalism, secularism & Humanism.
	9. Election violence and rigging.	9. Proper use of mass media & Electronic media to educate masses on Internal Security matters.	9. Secret Service Bureau.	9. Police public Relations & Peoples	9. Shift in economic policies.
	10. Collective violence & demonstrations.	10. Political dialogue and settlement.	10. Assam Rifles.	10. Support	10. Shift in social policies.
	11. Atrocities on weaker sections. SC/ST.	11. Public participation and awakening.	11. Home Guards	11. Support of mass media	11. Consolidation & updating of Laws & Acts relating to I.S.
	12. Women agitations.		12. Village Volunteer Force	12. Support of District & State Adm.	12. Role of Internation Institution.
	13. Drug Addiction.		13. Special Police Officers	13. Central Govt.assistance & release of funds.	
	14. Terrorism.		14. Community Policing in North Eastern States.		
	15. Narao-Terrorism				
	16. Communal violence & strikes.				
	17. Erosion of life values & value system.				
	18. Environmental Pollutions.				
	19. Subversive interventions by foreign powers & Govts.				
	20. Campus Unrest				
	21. Threats to VIP & VVIP				
	22. Private armies & Senas				
	23. Air Hijacking				
	24. Over Population.				

Extract from the Book "Police, Laws and Internal Security" By Dr. K.M. Mathur.

Appendix "B"

STEPS IN MANAGEMENT OF INTERNAL SECURITY

<table>
<tr><th colspan="3">MANAGEMENT OF INTERNAL SECURITY</th></tr>
<tr><td>Central Govt. level</td><td colspan="2" rowspan="3">Plural Executives</td></tr>
<tr><td>State Govt. level</td></tr>
<tr><td>District Adm. level</td></tr>
<tr><td>Step-1 : Identity & Survey I.S. Threats & emerging challenges</td><td rowspan="2">Economic Measures</td><td>Step-7 : Training of Police/CPOs</td></tr>
<tr><td>Step-2 : Planning</td><td>Step-8 : Motivation & Morale of Police /CPOs</td></tr>
<tr><td>Step-3 : Organising and developing Central Police trg. and State Police Forces</td><td>Political Measures</td><td rowspan="2">Step-9 : Control of movement deployment & OPS through control rooms.</td></tr>
<tr><td rowspan="2">Step-4 : Managing Information system and Intelligence sharing dessemination</td><td>Social Measures</td></tr>
<tr><td>Edn. Reforms</td><td>Step-10 : Media Management.</td></tr>
<tr><td>Step-5 : Staffing and personnel Policies</td><td rowspan="2">Psychological OPS</td><td rowspan="2">Step-11 : Civic action and Public support.</td></tr>
<tr><td>Step-6 : Coordination of deployment and OPS</td></tr>
</table>

REFERENCES

1. Peter F. Drucker, *Management Tasks, Responsibilities, Practices*, Allied Publishers Pvt. Ltd., New Delhi 1993, Reprint 1980 P. 5

2. Peter F. Drucker, Preface, *The Alternative to tyranny ; management; tasks Responsibilities and Practices.*

3. K.F. Rustamji, *Need for New Security Attitude, Indian Express*, 13 October 1986.

4. Harold Koontz, Cyril O Donnel and Heinz Weihrich-Management. MC Graw Hill International Book Company, Eight Edition 1986, P. 342.

5. N.S. Saksena, No Security Experts in the Country, *Times of India* 20 October 1986.

6. Lok Sabha proceedings- *Indian Express* 30 July 1993. "CBI to take over probe into bomb blasts Pilot".

7. Rao S.R., Lothal and the Indus Civilization, 1973 Also encyclopaedia of Police in India edited by Ghost and Rustamji, Ashish Publishing House, New Delhi 1993, p.4.

8. For details see Kautilya- Arthasastra 1.4.3, Santiparva (Dutta) LXIX; Manu- IX- 294; Sukra I ; 60-61; IV 1257-1258.

9. For further details see Dr. S.D. Trivedi, *Origin and the Development of Police Organisation in ancient India - in Encyclopaedia & Police in India.* 1993, p. 3-15.

10. R. Sharma Shastry, *Kautilya's Artha-Shastra*(1915) Quoted by K.M. Mathur in the problems of Police in Democratic Society RBSA Publishers Jaipur 1987, p. 88-89.

11. K.M. Mathur *Police in India - Problems and Perspectives*- Gian Publishing House Delhi 1991, p. 30.

12. P.B. Gajendragad Kar: *The Historical Background and the theoretical Basis of the Hindu Law*: AIR Journal February 1963, p. 19(21).

13. Dr. K.M. Mathur- *Policing for Internal Security in Adiministrative change* Vol. XIX No. 12 July '91 June 1992 (Edtd A.B. Mathur) p. 83.

14. K.M. Mathur, *The Problems of Police in a Democratic Society*- RBSA. Publishers, SMS Highway, Jaipur 1987, p.90.

15. For Similiar views *see* Dr. K.M. Mathur: *Concerns and constraints in Administration*-RBSA Publishers SMS Highways Jaipur 1991, p. 194-195.

16. V.M. Tarkunde, *Police and the Human Rights Hindustan Times* 29 April 1992.

17. Peter F. Drucker, *Management Tasks, Responsibilities Practices* Allied Publishers Pvt. Ltd., New Delhi Reprint 1980 , p. 121.

18 Peter F. Drucker- Ibid p. 123-125.

19. Peter F. Drucker- Ibid p. 128.

20. Dr. S. Subramanian, *Planning for Emergencies*- The Tribune April 1, 1993.

21. Lt. Gen. A .M. Vohra (Retd) *Changing Concepts of Security, Hindustan Times*10 July 1993.

22. *Times of India* 9 July 1993. Steps to Curbe Insurgency in North East.

23. Dr. K.M. Mathur, *Internal Security challenges and Police in a Developing society*- RBSA publishers Jaipur 1989,p. 313.

24. For similar view *see* N.S.Saksena India towards Anarchy 1967-1992. Abhinav Publications, New Delhi 1993, p.109.

25. *Encyclopaedia of Police in India*, Edited by S.K. Ghosh and K.F. Rustamji- Astush Publishing House, New Delhi 1993, p.132.

26. " I.B. To be modernised", Press Report in *Indian Express* Jan 12, 1989.

27. N.S. Saksena, India- *Towards Anarchy 1967-1993*-Abhinav Publications, New Delhi 1993.

28. *Indian Express*, 30 July 1993. Ahmedabad p.5.

29. Dr. S. Subramanian, *CPO Personnel Policy Needs Review, Hindu*.

30. K.F. Rustamji, Need for new security attitude.

31. IIPA New letter Vol. XXXVII August 1993 No. 8 Editer T.N.Chaturvadi, p.8.

32. Pilot seeks weekly law, order review- *The Times of India* 24th Aug. 93. New Delhi, p.7.

33. Dr. K.M. Mathur, *Internal Security challenges and Police in a Developing Society*- RBSA publishers Jaipur 1989, p.256.

34. K.L.Khanna, Maintaining Public Peace- Abuse of para-military foces, *Timesof India* 17 August 1981.

35. Dharma Vira (Chairman) National Police Commission sixth Report para 47, 14 p.25.

36. For further details see Dr. K.M. Mathur- *Administration of police Training in India-* particular chapter 9 part-II- ISA, Mt.Abu, Gian Publishing House , Delhi 1987, p.- 320-340.

37. William G.Ouchi, Theory 'Z'- How American business connect the Japanise challenge Quoted by Dr. K.M.Mathur- *Police in India- Problems & perspectives* 1991, p. 171.

38. Tavleen Singh, Capital Nates- In the valley for fear- *Indian Express* 28 February, 1993.

39. N.S. Saksena. *Roots of Terrorism in Punjab- Times of India* Dec-5, 1983.

40. Indian Police Journal Vol. XXXVI No. 3 July September 1989, p.9.

41. S.K. Ghosh, *Social order in India-* Ashish Publishing House, Delhi 1990, p.156.

42. K.F. Rustamji, *Tackling terrorism, Hindustan Times* 30 March, 1990.

43. *Ibid.*

44. Rakesh Gupta, Tackling Political terrorism- New Delhi Edition- *Hindustan Times* 29th July 1993.

45. North-East in Turmoil Lack of perspective at the decision-making level by Sunanda K.Dutta Ray *Indian Express* 17th July 1993.

46. For Similar views see Badruddin Tyabji-Paying the Press for enforcing law.

47. Dr. Krishna Mohan Mathur concerns and constraints in Administration, RBSA, Publishers, SMS Highways Jaipur 1991.

48. Dr. K.M. Mathur, *Police, Laws and Internal Security*, Gian Publishing House, New Delhi, 1994.

49. *Hindustan Times* August 13, 1993.

50. K.F. Rustamji, *Need for New Security Attitude- Indian Express* 13/10/1986.

51. Dr. S.Subramanian, Para- Military Forces- *Modernisation a must tribune* Chandigarh 3 May 1993.

52. For details see Dr. K.M. Mathur *Swatantra Bharat Meen Janta Ka Uttardayatwa Tatha Police Kee Bhoomika-* BPR&D, MHA, New Delhi 1991, p. 275-330.

53. *Rs.10 crore to modernise* T.Nadu Police Force- *Hindu Friday* August 6, 1993.

54. See "CBI to modernise probe techniques"*Indian Express* 7.9.93.

55. N.S. Saksena, *India: Towards Anarchey 1967-1992* Abhinav Publications New Delhi 1993 p.8.

56. K.F. Rustamji- *The Wrong tests of policing.*

57. For details see J. Sri Raman- Cult of the super cop. *Hindustan Times* 17 July 1993.

58. J.Sri Raman, *Cult of the super-cop. Hindustan Times* 17 July 1993.

59. K.F.Rustamji, *Police Indiscipline- Everyone to Blame. Hindustan Times* 5 August1988.

60. P.R. Raj Gopal, Violence and response, Delhi Uppal Publishing House 1988.

61. For similar views see G.C. Singhvi, Let us have Indian Police Service Cadre for Central Police Organisations also- Indian Police Journal January-March 1984, 3-7.

62. K.F. Rustamji, Police Administration and Insurgency in India- where we Defaulted- Tour note No. 171 Trishul Vol. V. No.1,p.48.

63. Major Joshi, *Kashmir in Agony- Imperfect instruments at work-times of India* 11 August 1993.

64. For similar views see- Dr (Mrs) Anjali Nirmal, *Role and, Functioning of Central Police Organisations*, Uppal Publishing House, New Delhi- 1992, p. 422-449.

65. Justice V.K.Krishna Iyer in Sunil Batra's case (No 2) AIR 1980 SC 1579.

66. For details see State Police to look after VVIP Security- *Indian Express* Sept, 6, 1993.

67. Lok Sabha Questions, *Indian Express* 30 July 1993-p.5.

68. Aircraft Hijacking and other criminal acts against Civil Aviation-Statistical and Narrative Reports- FAA May 1986.

69. Steps on to tackle threat to Envoys, Rajya Sabha Proceedings *Indian Express* 5 August 1993,p.10, Hyderabad Edition.

70. See Lt.Gen. V.K.Nayar, *Threat from within*, "Lancer Publishers Pvt. Ltd., New Delhi 1992,p.246.

71. K.P. Rustamji, Bureaucracy, *Police Administration and Insurgency in India*- Tour Note, 171.

72. See "24 more RR battalions to be raised", *Indian Express* Sept. 7, 1993.

73. A.G. Noorani- *Towards a National Security Council, Indian Express* 25th January 1990.

74. L.P.Singh (ICS Retd), *The Fourth Sardar Vallabh Bhai Patel Memorial Lecture*, Oct. 31, 1987.

75. K.F. Rustamji, Need for new Security attitude- *Indian Express* Oct. 13, 1986.

76. For details see 'Threat of Missing arms, UNI-The Tribune 3 September 1993 Chandigarh p.1.

77. Coomi Kapoor, *Our Intelligence Agencies- The Illustrated Weekly of India* Oct 14-20, 1990 p.12.

78. For further details see Coomi Kapoor, Our Intelligence agencies- The *Illustrated Weekly of India*, Oct 14, 1990 p.12.

79. Dr. K.M.Mathur, *Internal Security challenges and Police in a Developing Society*, RBSA, Publishers Jaipur, 1989 p. 46

80. Dr.K.M.Mathur, *Police, Laws and Internal Security*—Gian Publishing House, New Delhi 1994, See chapter Policing for Internal Security.

81. Prime Minister Shri P.V. Narasimha Rao address to Civil Servants on January 30, 1993.

2

Improving Police Performance Through Training— Search For Thrust Areas

Peter Drucker has said: "The prosperity, if not the survival of any (organisation) depends on the performance of its managers of tomorrow."[1]

The twenty-first century is knocking at our doors, but we do not really know how to greet it. What challenges, opportunities, uncertainties and tasks would it bring ? If we only knew what the twenty-first century holds for us, we could prepare ourselves for it. As Police administrators, we have devices that allow us to see what lies ahead of us as long as the road is straight, as long as there is continuity. We know how to extrapolate from the present into the future and we think we know to handle probabilities and future tasks. Even today there is a considerable gap between what the police agencies can do and what they actually do in order to deal with various tasks in an optimal manner. For improving police performance, identification of grey areas where police performance is weak or wanting, is necessary and present practices of, what Lindblom labelled "muddling through" is not conductive from a management point of view for the organisation.[2] State Police performance in India has fallen short of public expectations due to various constraints and handicaps faced by the civil police.[3] Political interference, low social status, outdated methods of work, inadequate training, low level of motivation, absence of adequate grievance redressal machinery, the Police Chief's helplessness, distracted effects of labyrinthine laws and rules, erosion in hierarchical control, growing indiscipline in ranks, poor leadership and rampant corruption are some of the causes ultimately jeopardising the performace and image of the civil police.[4] Police performance needs to be analysed at a macro-level by utilizing research tools and observational studies besides carrying out a review of available literature. Historically police performance measurement, in a generic sense, can be traced back to Sir Robert Peel.[5] According to David Bayley performance goals are defined primarily in terms of completing specific jobs, such as making arrests, regulating traffic, clearing drunks from the street and solving sensational crimes.[6]

Criteria for Police Performance

Police performance is generally assessed by the following criteria:

1. Population served for police employee and the cost incurred in terms of money and resources.
2. Crime rate and volume and prevention of crime by police patrols and surveillance.
3. Conviction rate of reported crime with reference to police investigations.
4. Arrests made by police for crime.
5. Percentage of arrest that leads to conviction.
6. Average response time for emergency calls.
7. Percentage of crime solved in less than X (given) days and weeks.

8. Percentage of population having a general feeling of security and safety.

9. Percentage of population expressing satisfaction or dissatisfaction with police services and delivery system.

10. Crime rate of certain offences and percentage of criminals apprehended and convicted.

11. Traffic control duties and total traffic violations in proportion to volume of traffic and number of vehicles.

12. Proportion and percentage of total hours policemen spent in a year on investigation work, service calls, crime prevention, traffic duty, VVIP security duty and law and order duties.

13. Performance in terms of anti-terrorist operations/ counter-insurgency operations carried out by the police and their success/failure ratio.

14. Performance of police in social service areas and in enforcing social legislation.

15. Time and manpower spent by police on election duties related to democratic rights of the citizens.

16. Performance of police on areas belonging to social responsibilities of the police.

17. Manpower and time spent on public relations and social service work.

18. Manpower and time spent by police in controlling and containing riots, disturbances, conflicts and other law and order duties.

The basic and fundamental problem regarding the police today is how to make them function and perform their duties as an efficient and impartial law enforcement agency, fully motivated and guided by the objectives of service to the public at large, upholding the constitutional rights and liberty of the people and at the same time maintaining the internal security of the Country.[7] Police performance has both qualitative and quantitative connotations. Goldstein asserts that police tend to measure their performance in terms of the frequency with which they employ easily quantifiable means of solving a problem rather than in terms of degree (quality) to which the problem is solved.[8] Traditional measures of police performance stress the apprehension of offenders and the deterrence of crime but numerous recent studies show that police do much more than fight crime or maintain internal security. Recent studies call for a reorientation in police performance assessment.[9] Indian Police must evaluate its performance periodically and must prepare itself through training to provide police service of the highest quality to the community and the nation. For achieving good quality policing (GOP), the values, the roles, motivation, rewards and intricate inter-personal relationships that comprise law-enforcement must be strategically and systematically transformed to make the police service, democratic, professional, humane and pro-active in police operations.[10]

The Police in India have to realise that the efficient performance of their duties will depend on the extent of ready cooperation they receive from the public.[11] People in India generally believe that members of the police force are "incompetent, cruel, normless and even corrupt. They are benefit of moral values".[12] Policeman has to perform his duties very judiciously. The citizenry cries for more stringent law enforcement yet when stringent law enforcement is used there are often cries of police brutality and harassment.[13]

Training

Recent experience of some countries indicate that training created the opportunities not only for improved individual performance but also had great potential for organisational development.[14] Conceptually Clark Hull is a major contributor to the analysis of the factors in performance.[15] Performance of an individual depends on many factors such as level of his skills, experience, training, age, level of motivation, organisational climate, level of job satisfaction, state of equipment available, level of technology used and overall other environmental factors. Training is basically a planned organisational function which identifies the current and future performance needs of the employees and provides them the knowledge, attitude, skills, habits and the techniques required to equip the employees for an efficient and effective performance of their presents and future jobs. Effectiveness of training is determined ultimately by the improvement in the employees performance and their behaviour. The thrust of the training should be on moulding a raw material into a fine and finished product capable of performing its assigned roles and responsibilities with right attitudes, right behaviour and right habits. Good and effective training can cultivate in trainees right attitudes to work, right knowledge of duties, right behaviour with the people, right skills and techniques to perform their duties in a manner which are compatible with the nation's interest and democratic ethos.

Evaluation of Police Performance

Performance is to be indentified both in terms of quality and quantity. Police training should provide officers with self motivation to perform for the purpose of achieving organisational goals and missions, achievement of self maintenance, growth and achievement of social satisfaction. In India and other Countries, the quality of police performance varies enormously since police in different Countries have different socio-political backgrounds. India has state controlled police, Japan has succeeded in standardising performance while decentralising command. The average Japanese police force—one in each prefecture—contains on the average five thousand officers and covers about 2.5 million people. In U.S.A. there are about twenty five thousand police forces, each containing on the average eighteen officers and covering eighty four hundred persons. In 1973 there was one policeman for every 585 persons in Japan and one for every 445 persons in U.S.A. The number of police personnel per 1000 population in 1991 is only 1.4 at All India Level. No. of Policemen per thousand population in Nagaland is 13.0, Mizoram 6.3, Manipur 6.2, Sikkim 5.9, Arunachal Pradesh 4.4. while it is 0.9 in Bihar. In India density of police personnel per 100 Sq Km is 35.1 and police strength is 78.4 percent of the total strength of 11.5 lakh at All India Level.

In India, Japan and U.S.A, performance of the police differs substantially due to their different roles, structures and mode of external regulation. Police personnel in different Countries for three different years are as under:—

Table showing Police personnel (in 0001)

Sl.No.	*Country*	*1982*	*1984*	*1986*
1.	India	932.9	1007.7	1032.3
2.	Japan	252.0	253.6	256.5
3.	U.S.A.	514.3	611.5	629.7
4.	U.K. England	186.5	188.2	191.0
5.	France	196.2	197.4	199.7

As regards workload it is 1.9 IPC cases per civil policeman at All India Level. Comparative crime figures of some countries of the world are as under:-

Table showing Total crimes per 100,000 of Population and other crimes in certain countries in 1980

Sl.No.	***Country***	***Total crimes***	***Murder***	***Rapes***	***Kindnapping***	***Robberies***	***Theft***
1	India	473	3.2	0.7	2.0	3.0	87.0
2	Japan	1163	1.4	2.2	0.1	2.0	999.0
3	U.S.A.	5840	10.1	36.1	N.A	N.A	5265.0
4	U.K. England	5128	1.6	2.5	0.1	N.A	4156.0
5	France	4884	N.A	3.5	N.A	9.0	2988.0

Source-Crime in India 1991- National Crime Records Bureau

In the context of the present study, police denotes not only civil police but also district armed police and all Central Police Organisations. Central Reserve Police Force, Border Security Force, C.I.S.F., R.P.F., I.T.B.P, Intelligence Bureau and Research and Analysis Wing, are all Central Organisations performing police duties and assisting civil police to meet the complex challenges of internal security and crime control. Justice S. Natarajan has mentioned the following three factors to be taken note of before an evaluation is made of the performance by the police.[16] Firstly, the nature of duties performed by the police has resulted in a different scale being used to judge their performance of duties. Secondly, due allowance has to be made for mental attitudes of policeman being different on account of the nature of the duties performed by them. Thirdly, the mental stress and tension to which they are subjected have also to be included in reckoning while evaluating the quality of their service and the standards of perfection achieved by them. Broadly stated, the police performs the following functions:

1. Prevention of crime;
2. Detection of crime;
3. Traffic control;
4. Maintenance of order;
5. Internal Security;
6. Other specific security tasks.

In the changed circumstances of our society, a wholly law and order oriented force has to be transformed into one, which, while retaining a keen appreciation of its legal responsibilities to safeguard life and property, has also an understanding of the larger social issues involved in its day to day work.[17] In India, police constable and Head constable constitute roughly more than 90 percent of any police force. Therefore police training should get its focus on the training at the grass root level in the police department.[18] Training should aim at producing "educated police service" because more than in any branch of public service, the personal character of the police work makes the accomplishment of its purpose dependent on the quality and spirit of its personnel, on the preparation of its members for the performance of their tasks in a dignified manner. Police officers have not so far developed an understanding of the social purpose of their activity, a sensitivity to trends and forces at work in the environment in which they work, and attitudes in consonance with the social justice with special reference to the weaker sections of the community. While performing their duties, they are generally "partial towards the rich, the influential, politicians and henchmen of politicians. Policemen are said to be rude and even brutal in their behaviour. The discourteous behaviour of policemen was not confined to criminals only".[19] A research survey carried out by the author 60.48 percent respondents rated police image as very bad and 27.62 percent as satisfactory.[20] Regarding reasons for dissatisfaction with police performance, 21.43 percent respondents found corruption in police, 18.58 found incorrect behaviour, 13.33 percent found police not committed to their job and 11.90 percent respondent found police indifferent to the people.[21] The view still persists that the police force functions as an engine of oppression for putting down the people at the behest of the party in power.[22] Effective performance by the police depends on the following factors.[23]

1. Quality and Quantity of staff and their time management.

2. Legal framework and social milieu which forms working environment.

3. Basic training, In-service periodical training and orientation.

4. Organisational infra-structure, equipment and logistics.

5. Financial support and economic feasibility.

6. Social value system and orientation and their support to police in role performance.

7. Organisational environment and sub-culture.

8. Police leadership at various levels.

9. Level of motivation and value-orientation of policemen.

10. Priorities in law enforcement and role of personal discretions.

11. Level of professionalism and organisational development and level of commitment.

12. Organisational health and discipline.

Never was the need for training brought out better than in the police failures in the last few years.[24] Aberrations of police behaviour are generally the following:-

(a) Misbehaviour with complainants; (b) Misbehaviour with people of low status; poor economic background and weaker sections; (c) Illegal detentions; (d) custodial violence and rape; (e) Burking of crime; (f) false implication of innocents; (g) Fabrication of false evidence; (h) Excess during crowd control and anti-insurgency operations; (i) Corruption and nepotism; (j) Nexus with criminal and politicians; (k) Organisational deviance and false encounters, (l) Ill-treatment with women; (m) Succumbing to political interference (n) indifference & dereliction in normal duties. It is a very long list and good training alone cannot change the behaviour pattern of the police in India.

Appraisal of Police Performance

A study carried out by Shri J.P. Singh, Prof. Organisational Behaviour, Indian Institute of Management, Ahmedabad about police performance indicates that Police performance in its various dimensions varies as shown in Figure-1 below:-

Figures showing Police Performance & Perceived percentage of police effort spent on various job dimensions.

Very Effective	5		
		4.61 Providing VIP Security	2%
		4.15 Maintaining law & order	48%
Somewhat effective	4		
		3.46 Gathering intelligence	10%
		3.38 Preventing & Detecting crime	30%
Neither Effective nor ineffective	3		
		2.69 Social Legislation enforcement.	5%
		2.31 Enforcing rule of law	5%
Somewhat Ineffective	2		
Very Ineffective	1		
			100%

Since the above Performance appraisal is based on the collective thinking of only 13 Police officers who had gathered for a training programme from all over the country it has very limited validity and the five-point effectiveness scale given in the figure can be easily contested by Police officers who are in the field. The study has limited scope. The author has also indicated the extend of undesirable behaviour prevailing in the Police force giving perceived public image and perceived self assessment[25] as given in the table showing ranking.

Table 1

Rank	*Perceived Public image*	*Rank*	*Self-Assessment*
I	Corruption in Police force	I	Pilability to political whims.
II	Pilability to political whims	II	Time taken in disposal of complaints.
III	Highhanded behaviour and public harassment	III	Criminality in police force.
IV	Lack of fairness in disposal of complaints	IV	Highhanded behaviour and harassment of public.
V	Time taken in investigating crime	V	Lack of human respect in handling crowds.
VI	Time taken for disposal of complaints	VI	Suppression of crime.
VII	Lack of human respect in handling crowds	VII	Corruption in police force
VIII	Suppression and minimization of offences	VIII	Time taken in investigating offences
IX	Lack of courtesy in treatment of complainants.	IX	Lack of fairness in disposal of complaints
X	Criminality in police force	X	Lack of courtesy to complainants.

Above given undesirable behaviour helps us in identifying areas where training is needed for improving performance. The matrix given in the coming page gives a non clear picture.

MATRIX REGARDING IMPROVING PERFORMANCE THROUGH TRAINING

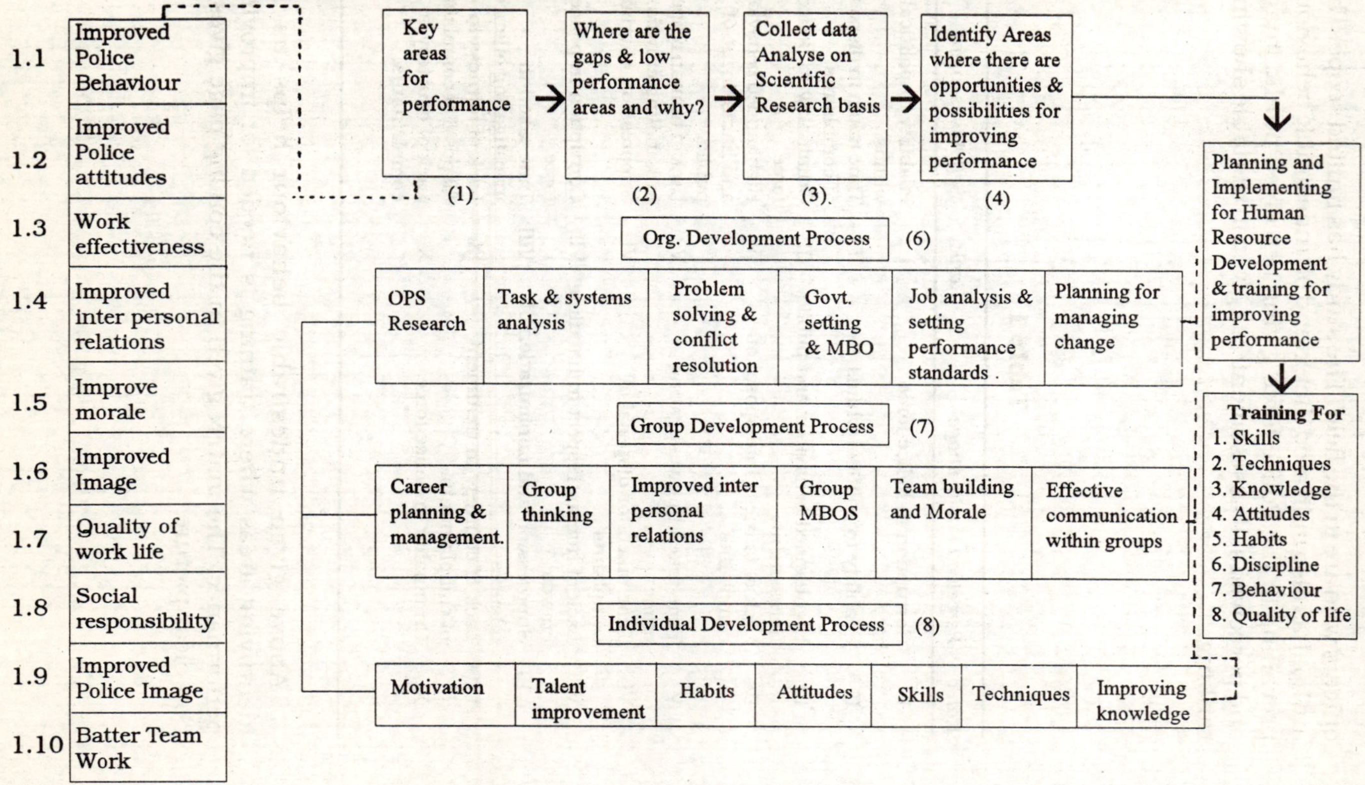

Case Studies of Successful Police Performance and Areas for Improvement

For effective and proper evaluation of police performance both Micro and Macro level case studies are needed. India has 25 States and 7 Union Territories and Police performance at both Micro and Macro level give a picture of both success and failure on the part of the Police. Generally police successes go unrecognised and unrecorded. There are many areas of police performance like prevention of crimes, collection of intelligence, surveil lance which cannot be noticed by a normal citizen. Generally many good works done by the Police goes un-noticed. In Bihar on April 13 at least 11 extremists of the Maoist Communits Centre (MCC) were killed in a gun battle with the police at Madgarh village in Gaya district in which eight policemen were also injured. In the 'Operation Flushout' the Bihar Police seized a cache of arms and ammunition. The Police had launched the operation Flushout in the Central Bihar Country side on April 7 ' 94 following a series of massacres by armed MCC Squads in the villages of Jehanabad and Gaya District. This incident indicates the effective performance of Bihar Police. In another incident on April 13 in U.P. a 12 year old boy, nephew of the BJP Meerut Cantt, MLA was rescued by the police after an encounter in which three of his kidnappers were gunned down by the police. SSP Mr. B.S. Sidhu said "his men encircled the kidnappers after a long chase, opened effective fire and killed three offenders. The kidnappers were demanding a sum of Rs. 50, 000/- from the parents of the boy". In another report the U.P Police killed in an encounter a dreaded criminal, Mahinder Fauji who has 52 cases against him including kidnapping, murder and dacoity in Bulandshar district.

It is a matter of great satisfaction for all the citizens of India that Indian Police, consisting of CRP, BSF, State Police and other security forces could completely control and contain the terrorism of Punjab, Naxalism in West Bengal and many other serious law and order situations in other parts of the country. It has so far successfully conducted all the elections both for Lok Sabha and State Legislature with great success in spite of being a very demanding and challenging task (Mathur 1994). Thousands of such successful cases can be listed where police has performed its job extremely well. The above mentioned three cases have been taken from one 'Hindu' of 14th April 1994. If cases of all good works done of a year are collected the list can be quite impressive. Such good cases must be highlighted in the press. Indian Police must do some serious self introspection to improve its images by controlling its temper during provocations and by eschewing mal-practices. There is however great need to eschew the following mal-practices:

(i) Third degree method of investigations.

(ii) Ill-treatment of persons given to police custody.

(iii) Padding, concoction and fabrication of evidence in investigation.

(iv) Burking and minimisation of offences.

(v) Partisan attitude during riots and disturbances.

(vi) Nexus with criminals, smugglers and other anti social elements.

(vii) Corruption and extortion of money from small shop-keepers and people of ordinary means.

(viii) Arrogance and trigger happy attitude.

(ix) Excessive and unjustified use of force.

(x) Dereliction & neglect of duty and non-performance of duty.

Training for Improving Performance and Areas for Consideration

Committee on Police Training (Gore Committee has suggested the following considerations in the training of the Police.[26]

(1) Loyalty to the Constitution, commitment to the goals of the nation and the concept of an egalitarian society and the need for national integration.

(2) Awareness of the problems that arise in the wake of the developmental process including conflicts, social disorganisation, scarcity and control, regional imbalances etc.

(3) A deep social awareness for comprehending and reacting to complex situations.

(4) Development of analytical and innovative skills since situations will continue to change and no readymade solutions can be prescribed.

(5) A new orientation in dealing with masses, who come from various strata of society.

(6) Need for the application of scientific techniques, management concepts and skills and constructive attitude and values in police work.

According to Japanse "ZEN approach " the purpose of training is continuous improvement in the performance of whatever one does.[27] In Police Organisations all ranks should regularly undergo periodical refresher training. The trainers should explain the trainees,"why the activity is performed, demonstrate it, have trainees practical it under supervision and criticise the performance until it is mastered.[28] According to I.L.O. document "Training challenge of the 1980s", training is an important key to unlocking the potential for an improved quality of life. Even after two decades of the Gore Committee recommendations, there is no noticeable change in the police performance for the better. Indiscipline and even criminality in police appears to be increasing.[29] There were 69 custodial deaths in 1990, 50 in 1991, 58 in 1992. Cases of policemen involved in rape cases were 37 in 1990 and 83 in 1992.It is ironic and tragic that in the hallowed land of Gautam Buddha and Mahatma Gandhi, even after fortyfive years of independence, Police stand in the dock charged with deviance, marginal crime, brutalities, illegalities and crime against humanity, often committed by the educated police officers under the mistaken zeal of protecting the society or righting the crime.[30] A research survey carried out by the author reveals that people are not satisfied by the performance of the police. Reasons given by the respondents for unsatisfactory police performance are given below in tabulated form[31]:

Table showing reasons for unsatisfactory Police Performance

Sl.No.	*Replies of respondents*	*Number*	*Percentage*
1.	Police has too much corruption	45	21.43%
2.	Behaviour with people is not good and courteous	39	18.58%
3.	Police is indifferent towards public	25	11.90%
4.	Police is not duty conscious	28	13.33%
5.	All reasons enumerated above	73	34.76%
	Total replies received	210	100.00%

The researcch survey carried out by the author indicated that 60.48 percent respondents considered police image as "Very poor" while 27.62 percent considered it satisfactory. Police image closely follows police performance. Police has been subjected to political pulls and pressures. In a 'soft state', collusion between police officers and power elites create a phenomenon of social indiscipline and a general attitude of disregard for laws and rules. Political and administrative manipulations of the police have damaged its image and completely eroded its political neutrality.[32] The capacity of police officers to resist its misuse depends on the quality of its personnel, their training and general organisational climate. Misuse of state intelligence agencies by politicians in power can be curbed only when police leadership is of high calibre and moral courage. Training can play only a marginal role.

Training as a Concept

Training is a deliberate and planned process of teaching and learning wherein knowledge, skills, techniques, attitudes and experiences are acquired by the trainees with the help and guidance of the trainers in a given learning environment. Training represents an intervention strategy with, inter alia, the following overall objects, namely: (a) checking and preventing obsolescence at both organisational and individual levels; (b) Curing pre-active shortcomings of knowledge and professional skills, techniques and procedures, (c) shaping and making adjustments with fast changing socio-technological, environmental changes and demands; (d) promoting and developing new outlook, and ethnological version of quality, excellence and accomplishment in one's profession; (e) transforming and making a total man with new professional and cultural attributes and vision; (f) providing the opportunities for the fullest development of the individuals and the organisation over a period of time. Training is a continuous and systematic development of individuals and training generally include the following (a) Basic training at the induction level, (b) Individual skills and job-training, (c) specialised training, (d) Promotional training (e) Collective training (f) Reorientation training (h) Refresher training/ Rotational Training.

Training, particularly in police organisations has to focus on improved performance and actual training to deal with various complex situations. Training has to be goal-oriented with emphasis on self-motivation of the trg. Training in Police should be based on "action-learning". State Police Organisations and Central Police Organisations should reorganise and restructure their training efforts for improving their performance and behaviour. Training is a continuous process and a organised system of rational arrangements of inputs, technology, people, material, events and processes designed to elicit behavioural outputs which produce further social and economic outputs increasing organisational effectiveness and efficient organisational people. Training as a system has the following components as given in the figure below:-

FIGURE 1
COMPONENTS OF A TRAINING SYSTEM

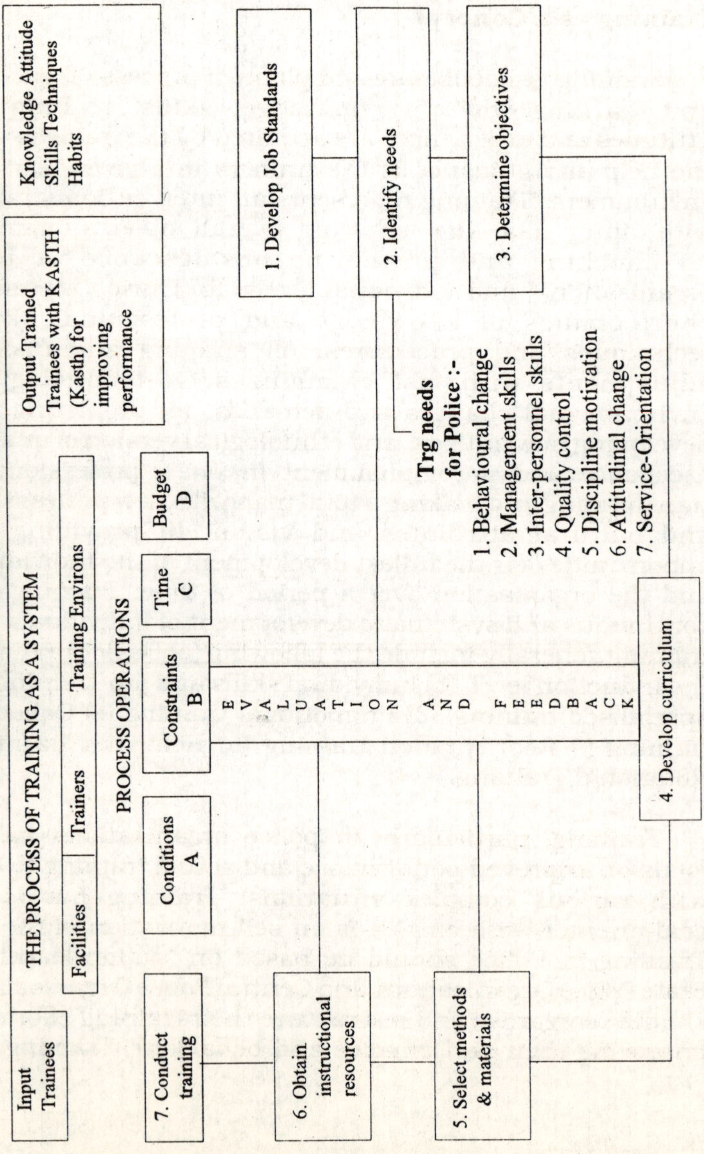

The methodology of training in police has to be used as correctives to behavioural tendencies which may be unconsistent with the present day needs. Similarly the environmental distortions and the psychological shortcomings in any class of policemen will have to be discovered and corrected during the course of training.[33] All this will require the building up of police training institutions on uptodate modern scientific lines with dedicated and qualified faculty members and experts of criminology, psychology, behavioural sciences and management as permanent members of the staff. It is only then that better results can be expected. Since the levels of political, social, economic and technological awareness of the people will be higher in the twenty first century. Police Organisations will have to improve quality of training, level of police effectiveness and quality of work life. For twenty-first century, better commitment to the values of life, more effective managerial skills and more humane treatment to the people by the PMF is expected through more realistic and job-enriched training. Training for Central Police Organisations will have to include quality of work life (QML) programmes so that police personnel develop knowledge, attitudes, skills, techniques and habits that will make them more professional, more committed to perform their tasks and jobs in an appropriate manner. The future challenges of twenty first century can be efficiently handled by the Central Police Organisations and State Police should prepare themselves for the challenges and equip themselves with appropriate technology skills and knowledge. Each Central Police Organisation/ State Police will have to identify its goals and missions for the twenty first century and thereby identify the development needs of the people in the organisation. Organisational development and individual development will have to be planned as suggested in Figure-2.

FIGURE-2

H. R. D. FOR IMPROVING PERFORMANCE

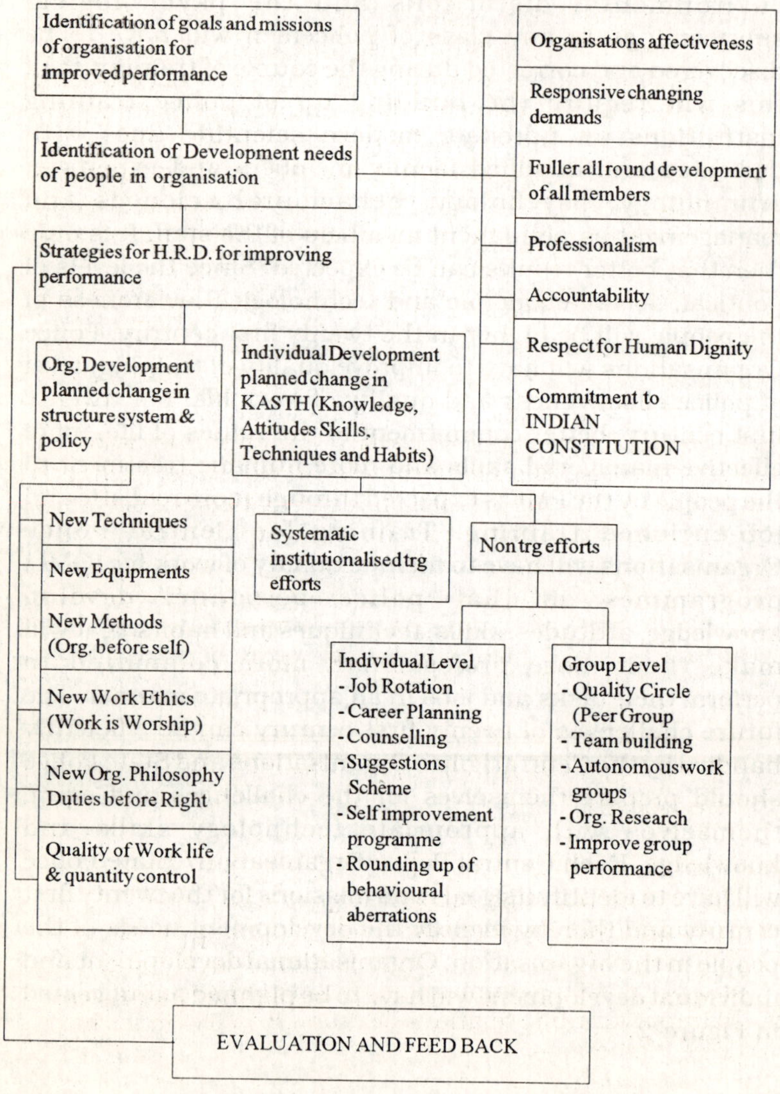

The Thrust Areas for Police Training

For 21st Century, Indian police must train and prepare itself to provide total service of the highest quality to the community by effective, efficient and good quality policing. (GQP). For achieving good quality policy (GQP) the values, the roles, motivation, rewards and intricate net-work or relationship that comprise law enforcement must be strategically and systematically transformed to make police service, democratic, professional, humane and pro-active in police operations.[34] The concepts and practices of Quality circle recognised that people are "Number one resources" of an Organisation and performance of the Organisation is determined by the ability and motivation of the individuals and effectiveness of their working in teams. Police leaders have to recognise that "social and psychological factors influenced performance and productivity more than the physical working condition".[35] In order to achieve quality of work life, the entire range of Indian thoughts from Rigveda to Bhagavadgeeta highlight that the most super-ordinate character of work ethnic is sacrifice with a sense of devotion to one's duty. The Indian psycho philosophy provides the following three guidelines on how to work,[36] "Yogastha Kuru Karmani (perform your duties dwelling in yoga relinquishing attachment)-Yogah Karmasu Kaushalam (skill in action lies in the practice of Yoga)- Tasmat Sarveshu Kaleshu Yoga Yukta bhavurjuma (at all times be established in Yoga in the form of equanimity)"

The concepts of quality circle should be applied in police with the following aims.[37]

"(i) Team work
(ii) Motivation (through recognition)
(iii) Opportunities for development of leadership at all levels.
(iv) Promote participative culture leading to advantageous and purposeful communication within the police.
(v) To improve public relations because, quality circles have three elements—
    (a) Quality
    (b) Customer orientation
    (c) Respect for humanity".

Such quality circles in police organisations will safeguard and "protect human Rights and will stop all abuses & violations of human rights. Public interest litigation is a challenge and opportunity to the police to make basic human rights meaningful to the deprived and vulnerable sections of the society and assure them social and economic justice which is the basis of our constitution.[38]

Future Training Requirements

Some of the important focus area for police training can be as under:-

(1) Removing the traditional and outdated culture of secrecy surrounding the police agencies and opening its operations upto the public as far as possible keeping in view the national interests.

(2) Bringing about radical changes in present performance appraisal systems and bringing in modern systems and bringing in modern approach to evaluation in performance assessment of personnel;

(3) Improving internal communications through informal open staff meetings; employee involvement in planning and implementation activities;

(4) Establishing more healthy and national personnel policies and allocating more resources to human resource development.

(5) Building up police as a human service agency rather than a criminal justice agency by revolutionalising its working philosophy and objectives;

(6) Allowing all ranks of police to go in for more correspondence courses in liberal education by providing study leaves and educational grants;

(7) Developing a system where all ranks get atleast one promotion after every ten years of service and thereby allowing police personnel to go up in the ladder.

(8) Providing better motivational strategies and reducing organisational rigidities.

(9) Building up a more relaxed, humane and democratic work environment which will reduce job-stress and provide better job satisfaction to the police personnel.

(10) Immediate and full implementation of all recommendations of Gore Committee on Police Training and National Police Commission. It will include modernisation of Police, building up of good Police Public Relations, adequate housing and welfare facilities for the Police personnel and better working conditions.

(11) To improve systems of selection recruitment, promotion, training and rewards so that police personnel improve their quality of life.

(12) Taking up "Organisational Development" and thereby bringing quantitative as well as qualitative positive changes in work environment and work-culture.

(13) Modernisation, specialisation, and professionalism must be accepted as necessary requirements of police organisation.

(14) Police should be an integral part of the National Planning process and long term perspective planning for policing the future to meet the emerging challenges of 1990s must be worked out by the police leaders, social scientists and HRD consultants in consultation with States and Central Government and multi-prolonged attempts should be made to develop the human resources available to the police organisations of the Country.

(15) There is an urgent need for disciplining police today. The cumulative effect of the law's indifference decline in the influence of the senior officers, and the new assertiveness of the lower ranks is promoting indiscipline and the use of unfair methods to control crime. Both police morale and discipline are required to be maintained at very high levels.

Constraints and Limitations of Training

As Lynton and Pareek have noted: "The training apparatus and its costs have multiplied but not the benefits".[39] Even the severest critics of training will readily admit that "while training can not guarantee success, its absence greatly increases the likelihood of failure".[40] Training is an essential input for improving performance. Training is neither a panecea for all ills nor it is a waste of time.[41] There is a need for a far greater understanding of training in its wide sense and in all its forms; to know when training can help and when it cannot; what type may be appropriate, how to improve its effectiveness and the reasons why training has produced such disappointing results over the past ten to twenty years.[42] It is not realised adequately that change in attitudes and behaviour can not be easily brought about by a training effort alone.[43] Gore Committee on Police Training has rightly observed that training is only one of the important factors which determine the efficiency and effectiveness of an organisation. The expectation that training can cure all the problems of an organisation is unrealistic as there are many factors that training can not remedy.[44] Training can not neutralise unwise promotions or ineffective methods of work nor can it replace intelligent supervision, favourable organisational conditions, individual willingness to accept responsibility. Training alone can not bring and sustain attitudinal change and behavioural modifications unless organisational climate, environmental conditions and organisational structural system can further support and nurture such changes. Organisational climate can create an environment which could sustain attitudinal developments and rectifications of aberrations of police behaviour. Administrative deficiencies, role dilemma, systems defects and resources inadequacy are four maladies which can not be cured by police training alone.[45] Lack of motivation and behavioural aberrations of the police personnel are areas where training can play a positive role only when organisational climate and working environment can provide positive reinforcement and desirable institutional support. "Training programmes do not solve such administrative deficiencies as defective administrative structure, cumbersome rules and procedures, lack of resources and so forth".[46] Training is a limited instrument.

It is just one piece in the puzzle for improving performance. Other pieces of the puzzle must be secured and put into place.[47]

Training is also not able to improve performance of police officers because in most of the training institutions, it is conducted in an unsatisfactory manner. The majority of police training programmes are superficial, rushed, poorly conducted and managed, often establishing a negative attitude towards job and society. Police Trainers have hardly any interdisciplinary approach and most of them are not qualified as trainers. As rightly observed by Shri D. C. Nath-the biggest casualty in the training institutions is the selection of faculty members. Most often those who should be kept far away from police training find place in training institutions".[48] There is at present a very wide gap between what is expected of police performance in the field and what is really being taught in police training institutions. Linkage failure makes trainees unprepared for role conflicts, work pressures and vested interests which they face in real life situations.[49] The effectiveness of police training also depends on other factors as level of motivation & morale in the police, organisational culture, leadership and value profile of superior officers, politico-legal framework and environmental factors.

Area for Improving Police Performance—Training Needs

1. Police Behavioural modification

Police Behaviour in India needs modifications and radical changes in view of the democratic, pluralistic nature of Indian society. Police should shed off its negative patterns of behaviour and should adopt positive patterns of behaviour as given below:-

Negative behaviour to Positive behaviour

1. Reactive response	—	Positive proactive response.
2. Indifferent attitude	—	Sympathetic attitude.
3. Corrupt practices	—	Honest and upright practices.
4. Brutal behaviour & use of third degree mehtods of interrogati on.	—	Courteous and police behaviour and use of scientific methods of interrogation.

5. Violations of human Rights.	—	Respect and protection of human rights
6. Biased & Partisan attitude during communal riots & other law & order situations.	—	Impartial & fair attitude during communal riots & other law and order situations.
7. Abusive & indecent language & gestures	—	Decent and respectful
8. Aggressive and hostile behaviour	—	Courteous and considerate behaviour.

2. Motivation and Reinforcement for good performance.

3. Internal Security management including anti-terrorist operations, psychological warfare, VVIP security, handling of riots and disturbances should get its due importance.

4. Crime prevention and crime control should get their proper places in police performance priorities.

5. Enforcement of social legislations should make police an agent of social change.

6. Building up good public relations and winning the confidence and spontaneous support of the citizens should get the highest priorities in police performance.

7. Police force will have to imbibe a culture of "service" to the weaker sections of the society to the needy & poor, to the old and handicapped and to the common man. Police have to develop "Service-orientation".

8. For improving police performance in rural areas rural policing should be increased in strength and quality.[50] Police stations all over the country need restructuring and more physical facilities.

9. Modernisation, better weapons, better equipment and communication system, better transport facilities and sound personnel policies can enable police personnel to improve their performance both in terms of quality and quantity.

10. Only better quality of intake of police personnel can improve police performance because police performance depends largely on the quality of police personnel selected and recruited in the form at various levels. Training, motivational techniques of police leaders, environment factors and organisational culture are important factors effecting police performance.

11. Police performance can not improve unless police personnel are provided adequate housing facilities, better motivation to work and better working and living conditions. The National Police Commission has rightly observed a mere change in the training schedule will not bring about the necessary improvement in their motivation or performance unless some more serious deficiencies in their living and working conditions which have long been neglected are immediately taken up and remedied. Organisational and procedural reforms should be made for modernisation of police organisations, police equipment, police training, police system in the context of newer challenges of development and change.[51]

12. The Police should formally participate in Community planning in all cities and towns.

Recommendations for Effective Training for Improving Performance

1. Suitable officers of the Police Organisations should regularly be sent abroad for training so that they may widen with their vision outlook and mental horizon and benefit for specialised training programmes of various training institutions abroad.

2. Many training institutions of police are having specialised training programmes. Course capacity of such programmes should be fully utilized by deputing officers of other police organisations.

3. There should be more free flow and exchange of faculty staff between different training instituions.

4. Research on various problems and challenges of the police should be conducted by the universities and all CPO academies should be recognised research centres for enabling M. Phil. & Ph. D. students to carry out research on both conceptual and operational problem areas. Bureau of Police Research and Development has already started Ph. D. research fellowship scheme but more fellowship should be made available.

5. BPR&D should start an audio-visual and film making department by hiring specialists so that training films may be produced for various police training institutions.

6. Vertical interaction programme should have regular interactions with the officers of Central Police Organisations so that they feel more integrated with the State Police Officers and more cordial understanding may emerge.

7. Training literature produced by various Central Police Organisations should be freely exchanged with State Police and such training material must be properly documented, evaluated and improved upon with the assistance of research scholars and universities.

8. Correspondence course should be started by the Training Directorate of Police Organisations for their officers and men so that their knowledge is kept uptodate.

9. Regular training seminars, and conferences should be organised on all India level to identify new areas for research and study. Officers of Central Police Organisations and State Police Organisations should jointly conduct training symposium, seminars and workshops on regional basis to enable greater participation from officers.

10. Centres for Excellence in various fields of training should be created in police organisations with adequate infrastructure and motivated facility members.

11. Training of Police officers should aim at improving the performance and developing a total man with a new cultural attributes operating in the realm of personality, character and behaviour and thus serve the people of India as truly "Peoples' Police" ensuring a mutually supportive police-public relationship with a firm commitment to secularism, socialism, democracy, social justice and modernisation. Career management of all ranks of various Police Organisations on scientific lines should be ensured by deputing them regularly on various earmarked courses. Career planning and training have to be harmonised in all the Police Organisations.

12. Police training, as is done today in India, certainly needs to shift its gears in a big way so that it may properly focus on improving police performance and prepare the Indian Police to meet the complex challenges of the twenty-first century.

REFERENCES

1. Peter Drucker — *The Practice of Management* (New York, Harper and Row , 1954) P-182.

2. Charles Lindblom — *The Policy-Making Process* (Englewood Cliffs, N.J. Prentice Hall, 1980).

3. Krishna Mohan Mathur — *Policing for Internal Security-Administrative Change* - Jaipur, Vol. XIX, No. 1-2, July 1991-June 1992, P-89.

4. Krishna Monan Mathur — *Police, Law and Internal Security*, New Delhi, Gian Publishing House, 1994, P-19.

5. T.A. Critchley — *A History of Police in England and Wales*, 1972, P-47-50.

6. David H. Bayley—*Forces of Order-Police Behaviour in Japan and United States*, California, 1976-P-195.

7. Krishna Mohan Mathur—*Police Laws and Internal Security*, Gian Publishing House, New Delhi, 1994, P 22-23.

8. Goldstein H—*Policing a Free Society*, Cambridge, (1977). Improving Policing, a problem oriented approach. Crime and delinquency (1979) 25, 236, 258.

9. Stepher Mastrofski — *Police knowledge of the Patrol Beat* —A performance Measure in Police at work. Policy Issues and Analysis (Edited) Richard R. Bennett. Sage Publications, New Delhi, 1983, P-45.

10. Krishna Mohan Mathur — *Indian Police Role and Challenges*, Gian Publishing House, New Delhi, 1994, P-286.

11. From Principles of Police Conduct quoted in the report of the Delhi Police Commission 1966-68. Ministry of Home Affairs, Govt. of India.

12. P.D. Sharma—*Police, Polity and People in India*, Uppal Publishing House, New Delhi, 1981.

13. Carl Wetherman and Irwing Piliavin Gang Members and the Police, Berkeley, 1967.

14. Improving the Organisation and Administration of Agricultural Development in the Near East-Report of a Regional Expert Committee held in Nicoisia, Cyprus, Dec. 1980, Rome FAO, 1981, P-89.

15. Hull C. L. *Principles of Behaviour* (1943), Behaviour postulates and corollaries (1950) Essentials of Behaviour 1951-New Haven, Yak University Press.

16. Justice S. Natrajan - *Evaluation of Police Performance —Indian Police Journal* , Vol. XXXVI, No.4, October-December 1989, P-46.

17. M.H.A. G.O.I Report of the Committee on Police Training (M.S. Gore) P-115.

18. R.S. Kulkarni-*Training at the grass root level in the Police department-in Training in Government*—objectives and opportunities-Edited by A.P. Saxena-Indian Institute of Public Administration, New Delhi, 1985. pp. 212-217.

19. Fifth Report of the National Police Commission, Govt. of India November 1980, P-48.

20. See Krishna Mohan Mathur—*Swatantra Bharat Mei Janata Ka-Dauitwa Aur Police Ki Bhoomika* (1991) - BPR&D MHA Publication 1991, P-267.

21. Krishna Mohan Mathur —*Swatantra Bharat Mein Janta Ka Dauitwa Aur Police Ki Bhoomika* (1991), P-267.

22. Justice S. Natrajan — *Evaluating Police Performance Indian Police Journal,* Oct-Dec, 1989-Vol. XXXVI No. 4, P-43.

23. See K.M. Mathur, *Police in India—Problems and Perspectives*-Gian Publishing House, Delhi 1991, P-306-307.

24. K.F. Rustomji—*The Imperatives of Training.* SVP NPA Magazine Jan-June, 1993, P-4.

25. J.P. Singh — *Effectiveness of Police performance*—Indian Police Journal, Vol XXXVI, No. 1, January- March 1989, P-10.

26. Ministry of Home Affairs G.O.I — Report of the Committee on Police Training, P-115.

27. Parkinson and Rustomji — *Realities in Management.* P. 88-89.

28. Koontz and O Donnel —*Management. A system and contingency Analysis of Managerial functions,* P-522.

29. Dr. K.M. Mathur — *Concerns and constraints in Administration* — RBSA Publishers, Jaipur, 1991, P-193.

30. K.M. Mathur — *Indian Police Role and Challenges*, Gian Publishing House, New Delhi, 1994, P-68.

31. For further details see research survey in Dr. Krishna Mohan Mathur— *Swatantra Bharat Mein Janata Ka Dauitwa Aur Police Ki Bhoomika* (Hindi) Bureau of Police Research and Development, MHA New Delhi-1991P.267.

32. For further study see — K.N. Prasad-*Political and Administrative Manipulation of the Police*, Bureau of Police Research and Development New Delhi , March , 1979.

33. Govind Narain—*Training the Police for better performance-The Indian Police Journal* , Vol. XXVII, No.1, July-September, 1980, P.10.

34. Dr. K.M. Mathur — *Indian Police—Role and Challenges*, Gyan Publishing House, New Delhi, 1994 P.286.

35. Mayo E. *The Human Problems of an Industrial Civilization*, New York, MacMillan, 1933.

36. S.K. Chakraborty— *Managerial effectiveness and Quality of work life, Indian Insight*, Tata Mc Graw Hill, 1987.

37. T. Ananthachari— *Quality Circle-An Instrument to Improve Police Efficiency*. The Indian Police Journal, Vol.XXXX , No.1, January , June 1993, P.22.

38. Chief Justice P.N. Bhagwati in *Bandhna Mukti Morcha* Vs Union of India AIR, 1984, SC 803.

39. Roy P. Lynton and Udai Pareek —*Training for Development*. Illnois, 1973, P.3.

40. Paper from a Common Wealth Workshop Colombo Srilanka 1979, London. Common Wealth Secretariat 1980-P.9.

41. Lynton and Pareek—Training for Development p.4.

42. Wym Reilly—*Training administrators for Development*. London Heineman, 1973,p.2-3.

43. Hari Mohan Mathur—Some avil service attitudes inappropriate in the Development Context—Using Training as a correctional Device—Proceedings of the Annual Conference on Training, New Delhi GOI MHA., 1976.

44. Report of the Committee on Police Training-MHA GOI, P.13.

45. Dr. K.M. Mathur—*Administration of Police Training in India*, Gian Publishing House, New Delhi, 1987, P.44.

46. Carlos P Ramos— "*Identifying Training Needs and methods in the context of Management Development in Inayatullah ed.* Management Training for Development: The Asian experience (Kuala Lampur-The Asian Centre for Development Administration, 1975), P.234.

47. Ali Berkman—"Comments" in Swerdlow and Ingle-Public Administration Training for the less Developed Countires, P.69.

48. D.C. Nath-Police Training-Thrust Areas-SVP NPA Magazine, Vol. 45 No. 1, Jan-June, 1993, P.18.

49. For Evaluation of Police training see Dr. K.M. Mathur. *Administration of Police Training in India*, Gian Publishing House, New Delhi, 1987 PP. 246-248.

50. K.M. Mathur — *Police, Law and Internal Security*, Gian Publishing House, New Delhi , 1994, p.319.

51. Dr. K.M. Mathur, *Internal Security Challenges and Police in a Developing Society*, RBSA Publishers, Jaipur, 1989, P.274.

3

Rural Unrest and Agrarian Movement in India

During the last four decades, there have been growing tensions among different social groups especially in the rural areas which are manifested in the form of protests, movements, conflicts and violence. There is an urgent need to critically examine the nature, magnitude and coverage of rural tensions in depth with a view to studying the social problems manifested in them and to suggest remedial measures at the policy level so as to minimise rural tensions. In India there are nearly 5,75,936 villages out of which 3,18, 633 villages have a population of less than 500 people and the rest have a population of over 5000 people although there has been a steady exodus of the village population into towns and cities. According to the latest 1991 Census 74.3 percentage of the population in India is Rural and 25.7 percent is urban in nature. In rural India one can easily find the yawning gap between the rich landed classes and the landless or the marginal peasant classes. Rural unrest is generally manifested in various caste conflicts, atrocities on weaker sections of the society, party conflicts or factional fights between various group of people in rural areas of the Country. During the last three decades the profile of rural society in India is fast changing and the rural India is gradually becoming a vast cauldron of boiling lava of tensions, antagonisms and conflicts. In rural India, adult franchise, rural development programmes and the dialectical inter-connection between the various sectors of the social structure such as class, caste, politics, education, culture etc. have started a fundamental process of agrarian transformation at a very high rate resulting in a gigantic upheaval. Introduction of the Panchyat Raj, extension and improvement of agricultural techniques and expansion of roads, railway tracks, measures of land reforms and developmental programmes of rural areas have brought about a new mass awakening in rural India. The persistence of serious-economic inequalities, creation of a new political dynamics of power and ineffective implementation of land reforms have given rise to rural unrest.

In rural India, land is the most important factor in the socio-economic power structure. According to the 43rd round (1987-88) of the National Sample Survey Organisation approximately 33 percent of the population in rural areas is generally landless, unemployed and poverty-striken, living below the poverty line. Forty percent of the rural households at the bottom own five percent of the assets as against the top five percent who own about 46 percent of the assets. All India report on Agricultural Census (1985-86) says that the marginal farmers who constitute 59 percent of the total farmers, operate only 13 percent of the total area. Scheduled Castes constitute only about 12 percent of the total farmers and are dominated by sub-marginal farmers who operate only 7.7 percent of the total area. In India 23 percent of the total households are agricultural labourers who get less than 180 days of employment in a year.

Peasants Movement in India

It can be broadly divided into five phases—

1. The Initial Phase (1857-1921)— sporadic growth of peasant movements in the absence of proper leadership.

2. The Second Phase (1923-1946)— marked by emergence of the class conscious peasants- it was led by people who gave priority to Kisan problems in the struggle for national liberation.

3. Post Independence Phase (1947-1967)— failure of Ruling party to resolve the basic problems of toiling rural masses. :-

   (a) Awareness and feeling of power.
   (b) Involvement. Political Motivation.

4. The Phase of Armed Revolt & political protests-Led by predominantly left Political parties like CPI (ML), CPI characterised by high level of politicalisation.

5. The Fifth Phase can be broadly termed as reorganisation of middle class and rich peasants to extract political mileage from their peasant movement.

Above classification of agrarian movement of peasants is very broad since various agrarian movements are generally politically motivated and do not really represent the genuine interests of the rural poor.

Peasant movements and uprisings after 1857 (particularly Indigo revolt of 1859-60 in Bengal) and agrarian unrest during the 1870s and early 1880s are all part of India's struggle for Independence and a very authentic account is available in Bipin Chandra's book India's struggle for Independence.

Peasant movements in the 1930s and 1940s brought a new and nation-wide awakening of Indian peasants to their own strength and capacity to organise for the betterment of their living conditions. It covered large areas of the country particularly U.P., Maharashtra, Punjab, Kerala (Malabar), Andhra Pradesh, Bihar and Bengal, The main focus was on mobilisation through meetings, demonstrations and rallies, involvement of members in Kisan Sabhas.[1] According to

Dr. Sunil K. Sen, Professor of History, Ravindra Bharati University "The peasant movement has come face to face with a dilemma that arises out of the increasing penetrationof capitalism in agriculture" and state intervention is of crucial importance.[2] The CPI launched Bhartiya Khet Majdoor Union in 1968 and by 1975 Khet Majdoor unions had been formed in most of the states and the membership had increased from about four lakhs in 1970 to more than one million in 1975-76. The agricultural labourers hardly organised wage struggle in U.P., Haryana, M.P., Rajasthan, Gujrat, Karnataka & Assam although wages remained low in these regions. In fact minimum wage legislation was not enforced in most of the States.[3] This is a potentially important area which needs our attention and concern. "It was in the Mahatma Gandhi era that the Congress embarked upon peasant mobilisation. The general spirit of defiance of authority generated by the nationalist movement from 1920 onwards and the Gandhi's charisma surely promoted the growth of peasant movement almost throughout the country. The techniques of peasant mobilisation evolved by Gandhi—meetings, processions, signature campaign, Satyagraha—corresponded to the agrarian programme of the Congress that included reduction in rent and revenue, abolition of feudal dues and levies, fixity of tenure and moratorism on debts".[4]

During 1965 to 1975 the land struggle was simultaneously launched in fifteen states in which peasants occupied hundreds of acres of land. The land struggle gave a big push to the agrarian movement and brought the question of land reforms again to the forefront.

Land Struggle

States	Number arrested	Number killed	Area of land occupied (Acres)
1	2	3	4
1. West Bengal	5000	14	27800
2. Bihar	3137	3	35365
3. Tamil Nadu	13500	-	-
4. Uttar Pradesh	10000	5	26500
5. Punjab	7000	1	-
6. Maharashtra	7000	-	23000
7. Andhra Pradesh	9241	1	97600
8. Orissa	778	2	20800
9. Assam	-	-	50000
10. Rajasthan	2500	-	45000
11. Madhya Pradesh	1626	-	5000
12. Haryana	275	-	500
13. Karnataka	85	-	1000
14. Gujarat	1017	-	-
15. Tripura	-	-	400
16. Himachal Pradesh	56	-	1700

Food shortage and rising food prices, coming in the wake of stagnation in agriculture hit the rural poor in 1963-64; food riots occurred in towns and villages while the landlords and traders made bay.[5] In 1968-69 the agrarian struggle spread to Assam, Andhra, Bihar, Kerala, Madhya Pradesh and Orissa. According to report of the Ministry of Home Affairs 1970, the following breakup of the cases of occupation of land was reported for the States: Assam (5), Andhra (5), Bihar (3), Gujrat (1), Kerala (3), Madhya Pradesh (5), Maharashtra (1), Mysore (1), Manipur (1), Orissa (3), Punjab (3), Rajasthan (2), Tamil Nadu (2), Tripura (1), Uttar Pradesh(5), The main form of the struggle was occupation by hundred of peasants of forest land and government land. The Home Ministry came to the conclusion that land reforms had not benefited the actual tiller, share croppers had no security of tenure and were forced to pay exorbitant rent. It was conceded that development programme "so far implemented was still more favourable to the large owner-farmer than to the small tenant farmer; the share-cropper and the landless labourer have been more often than not, left out in the cold". The report noted that "disparities have widened, accentuating social tensions". The single biggest issue on which the peasants launched a series of movements throughout the Country since independence was "Land Reforms". The Ceiling laws passed by the state governments were successfully sabotaged by the vested interests.

In our contemporary society, rural unrest is evident in atrocities on weaker caste clusters in villages and in machoistic sexual exploitation of women in rural areas. The abolition of zamindari system, the decline of feudalism and the classical caste system in rural areas and the rapid socio-economic-political changes are producing unsettling effects on vast masses of rural population and throwing up uncouth and inadequately socialized political elites. Panchayat Raj institutions have unleashed the arrested processes of growth and change in villages of India. As an instrument of developmental[6] Panchayat Raj system generated factors and forces which lead to fresh tensions and new disorders, political and social.[7] The law and order situations in rural areas have deteriorated in the wake of introduction of Panchayat Raj bodies due to the following reasons:-

(a) Lack of respect for government authority.
(b) Negligence on the part of government officials.
(c) Over aspirations of emerging elite groups.
(d) Informal relations with policemen.
(e) Being the vote bank for senior politicians, the junior politicians expect political patronage from their seniors.
(f) Undue interference from politicians and administrative corruption in the body politics[8]."

The working of Panchayat Raj institutions has politicised the rural population and as a result the corruption, the crime and harassment of the people in general have on the increase in the rural areas.

Rural Violence Rises with Expectations

A social revolution is slowly gathering momentus in Indian 500,000 villages and rural masses are asking for a fair share of the economic cake. Promises and talks of rural development and village uplift and the pious pledges of land reform and green revolution, implemented half-heartedly if at all, have created lot of expectations in rural masses and now after 33 years of independence rural masses show signs of militancy and a new consciousness of their mighty power of the 1.5 million crimes registered during 1978, 20 percent or 300,000 involved in land disputes. Half of these land dispute cases were committed in Uttar Pradesh, Bihar and Tamil Nadu. The rising expectations of those living in villages in poverty and the deeply entrenched social hierarchy caste system have created rural tension on the caste lines. It is a manifestation of the deep malaise which is resulting in rural violence.

The Rural Scene in India

A tidal wave of farmer's protests is sweeping across India, threatening to wash away the fragile foundations on which Indian economy have been built up during the last three decades. A new breed of farmers has hit the streets in violent and non-violent agitation, demanding a fair deal from his complacent urban counterpart and the government. In rural India today, the poverty phenomenon is the resultant of forces such as land-owning pattern, collaborative mechanism building of local institutions by the dominant upper class caste groups, acquisitive power of the upper strata to monopolise the fruits of development schemes and projects; prevalence of socio-economic and cultural rights causing blockage in horizontal mobilization of the poor sections of the rural community; entrepreneurial ventures to 'mine' land causing ecological imbalance to tribal subsistence economy; the preference of planning administration in favour of agricultural growth to the neglect of development of landless labour and the prevalent economic and social illegalities, disabilities and indignities prevalently in vogue in rural India. Bonded labourers though officially abolished, according to one estimate were 8,25, 239 during 1977-78.[9] The States of Bihar, Madhya Pradesh, Uttar Pradesh, Haryana in the north and Karnataka in the south together contribute 85% of the bonded labourers who are in a state of de-facto slavery. Another survey conducted in five districts of Telengana region in Andhra Pradesh indentified 10,000 bonded labourers who are subjected to social and cultural deprivations and economic exploitation. Agricultural labourers and the poor peasants classes are being exploited and this is bound to create agrarian tension with the awakening coming up in the rural India. Dr. K. N. Raj has mentioned that 66 percent of land has been in possession of 15 percent of the rural households who also benefit from all credit sources to the tune of 16 percent. Estimates based on data available in the Nineteenth round of the National Sample Survey for 1964-65 reveal that about 37 percent of the rural population is "employed at work" and about 60 percent is not in the labour force. The remaining 3 percent include those 'employed not at work', 'unemployed seeking work' and 'unemployed not seeking but available for work'. Out of those who are employed at work only about 14 percent work for less than six days a week while about 78 percent work on all seven days of the week and about 64 percent of the 'employed at work' work for more than 49 hours per week. The dominant aspect of the mode of production in Indian agriculture, by and large, is semi-feudal, wherein the vast bult of poor peasantry is having dependence on rich peasantry, economically, socially and politically and the rich peasantry is playing a key role in keeping the system inimical to overall rural development during the last 30 years. The grip of the money-lenders and rich peasants, though reduced, has remained considerable over the Indian countryside. Poverty, hunger, inequality, exploitation coupled with the adult franchise polity and parliamentary democracy are bound to throw rural India in rural resurgence. Though there are regional variations and no sweeping statements can be made, some of the main trends of rural synamism of last thirty years are as under:-

1. The trend growth rate of foodgrains has been between 2.54 to 3.40 percent compounded [10] but the fluctuations have been high for most agricultural crops.

2. The quantum of unemployment and underemployment is staggeringly high and has grown over the last three decades.

3. The gains in agricultural output are being wiped out due to very large increase of the agricultural work force in the fast growing regions.[11]

4. Inter regional and interpersonal inequalities are increasing and growing and this trend has been further magnified after the mid-sixties.[12]

5. The economic trends of an ever impending crisis have resulted in a general state of tension in rural areas over issues of land, wages and market.

6. The status of women—by income, employment or any other criterion—has steadily deteriorated over the period under review.[13]

7. Economic and social inequity has been further accentuated due to a distorted taxation and subsidy structure with the incidence of direct taxes being very low and the subsidies being built into modern imputs being used essentially by the richer sections of the society.

8. There has been a general definite increase in the number of agricultural labourers and an increase in alienation from land of the smaller peasantry. The richer farmers have gained and the tendency towards pauperisation continued for the smaller and landless peasantry in most of the rural areas.

9. In rural areas hospitals and schools have sprung, production has generally gone up; road, transport, communication have had a varitable revolution as compared to the past; our consumption basket has been

widened and yet in spite of so many indicators of progress unemployment, underemployment, exploitation, inequality, hunger and poverty stalk the countryside.

10. While tension, conflict and social antagonism are the principal aspects of the rural scene today, the review of 30 years of development have proved beyond doubts the existence of certain disturbing trends which will pose a growing threat to 'political stability', Naxalite movement and the recent farmers agitations are the two examples. "While there has been progress, it has been insufficient in relation to needs and of course to aspirations".[14]

Rural unrest is clearly visible today in the states of Maharashtra, Tamil Nadu, Gujarat, Karnataka, Uttar Pradesh and Bihar. Though the farmers agitation is not uniform throughout the country, in the short span of six months it has developed certain characteristics which point out its remarkable nature[15]:—

1. The movement is better organised and more widespread in the agriculturally more advanced region of the country, like Vidharba in Maharashtra, the paddy surplus regions of Tamil Nadu and the oilseeds growing region of Gujarat.

2. The agitation is being built around concrete demands of two kinds: higher prices for their produce and lower costs for input like water, electricity, fertilisers and pesticides.

3. For the first time, farmers are looking for protection from the risks of seasonal far-level decision making and demanding assured prices over one or two years.

4. The struggle has shown a surprising degree of militancy. Farmers have braved police firings and they have blocked road traffic, waged no-rent struggles are refusing to pay taxes and bills.

5. The agitating farmers are demanding equality with urban population in the sharing of economic and social gains.

Raj Krishna describes "agrarian reforms" as a "sad history of broken promises." The main problem in agrarian reforms is the poor state of land records and non- implementation of land laws due to litigations. A Task Force appointed by the Planning Commission accepted that "in no sphere of public activity in our country since Independence there has the hiatus between the precept and practice, between policy pronouncements and actual execution been as great as in the domain of land reforms." The Agrarian Unrest in recent years got head-news when Maharashtra farmers' agitation over higher prices for certain commodities notably sugarcane and onions gained momentum. In Maharashtra, Shard Joshi is leading the farmers' agitation in the Nasik-Pune region for a hike in onion prices from Rs. 45.75 P. to 100/- per quintal and sugarcane prices to Rs. 30/- per qtl. from the present Rs. 19/-. Side by side, the six party front under the leadership of Sharad Pawar (Cong-U) took out a dramatic 'long march' from Jalgaon to Nagpur with over 8,000 farmers. In Tamil Nadu the bandh organised by Tamil Nadu Agriculturalist Association under the leadership of Naidu has resulted in death of eight and bringing number of people detained since the start of agitation to 8000. The movement is demanding Rs. 150/- per qtl. for paddy, writing off of loans and a year's moratorim on power due and six other demands. In Gujarat the demands of farmers for better prices for ground-nut and milk are being voiced by Krishi Rakshak Sangh. Two persons were killed in Mehsana districts by the police firing when Krishi Rakshak Sangh blocked roads/ railways and fought pitched battles with the police. In Karnataka the demands of the agitating farmers include support prices of Rs. 200 per qtl. for Jowar, Rs.150/- for Maize and Rs. 250/- for Wheat. In Bihar and U.P. also farmers are organising themselves for a better deal from the Govt. Planning Commission member M.S. Swaminathan said: "Basically the farmers are agitating for reasonable returns for their produce. The farmers feel that the finished goods they purchase are far more expensive and they are not insulated against the risks involved in their work". Sharad Joshi, the leader of farmers movement in Maharashtra wants to keep the agitation free from politics. According to him no political party can seriously be interested in farmers getting remunerative prices. All these political leaders and all these parties are part of the system which has been deliberately exploiting farmers since the independence in a new form of colonial exploitation".

An eminent social scientist M.N. Srinivas foresees a dismal scenario of rural India: "The fact that even in AD 2000 about 70 percent of the population is likely to be rural, will mean that India's villages will each become a mini-battlefield for Inter-caste conflict. Since resentment at the progress of the Scheduled Castes is not confined to the dominant castes, the conflict might bring together all the Caste Hindus, including those which are just above the untouchability line against the Scheduled Castes". Today India is living on a revolution caused by rapid political mobilisation of masses, creation of huge pressure groups at the regional and state levels, emergence of new group identities for gaining greater access to power educations and the professions, increased caste activity in politics, education and social life and the new participants in the modern democratic process. The introduction of protective discrimination has divided Indian society into various strata and disturbing the social harmony of the society in general. The widening gulf between the rich & the poor has resulted in increasing unrest in our villages and village societies are no longer communities with common interest and harmony. Rural India has been converted into arenas for warring factions, battle ground for the rich and the poor to fight each other.

During the last four decades the conflicts and contradictions inherent in the processes of change in India became manifest and sharp. The agrarian unrest manifested in the form of violence against the Scheduled Castes/ Scheduled Tribes in India is not a law and order or administrative problem. At bottom it is a socio-economic problem and arises out of the deeper processes at work in the economic, social, and political structures. The sharp increase in the scale and quantum of agrarian unrest in the more recent period is traceable to the differentiation and conflicts taking place in Indian rural society as a consequence of the various Institutional and technocratic attempts to transform the agrarian structure in a broadly capitalist direction.[16] There are more spectacular out bursts of agrarian violence, featuring for example, well organised killings of share croppers, marginal farmers, agricultural labourers belonging to the scheduled castes by caste Hindu landlords or rich peasants. Instances such as the Kilven mani Carnage in Tamil Nadu in 1968, Belchi in Bihar, Banda and Narainpura in Uttar Pradesh, Bidar in Karnataka or Kestara in Madhya Pradesh may be cited.[17] According to the latest estimates of the Government of India 50.82 percent of the rural population have been subsisting below "the poverty line continuously over a long period.[18] Rural areas are facing tensions due to the implementation of DPAP and IRDP programmes. For the country as a whole the following picture emerges in respect of agrarian tensions:-

Economic Tensions			*Socio Religious & Political tensions*	
1974	928	(29.9%)	2102	(70.0%)
1975	468	(13.6%)	2958	(86.4%)
1976	1019	(27.5%)	2690	(72.5%)

Agrarian unrest needs to be analysed from critical angle. According to 1981 Census the workers in the primary sector formed 70.68 percent (Cultivators 41.53%, Agricultural labourers 25.16 percent, household industry 3.99 percent of the total main workers. The agricultural workers constitute the poorest section in the country. Though nearly 80 million rural workers are classified as cultivators, their economic condition is not far from that of the 47 million agricultural labourers, since 17 percent of them have land holdings below one acre and nearly 60 percent have holdings below 5 acres as a result of which the cultivators also compete with the landless agricultural labourers in the rural labour market. Farmers' movements sprang up in the 1970s in various parts of the country as and when the farmers found themselves in "a crash-crunch or a debt trap".[19] The bitter fact about farmers' movement is that only the affluent ones have been cornering all the facilities granted by the Governments. Poor and marginal farmers have only been used as cannon-fodder. Remunerative prices for farm produce have enabled the holders of large agricultural lands to acquire financial and consequential political influence. The Karnataka Rajya Raita Sangha has shown the people that only agitational methods can yield results. Shrimati Indira Gandhi however openly held that "if we yield to such demands (being raised in such peasant agitations), the equilibrium in rural areas will be disturbed and there will be greater inflation and sharper polarisation between villages and towns. "Some how most of the recent farmers movements are disappointed and disgusted by the politicians for their personal gains and vested party interests leaving the farmers in the lurch after their own aims are fulfilled. The farmers agitations ultimately become an effective smoke-screen for the intensification of the exploitation of wage labour and atrocities on the rural and poor at one level and rising pressure for satisfaction of the sectional interests of surplus farmers at another. The surplus farmers at the same time pretend to stand up as undisputed leaders of rural society as a whole.

Another dimension of Agrarian unrest is the social conflict arising out of mal-treatment and atrocities on harijans and the weaker sections of the society. The assault on harijans at social, economic and political levels is the result of a complex combination of causes that are perpetuated in many ways. Though the figures are of 1977 and 1978, a comparative picture of the trend of atrocities in 11 states is indicated in the table below.[20]

Sl.No.	*State*	*No. of atrocities*		*Percentage of*
		1977	*1978*	*Increase/Decrease*
1.	Andhra Pradesh	102	110	7.84 (+)
2.	Bihar	681	1911	180.62 (+)

3. Gujarat	331	540	63.14 (+)
4. Karnataka	59	376	537.27 (+)
5. Kerala	233	767	229.18 (+)
6. Madhya Pradesh	3355	3240	3.74 (+)
7. Maharashtra	570	1046	83.51 (+)
8. Orissa	69	1359	5.65 (+)
9. Rajasthan	261	886	239.46(+)
10. Tamil Nadu	54	130	140.15(+)
11. Uttar Pradesh	4974	5660	13.79(+)

In 1981 the Government has recorded 11.743 incidents of atrocities in the first eleven months. In 1980 the number was 13.746 and in 1979 the figures were 13426 cases. In 1978 there were 15053 cases of atrocities against harijans. On June 17, 1988 an armed mob of 55 supporters of the Arvind faction of Mazdoor Kissan Sangram Samiti (MKSS) launched a surprise attack on the Harijan Toli of Nagwa of Nenhai village of Jahanabad district in Bihar and brutally killed, 18 harijans who belonged to Indian People's front (IPF). In 1987 about 20 people belonging to Alelchak Bhagaura and Chechani villages of Bihar were killed in caste-clashes and atrocities were committed on other villagers. The term atrocities covers cases of murder, rape arson and violence although the term has not been defined by the penal laws. National Police Commission has noticed the increasing awakening in the rural areas leading to bitter and brutal caste and class conflict. Rural unrest•can be anticipated in future as rural landless workers and small agriculturalists are now organising themselves demanding better wages and better prices for their products. It is anticipated that the most serious threats to law and order will in future arise in rural areas.[21] The problems of the north eastern region which have caused great concern to the Central Government during the last four decades since Indias independence are basically economic in nature and can be termed as peasant unrest or agrarian unrest in a limited sense. Insurgency, violence, ethnic conflicts seem to be the apparent causes of unrest in north eastern region but the basic cause is agrarian and economic in nature. Mizo unrest was the direct outcome of economic backward and famine conditions in 1965 and it can be to some extent called an agrarian unrest. In 1965 the district was hit by famine and within the next couple of years a full scale insurgency was on.[22] If we trace the genesis of unrest in Mizoram we find that it was in the year 1959 that there was a serious famine in Mizoram and in order to provide relief measures for the victims of the great famine a voluntary organisation known as Mizo National Front was formed. Thus Mizoram Insurgency was basically an agrarian unrest which got political, tribal and ethnic dimensions at a later stage. However agrarian unrest in north eastern region has been contained by various economic political and legal measures, under the I.R.D. Programmes 58.15 percent of the families could be assisted in the region by the financial institutions during the sixth plan period and subsequent five year plans. Agrarian unrest today represents the awakening among the oppressed about their rights and privileges and their preparedness to fight for them. They are no more prepared to suffer in silence and would rather prefer to take to arms. When the consciousness grows among the landless labourers about their rights, the tendency among the landlords is to meet it through strong arm methods. The lack of even basic amenities like roads, water supply, communication and jobs for the unemployed is also a factor accentuating rural violence and agrarian unrest. The criminalisation of politics, aided and abetted by the politicians, as evident during elections when booth-capturing becomes the order of the day, also accounts in its own way for the growing agrarian unrest. This is coupled with the easy availability of firearms and ammunition mostly of the illegal variety in many pockets of the states. Thus the entire social order today is aggravating agrarian violence in India.

The present police organisational structure is inadequate to meet the growing agrarian unrest due to the following main reasons:-

1. Strength of present rural police is inadequate.
2. The communication facilities in rural areas are poor and unsatisfactory.

3. Lack of effective leadership at middle ranks namely Inspectors and Sub-Inspectors.
4. Gross under estimation of future events and failure of intelligence planning.
5. Lack of commitment and motivation on Police forces.
6. Lack of adequate training and lack of preparedness to deal with agrarian unrest.
7. Lack of proper man power planning and misuse of available resources.
8. Partial attitude of Police officials.
9. Corruption in police force and arrogant attitude.
10. Poor system of communication with weaker section of society.
11. Inadequate representation of scheduled castes/ scheduled tribes and other weaker sections in middle and higher ranks.
12. Prejudiced and biased attitude of police towards poor and down-trodden.
13. Inadequate transport and non-availability of transport for emergency duties.
14. Lack of proper rapport and communication with representatives of farmers and other weaker sections of the society.
15. Agrarian unrest is considered as purely law and order problem and not a socio-economic problem.
16. Lack of proper orientation and briefing in rural police for such tasks and inadequate response.

Concluding Remarks

According to National Police Commission the first essential of police reform on the rural side will be to increase the spread of the regular police in the rural areas and reduce the gap in the density of police presence in the urban areas and the rural areas as compared to each other (NPC Vol.III P/ 20-15 page). Political will is needed to redress the grievances of the farmers. Agrarian unrest can be contained and controlled only by giving farmers their legitimate dues and much needed economic support by the Government. For example in Andhra Pradesh state was giving electricity at

Rs. 50 per HP per year to the Agriculturalists and supplying fertilisers and pesticides at 50 percent subsidy to farmers during natural calamities. Government of India has launched a number of economic programmes under twenty point programme for the amelioration of the economic condition of rural poor. Special programmes for the weaker sections are: the Small Frmers Development Agency (SFDA), the Marginal Farmers and Agricultural Labourer Development Agency (MFAL) and the Integrated Dry Land Agricultural Development. Bonded Labour System (Abolition Act 1976 has made all bonded workers free and discharged from any obligation to render bonded labour. The twenty point programme of 1982 emphasises on effective enforcement of minimum wages for agricultural labour. The above measures have to some extent checked and contained growing agrarian unrest in India. Agrarian unrest can be ultimately diffused through political, administrative and social measures aimed at bringing social harmony in rural areas and economic transformation of the undeveloped regions. A suitable strategy needs to be worked out by the state governments through intelligent use of radio, T.V. and Press to ensure that agrarian harmony is built up in rural areas through various socio-economic and political actions. Masses should be mobilised to keep rural fabric intact and help in building a violence-free rural India. A former Planning Commission expert on agrarian reform who drafted the well known Task Force Report has recently observed: "We are not likely to formulate and implement a meaningful anti-poverty programme until the numerically large poverty groups get themselves together organised and start influencing public policy.[23]

REFERENCES

1. Bipin Chandra & Others—*India's struggle for Independence* P. 343-355.

2. Dr. Sunil K. Sen—*Peasants movement in India-Mid nineteenth & Twentieth Centuries*-1982 , P. 252.

3. General Secretary's Report—Fourth Conference of Bhartiya Khet Majdoor Union 1977, P.28.

4. Dr. Sunil K. Sen-- *Peasants Movement in India*-1982, P.20-29.

5. G. Myrdal— Asian Drama Vol.2 pp. 1307-8, 1326-7).

6. N. Nath '*Area development planning at District and Block levels*-IJPA 11 (1965) P.74-5.

7. T.N. Chaturvedi—*Tensions in Panchayat Raj: Relations between officials and Non-officials*. Economics Weekly 16 (221) May 30, 1964.

8. S.N. Mishra—*The Panchayat Level*-SEMINAR 255 No. 80, P. 23.

9. Nitish R. De—*India's Agrarian Situation-Some Aspects of changing the context-in Agrarian Relations in India* 1979, P.238.

10. S.N. Misra—*(Alternatives in Agricultural Development)- Unpublished Report ICSSR* 1978.

11. G.S. Bhalla—'*Spatial pattern of Labour Productivity in Indian Agriculture*. JNU 1978.

12. P.K. Bardhan—*Poverty and Income Distribution in India*-1974.

13. Report of the Committee on the status of women in India- New Delhi 1975.

14. Arun Shourie— But what when is the Solution—Indian Express 29 Nov 1980.

15. The Angry Framer— *India Today*— Jan 16-31, '81 Vol. VI No. 2.P.32.

16. For further details see Govt of India First and Second Reports of the Commission for Scheduled Castes and Scheduled Tribes (1978-79).

17. Press dated 18th April, 1982 PPI and 6. Also M. Shivraman in H. Sharma and K. Gougha 1973 PP 246-264-Imperialism and revolution in South Asia (Monthly Review Press).

18. Government of India—Ministry of Home Affairs Annual Report of the Implementation of the Protection of Civil Rights Act 1955 for the year '80.

19. Shorad Joshi—*The Lessons of Meerut-Indian Express,* Sunday Magazine March 27, 1988.

20. For Further details and special report see *Indian Express,* Sunday Edition April 18, 1982, P.1.6.

21. Dharam Vira Report of the National Police Commission (Eighth Report) P. 20 Para 62.20.

22. 1. Banerjee—The Troubled North East Sunday (Calcutta) Vol. 12 No.5, 14-20 Feb 1988, P. 29.

23. See P.S. APPU "The Phoney War" -Reaction to poverty symposium Financial Express, dated 1 Nov. 1982 P.5. Also see The report of Task Force on Agrarian Relations in Kurukshetra Vol. XXVII No. 131 April 1979, P. 422.

4

Conflicts of Plural Society: Their Impact for Internal Security

In all societies there is conflict, tension and constant struggle for survival and material advancement. In all multi-ethnic societies, generally called plural societies, many types of conflicts emerge either explicitly or implicitly which have direct impact on internal security of the state system. Economic development on various regions of the Country has gone astray mainly because it has not been able to manage the major conflicts of a plural society in a desirable way and the manner of managing conflicts has led to the adoption of wrong priorities. The arena of conflicts that have arisen during the process of economic development and nation building in India, need to be analysed in depth and their impact on internal security has to be surveyed. Conflict management in a plural society wedded to the ideals of secularism, self reliance, democracy and social justice requires research and long term policy formulations.

Conflict — A Conceptual background

Conflict manifests itself in a variety of shapes, sizes and even disguises through the entire gamut of human inter-actions. Conflict usually refers to a process of interaction between individuals and troups or parties involving a struggle over claims to resources, power and status, beliefs and other preferences and desires. Conflict itself, is a form of sociation, is designed to resolve divergent dualisms; and in fact dissociating factors-hate, envy, need, desire-are the causes of conflict; it breaks out because of them. Conflict within a group may help to establish unity or to re-establish unity and cohesion where it has been threatened by hostile and antagonistic feelings among the members.[1] In all ages, in every type of social structure, there are innumerable occasions for conflict, since individuals and sub-groups are likely to make from time to time rival claims to scare resources, prestige or power positions. Internal social conflicts which concern goals, values or interests that do not contradict the basic assumptions upon which the relationship is founded tend to be positively functional for the social structure.[2] Conflict is conceived as a socio-psychological phenomena of deviance which is to be contained for ensuring structural stability of a plural society. Talcott Parson equates deviance and conflict when he says; "cultural patterns which either fail to define a minimum of order or which place impossible demands on people...... generate deviance and conflict".[3] Many classifications of conflict like the one attempted by Stuart Chase, Ross Stagner, Lassewell, Adorno, Boulding and Kardiner are either merely catalogue of contemporary conflicts or their analysis at the psychic level.[4] Karl Marx has given the most powerful and realistic approach to the problem in his books "The Communist Manifesto" (1939) and "A critique of Political Economy. George Sinmel, A.W. Small, Coser and Dharendorf have made valuable contributions with respect to the consequences of conflict rather than the process itself.[5] Karl Marx recognised that class conflict was bound to be political and "the struggle between class and class is a political struggle".[6] Karl Marx held that with the change of the economic foundation, the entire immense superstructure is more or less rapidly transformed. In considering such transformations distinction should always be made between the material transformation of the economic conditions of production which can be determined with the precision of natural science and the legal, political, religious, aesthetic or philosophic—in short ideological forms in which men become conscious of this conflict and fight it out... No social order ever perishes before all the productive force for which there is room in it have developed; and new higher relations of production never appear before the material conditions of existence have matured in the womb of the old society itself".[7] Briefly conflict theories are economic sociological, psychological and political—depending upon the emphasis assigned to the particular fact by thinkers. Social conflict has been defined as "a struggle over values, or claims to status, power and scare resources, in which the aims of the conflicting groups or parties are not only to gain the desired values, power or scarce resources but also to mentralize, injure or eliminate their rivals".[8] Social conflict may generally occur between individuals, between social groups, and between collectivities. Conflict is an important element of social interaction because inter-group as well as intra-group conflicts are perenial features of social life. Hegel, Karl Marx, Herbert-Spencer, Gustan Ratzenhofer, Lud-wig guinplowiez, Willian Graham Suinner are some of the well known social thinkers who have paid attention to social conflict. The struggle for power and influence is one of the themes of Pareto's theories as well as those of Sorel, Michels, and Hosca. Sinmal has carried out a classical analysis of various forms of conflicts and held that "conflict is a form of sociation" and that "a certain amount of discord, inner divergence and outer controversy, is organically tied up with the very elements that ultimately hold the group together. Robert Park (1924), Weber, Talcott Parsons, Gessic Bermard (1957) and Max Gluckman (1956) have analysed various aspects of social conflict including a conflict model of society. Talcott Parsons claimed that the Central problem of sociological theory was the "problem of order". Conflicts are power struggles carried out by various ethnic groups for winning political and economic power as a generalised means to persue goals, ideals or interests.

The concept of plural society

The theory of the plural society as a separate part of sociological theorising owes its origin to J.S. Furnivall.[9] M.G. Smith, used Malinowski's account of a socio-cultural system in describing the institutional structure of the separate ethnic groups in a plural society, and claimed that each group has a nearly complete set of institutions within itself, lacking only the political institution.[10] In a plural society separate ethnic groups are bound to have conflicts and are likely to break up unless one of the ethnic segments take over the dominating role and succeed in dominating others politically.[11] Furnival emphasised economic ties divorced from a normative context while Smith emphasized political ties but both thinkers did not develop a theory of conflict in a market place. According to John Rex, the ethnically plural society is a class society and the class struggle often takes an ethnic form. In a plural society conflicts over power and authority are the fundamental social processes as suggested in the Debrendrof thesis.[12] In plural societies, economic exploitation and political domination give rise to conflicts between various ethnic groups. India is a very good example of a plural society due to rich variety of pluralism. The fragmented plural society, then, is marked by a plethora of groups, the scarcity or absence of brokerage institutions, the short supply of coalition building skills necessary to organise political conflict, the eventual anarchy of instructured conflict as a result of primordial distrust, and typically, the initiation of rule by the military who possess a monopoly[13] on organisational and political skills. J.S. Furnivall introduced the concept of the "plural society" in 1939. Furnival defined a plural society as "comprising two or more elements or social orders which live side by side, yet without mingling in one political unit". He concluded that plural societies are qualitatively different from homogenous ones and that the different communities of the plural societies can meet only in the market place. Plural societies are inherently prone to violent conflict and the hall mark of the plural society is the practice of politics almost exclusively along the ethnic lines. According to Rabushka and Shepsle a society is plural if it is culturally diverse and if its cultural sections are organised into cohesive political sections.[14] In a plural society competitive politics is characterised by ethnic politics and ethnic nepotism. All Indian sociologists agree on the point that India is a plural society with unity in diversity. Prof Amartya Sen, renowned academician and economist delivering a lecture on "Indian Pluralism" in July 1993 at Delhi touched upon India's intrinsic cultural diversities, its inherent strengths and the need to practice and defend this pluralism against organised attack.[15] India's plurality was quite remarkable. "What is Central to Indian pluralism is its religious diversity, added to it is the diversities in art and music. "We are not unique in being diverse but there is something quite special in the tremendous extent of diversity in our traditions. Our religious diversity is a part of much wider experience, of which we can be legitimately proud.[16] The great thing about the basic "Hindu" heritage is not only that it is itself pluralistic but that it imparts this plurality to other ('non-Hindu') communities too.[17] The vast majority of Indians may be Hindus, but we have more than a hundred million Muslims, we have more Sikhs than any other Country, more Jains too and more Parsis as well. I don't believe there exists another country the religious diversity of which begins to match ours.[18] The main pluralities of Indian society can be explained by the following realities:-

(1) As many as 1652 languages and dialects are spoken in India while the Constitution of India recognises 18 major languages.

(2) India has an estimated tribal population of 51.6 millions in 1981. Major tribes of North Eastern States are Nagas, Angami, Semia Aao, Tangkul in Nagaland, Lushais chakma and Tripuries in Tripura, Lepchas in Sikkim, Kuki in Manipur, Khasis and Garos in Meghalaya, Jarwas in Little Andamans, Apatamis in Arunachal Pradesh, Abors, Mikirs, Khasis and plain tribal people in Assam.

(3) India has people belonging to almost major religious and sects.

Indian society is seen to be developing in the direction of a full fledged pluralist democracy. India is a plural society with a nearly unfathomable diversity of languages, sects, castes, ethnicity, religions, regions and cultures. In a plural society conflicts may develop around (a) conflicts over the inheritance of land, (b) quarrel over the adoption of sons, (c) quarrel over house sides and irrigation rites, (d) quarrel over sexual offences and (e) conflicts over castes. According to Dr Yogendra Singh conflicts and feuds by various groups can be analysed as under:-

(1) Inter-Caste feuds over the issue of land reported in 44% cases,

(2) Serious fights and court cases reported in 15.5%.

(3) Feuds and conflicts on the violation of the connubial rules of castes or sub-castes reported in 30% cases.

(4) Conflicts over the inheritance of property reported in 10.2%.[19]

According to Balmit Singh factional conflicts in rural society centre around the existing system of individual land ownership.[20] India is a meeting point of diverse racial strains and cultural traditions and one finds here the co-existence of different politico-economic formations. Pluralism in India is not only social and cultural but also historical and political.[21] At the same time there is an overwhelming sense of overarching shared civilisation and political experience among various communities, ethnic groups and other major sections of the population.

Conflicts as regular political phenomena in Democracy

Lewis Coser has distinguished between two types of conflicts—realistic and non-realistic. In realistic conflicts, the attainment of desired goals is more important than-the destruction of the enemy. In non-realistic conflicts, conflicts generally are not aimed at the attainment of concrete results but at the expression of aggressive impulse by one party and generally spills over in the form of violence of remonstrance and frustration on the third parties. Conflict is the conscious attempt to oppose, resist or coerce the will of another or others. Conflict is manifested in physical confrontations between collective actors if it involves actual or symbolic physical confrontation between groups expressing orresisting demands for change or is expressed in actual physical clashes (e.g. armed attacks, riots) or in a symbolic ones (e.g. general strike, civil disobedience, political protests). The political conflict theorists focus on the role of organised group conflict for political power to explain collective violence and revolutions.[22] Insurgency, guerrilla warfare, terrorism, revolutions coup-de'tat', and violent political movements are all forms of political conflicts having their impact on internal security. Conflicts can range from disturbing law and order or public order or internal security depending on the following factors:

1. The probability of the occurrence of disturbance to law and order caused by conflicts;

2. The potentiality of damage in terms of lives & property;

3. The intensity & effectivity of the conflict; and

4. The recurring nature of the conflict phenomena and its magnitude and dimensions.

Conflict is also at times struggle among groups over ideology or way of life or over power or scarce values which can be explained in terms of patterns of social structure. There are a number of points at which conflicts might occur within the system. One of the main reasons for conflict is the power difference between dominant and subordinate groups wherein dominant group possesses superior power in relation to the relative, carelessness of subordinate group. Weber contributed to the development of a conflict theory of society by introducing concepts of power, authority and social change. Mosca's theory of conflict centre around power struggle in the polity. According to him there is a ruling class in every society which constantly tries to monopolize political power at the expense of the lower class and this conflict produces an unending ferment of endosmosis and exosmosis between a class that rules and a class that is ruled. Powerful classes shape the legal structure to serve its own narrow interests. According to Neil J. Smelser, as propounded in his book "The Theory of Collective Behaviour", the manifestation of conflict, in collective behaviour occur only in the following six conditions:-

1. Structural conductiveness.

2. Structure straints.

3. A generalised belief.

4. Precipitating factors.

5. Mobilisation for action.

6. Ineffective social control.

Structural conductiveness refer to the structural contradictions which are the primary cause for conflicts and collective behaviour manifestations in the form of direct action, strikes and even riots.

Conflict is the outcome of a psychological feeling of relative deprivation. Relative deprivation can be understood as "actors" perceptions of discrepancy between their value expectations (the goods and conditions of the life to which they behave they are justifiably entitled) and their value capabilities (the amount of those goods and conditions that they think they are able to get and keep)". The psychological response to perceived relative deprivation is discontent or anger and that anger is a motivating state for which aggression in an inherently satisfying response. There are however four important societal variables namely "Coercive potential", institutionalisation, social facilitation and legitimacy of the political regime which determine the magnitude of the manifestation of the aggression into a civil strife. The figure shows casual model of civil strife.

Relative Deprivation	Coercive potential Institutionalisation Social Facilitation Legitimacy	Magnitude of civil strife

In the above given model coercive power includes the quality and quantity of coercive forces, the loyalty of the forces and the attitude they take in a particular context. Institutionalisation refers to the social, political, economic and other societal structures which minimise the intensity of strife. Social and structural facilitation comprises aspects of organisational and environmental facilitations of strife such transportation net. Legitimacy refers to the degree of popular support for the regime. Manifestation of group conflicts become civil strife and can take shape of turmoil, domestic conflict, conspiracy or internal war. The magnitude of a domestic conflict or civil strife depends on the following three factors:-

(a) *Pervasiveness*: The extent of participation by the affected population.

(b) *Duration*: The total span of time in terms of days and hours.

(c) *Intensity*: In terms of loss of property and life, total estimated casualties dead and injured and destruction of property in terms of quantity. Machiavelli, Bodin, Hobbes and Mosca have analysed conflicts in terms of power relationships.

Conflicts arise in every state in the distribution of scarce goods and resources between different groups. The conflicts between the centre and states arise on various economic, political and linguistic matters as their interests clash. States want to get more and more autonomy while Centre wants to remain strong and all powerful. Non-realistic conflicts arise when states demand more and more powers and autonomy in various fields while Centre wants more powers for the Union. In democratic form of government, according to Mosca, an organised minority imposes its will on the disorganised majority and this itself is a contradiction of political system because the ruling class tries to monopolise political powers at the expense of the other class of citizens.

According to some thinkers, conflicts arise when the individual freedom is completely subjudicated to the so called "national-interest", which in essence means the interests of the powerful elite ruling the country at times. Political conflicts arise over values and claims to status, power and scarce resources when the aims of the conflicting parties are not only to gain the desired values but also neutralise, infuse or eliminate their political rivals. Such conflicts are structural, long lasting and deep rooted.

Conflicts in the Political System having implications for Internal Security

In a federal system inter-state conflicts can arise over river water distribution, sharing of revenues, powers of the states, appointment of governs and over other economic social and political policies of the state.

Conflicts arise in the political system out of the structural contradictions in all political societies. The democratic system provides freedom for constructive conflicts, channeling the aggressive political impulses of men. Conflicts have to be resolved by legitimate means those formally provided and socially recognised. Naxalites and other Communist Marxist-Leninists groups have no faith in the present political system and are ready to overthrow it through a manifested conflict. In India we have both conflicts about the political system and also conflicts within the political system. In India today masses have developed a new cult of conflict, protest and violence. In India the conflict between the actual immediate interest of groups and their long range interest is not immediately apparent to the participants which they manifest conflicts in various forms under their power-crazy political leaders. India has inherited the legacy of Satyagraha from the father of the nation. Coercive public protests have assumed the following primary forms in India:-

(i) Processions and public meetings, assemblies.

(ii) Hartals (work stoppages), boycotts & strikes.

(iii) Fasts of political nature including other forms of civil disobedience movements.

(iv) Obstruction and gheraos and other forms of direct actions.

(v) Courting of arrest and violation of Section 144 CrPC.

(vi) Political riots followed by violence.

(vii) Political kidnapping and hijacking.

(viii) Political terrorism and political violence.

Political violence is one of the well known manifestations of conflict in the political system. Civil war, political terrorism insurgency, armed rebellion, street violence and political gang warfare are some of the well known forms of political violence. The Assam agitation and the Punjab agitation are two most well known political agitations causing violence of great intensity. According to Shri Y.B. Chavan there are four type of direct actions and conflicts which do take place in a political system.

(a) Wherein a group of persons take law into their hands and administer direct punishment to the supposed wrong-doer without going through the due process of law;

(b) Wherein a group of people (particular religion, economic or caste group) feels wronged and take vengeance against the other group by methods not permitted by law ;

(c) When a group of persons feeling aggrieved on occasions by the policy of the government or party in power launches organised defiance of law as a technique of solving the problems;

(d) Actions launched by the groups which are impatient to realize those natural urges which make them aspire for better form of economic society for better socio-political ideologies and are not patient enough to achieve them in accordance with time table. When there is contradictions in the working of parliamentary democracy, when the government itself is out to destroy the values of democracy, people get the right of direct action. There are large scale demonstrations, riots, violence in India but the Indian political system has acquired the capacity for sustaining and eventually resolving these internal conflicts without compromising its commitment to democratic norms. Political conflicts arise according to Trotsky when there are deep divisions among governing elites and leadership groups or when there is great erosion of confidence in the regime, its values and institutions, afflicting all levels of the populations including the government. According to Felkins Gross, conflicts arise in the political system due to the following reasons:-

(a) perceived political inequalition, infringement or rights, injustice or oppression;

(b) lack of adequate channels for peaceful communication of protests, grievances and demands (e.g. denial of franchise and other right of participation, representation or access to media):

(c) the availability of a revolutionary leader equipped with a potentially attractive ideology.

T.A. Critchley holds the view that whenever in a civilised political system, a substantive section of the community has reason to feel on racial, social or religious grounds that it is under privileged or otherwise deprived of elementary political rights, its political protest is likely to take the form of direct action (manifested conflict). Most of such conflicts have a major impact on internal security of the country. Dr. B.R. Ambedkar, in his prophetic observation at the time of making of Indian Constitution has said "In Politics we will have inequality .... We must remove those contradictions at the earliest moment or else, those who suffer from inequality, will blow up the structure of political democracy". The introduction of adult sufferage, alongwith huge plans of mass education and economic development have over-stirred the political system in India to the extent its inbuilt contradiction seem like recking the entire society in the absence of a requisite infrastructure. The political system's growth, with its teething troubles, is further accentuated by the over increasing regional imbalances in the economic field. Recently political agitations and public disorders have gained new dimensions, strategies, tactics and manifestations.

The rising expectations of the under-privileged citizens, the emergence of a new type of political leaders, spread of political consciousness in the society, lack of social discipline and the emergence of a "soft state" have further given rise to political conflicts of intense nature giving rise to public violence, communal, regional and linguistic agitations.

In every plural society conflicts over power and authority are bound to continue as they are structural in nature. Ideological conflict and power conflict can take manifestations in the form of political protests, direct action, terrorist activities to insurgency, revolt and even fulfledged revolution on the structure and nature of political system. In democratic system, conflict generally remains constitutional and open while in other forms of systems it at times becomes convert and revolutionary. Political conflicts have great implications for internal security and therefore required proper analysis and systematic study.

Sociological approach to conflicts

In plural societies, the structural differentiation in caste results from the urges for social mobility. Many sociologists have seen in the process of sanskritization a latent form of class-conflict which results because of the peculiar structural constraints of the Indian society. (Harold Gould 1961 E.R. Leach 1960 etc).[23] According to Pareto and Mosca, the dynamics in the structure of elites and the process of circulation among elites operates through conflict, intrigues and competition by which each section of elites tries to overthrow the power elites and occupy its position. In a system of social stratification of a plural society, it posits a permanent conflict between classes which have command over power and wealth and those who do not possess them.[24] In order to understand the dimensions of conflict within the frame of social stratification it is essential to realize that conflict and tension can only be examined with the help of concepts which have significant diacritical features of their own. Class conflict and caste mobility occur because there are full-fledged differences between castes. Conflicts arise on a far more general scale in caste societies because of the existence of multiple caste hierarchies which are all separate and equal and support their positions through their own caste ideologies.[25] The incidence of Caste conflicts and violence in recent times have not been confined to rural areas only but have taken place in urban areas of Gujarat and Maharashtra as well. Mobility, social stratification, mutual reinforcement of economic and social inequalities and culture and ideology of repression in promoting and aggravating conflicts need special focus today.

Factors responsible for conflict in India

Primarily the roots of conflict lie in the exploitation or attempted exploitation.

(1) Caste system with its prejudices against lower castes has aggravated the tension and conflict.

(2) Democratic system has given way to rising aspirations of the people and the feudal outlook of the people are responsible for conflicts.

(3) Complete absence of the culture of communication and accumulating girevances of the people give rise to conflicts. Psychological factors give rise to conflict.

(4) Indian economic system is partly responsible for many conflicts.

(5) Political system of India with a federal polity with a written constitution has given rise to conflicts.

(6) Unresolved and unjust wage system, unscrupulous exploitation of the working classes and growing criminalisation has resulted in conflicts.

(7) Conflicts are emerging due to the development process in a developing society.

(8) Religion and communal bias and prejudices are causing conflicts.

(9) Conflict can be due to generation gap.

(10) Fanaticism and schismatic beliefs can give rise to conflicts.

Ethnic conflicts in India and their impact on Internal Security

In North-Eastern States of India like Nagaland, Tripura, Mizoram and Manipur following types of conflicts are noticed:-

(1) Diffused conflict at the ideational level,

(2) Conflicts within the tribal communities.

(3) Between different communities.

(4) Between tribal communities and the State.

These four types of conflicts are not wholly exclusive. From times memorial, conflicts of economic interests have perhaps been the most obvious aspects in North Eastern States of India. Even today economic conflicts continue to dominate other type of conflicts either explicitly or implicitly. There is a competition for and exploitation of, source resources, encouraged by a political system which promotes concentrated extraction and profits for a few. Diffused conflict at the ideational level arises with the need of recognition of identity of each ethnic group. While non-recognition of at least some ethnic identities in India as indigenous population will accelerate the conflict, even formal recognition will not clinch the issue.[26] Ethnographic accounts are replete with intra-tribal conflicts related to the question of control and management of load in the tribal areas of north east India.[27] Inter Community conflicts in tribal areas of north eastern states are quite common. Self styled ethnic extremists have continued gruesome killings in Manipur. In August 1993 as many as 50 people including women and children were killed in ethnic conflicts and whole villages were put to the torch. In August 1993 ambushes killed 6 army and two CRP Jawans. Over a hundred people have been killed in clashes between Tangkhul Magas and Kukis in recent weeks of Sept. 1993. On 15th September 1993 suspected extremists belonging to a particular community massacred 90 Kukis and laid waste their villages at Zoupi and surrounding areas in Manipur's Senapati district. It is difficult to disentangle the tribal conflicts between Nagas belonging to National Socialist Council or Nagaland (Muviah group) and the Kukis organised by well-equipped Kuki National Army and both groups make their claims over control of territory in Manipur. Manipur State Govt. is a helpless spectator to this ethnic conflict.

In clashes between Nagas and Kukis in Manipur 113 persons have been killed, 75 injured and 1067 houses gutted or damaged between January and August 11, 1993.[28] To enforce effective counter-insurgency operations, Army was inducted in Manipur in May 1993 with the support of the State Police and Centre Para Military Forces. Conflicts in tribal areas involving tribal communities and the State are found in almost all north east states which have non-ethnic conflicts with insurgent activities rocking the state frequently.

In a plural society, there are bound to be differences, frictions and conflicts due to political, socio-economic, ethnic and religious reasons. Due to lack of vision and political expediency, conflicts are not being resolved and managed in time. Most of the problems are glossed over till they emerge in their violent and extremist form causing serious threat to the internal security of the country. Many ethnic conflicts are due to unbalanced economic growth and question of ethnic identity. In the North East India, the question of identity, perpetuated isolation and lack of economic development, required a well planned graduated and wholesome approach to modernisation. "Ethnic conflicts are common in all ethnically plural societies and it has been extremely difficult to create harmonious relations between clearly different ethnic groups".[29] Absence of a declared policy results in disjointed responses, by the politicians, the bureaucrats and the managers of internal security. It is therefore essential that it is within the knowledge of all responsible for its implementation.[30]

Naxalite Movement—A manifestation of conflict

Naxalite movement which was started in 1967 in West Bengal, gradually spread to Andhra Pradesh, Orissa, Bihar and Kerala with sporadic activities in the States of Punjab, Uttar Pradesh, Assam, Tripura, Maharashtra and Tamil Nadu. Agrarian unrest, and conversion of CPI (M) into a revolutionary party believing in annihilation of class enemies were the twin causes of Naxalite movement gaining mass appeal. Due to failure of leadership and unrealistic analysis of socio-economic-political reality of India, movement has gradually died out except in Andhra Pradesh. The Naxalite movement in Andhra Pradesh has taken a very violent conflict form and has seriously jeopardised the internal security of the State.

Industrial Conflicts and Disputes

Industrial conflicts and disputes are the product of industrialisation and are recurring phenomena in all plural societies which are trying to develop their economies through a process of industrialisation.

Industrial conflicts and disputes

(Figure in thousands)

Year	*No. of strikes.*	*Disputes lock-outs.*	*Total*	*Workers Involved*			*Mandays lost*
				Strikes.	*Lock-outs*	*Total*	
1980	2501	355	2856	1661	239	1990	21925
1981	2245	344	2589	1261	327	1588	36583
1982	2029	454	2483	1191	278	1469	74615
1983	1993	495	2488	1167	294	1461	46858
1984	1689	405	2094	1726	223	1949	56025
1985	1355	400	1755	878	201	1079	29240
1986	1458	434	1892	1444	201	1645	32749
1987	1348	451	1799	1495	275	1770	35358
1988	1304	441	1745	937	254	1191	33947
1989	1307	389	1786	NA	NA	1351	32690
1990	1459	366	1825	NA	NA	1308	24090
1991	NA	NA	1428	NA	NA......	991	15729

(Source: CMIE August 1992)

The noticeable feature in the last few years is that the incidence of industrial conflicts seems to have begun an upward climb from the second half of the 1991. The latest economic survey of the Govt of India observes that from the second half of 1991-1992 there was a sharp upward increase in the number of mandays lost due to industrial unrest caused by conflicts. Industrial conflicts create serious problems of law and order and when prolonged for many days and months they impinge on internal security of the country.

Manifestations of violent social conflicts and their impact on Internal Security

Caste riots are not uncommon in India and especially during the last three decades there have been a number of such riots in rural areas of the various parts of the Country. Caste riots are primarily rooted in disputes over land and wages and sometimes in deep-rooted caste prejudices among the upper castes on one hand and social mobility of SC/ST on the other. Some studies indicate that caste conflicts were mainly over the scarce resources and employment opportunities. In Gujrat State intensity of Caste conflicts was found in Ahmedabad, Mehsana, Kaisa and Baroda districts. Caste conflicts and caste violence in Gujarat can be judged by the figures given below-:

Intensity of Caste Conflicts in different Districts of Gujrat[31]

S.No.	*Districts*	*Killed in firing*	*Injured in firing*	*Days of continued disturbance.*
1.	Ahmedabad	18	29	10
2.	Mehsana	8	11	12
3.	Kaira	5	12	7
4.	Baroda	2	7	11
5.	Surat	-	-	7
6.	Sabar Kanta	1	-	1
7.	Jain Nagar	-	-	3
8.	Raj Kot	-	-	3
9.	Bhavnagar	-	-	3

Caste conflicts and atrocities on lower castes SC/ST have been estimated to be 40,000 during 1966-76 and during 1976-78 this figure exceeded 17000. Caste conflicts in urban areas are generally related to the mobility of the scheduled castes and scheduled tribes. Indian society is having various types of social conflicts in almost all the states. Articles on violent social conflicts published in "India Today" from 1980 to 1988 can be classified as under:-

The Frequency distribution of articles on violect social conflicts published in India Today-1980-89 by the type of conflicting groups.[32]:-

Type of Conflict	*1980*	*81*	*82*	*83*	*84*	*85*	*86*	*87*	*88*	*Total*
1. Hindu Muslim	2	4	3	6	1	2	8	5	5	36
2. Hindu Harijan	3	5	4	2	-	1	1	1	2	19
3. Tribal Non -Tribal	16	6	8	5	11	8	7	11	13	85
4. Hindu Sikh & Sikh Terrorism	-	3	4	10	19	9	15	9	17	86
5. Other violent ethnic conflicts	8	4	4	7	3	10	2	2	2	42
6. Non-ethnic violent conflict including Naxalites	2	8	2	2	1	1	5	2	2	25
Total	31	30	25	32	35	31	38	30	41	293

Geographically Hindu Muslim violent conflict have mainly affected U.P, Assam, West Bengal, Bihar, Gujrat, M.P. and Maharashtra, Karnataka, Kerala and Andhra Pradesh. Political violence and conflicts have been increasing in India and political murders have been reported in all states during the last ten years. In 1988 in West Bengal alone there were 182 murders. Caste conflicts and violence in Bihar and U.P. are generally over the issues of wages, sharecroppers, social oppression, land disputes and retaliation. The 6th December 1992 Ayodhya incident has sparked of serious communal conflicts resulting in violence taking a very heavy toll in cities as can be seen in the table below.[33]

Major Cities		*Killed*	*Injured*
1.	Bombay	500	1000
2.	Surat	184	60
3.	Bhopal	139	450
4.	Calcutta	25	50
5.	Kanpur	62	118
6.	Ahmedabad	150	700
7.	Hyderabad	13	50
8.	Mysore	9	260
9.	Banglore	28	150
10.	Total in major cities	1100	3378
11.	Total Post-demolition violence victims in India	1700	5500

The Statewise break up of communal conflicts resulting in deaths and injuries caused after 6th December 1992 at Ayodhya as shown below indicate the intensity of the communal violence in India.[34]

Sl.No.	*State*	*Total Toll*	*Property damaged*
1.	Maharashtra	259	3.9 crores
2.	Uttar Pradesh	170	5.5 crores
3.	Gujrat	208	7.25 crores
4.	Rajasthan	49	7.37 crores
5.	Karnataka	78	5.97 crores
6.	Madhya Pradesh	133	1.05 crores
7.	Andhra Pradesh	20	6.00 Lakh
8.	West Bengal	27	N.A.
9.	Bihar	40	N.A.
10.	Kerala	21	1.5 crores
11.	Assam	115	49.0 Lakh
12.	Orissa	02	6.00 Lakh
13.	Tamil Nadu	02	70.00 Lakh
14.	Haryana	01	N.A.
15.	Chandigarh	15	N.A.
16.	Delhi	17	N.A.
17.	Jammu & Kashmir	7	N.A.

It is noticed by all enlightened persons that social conflicts, violence and destruction of property are gradually increasing in our plural society. Conflict in Indian society has apparently been intensified by the Ayodhya outrage in a substantial manner. While there are some whispered reference to the possibility of the exacerbation of extremism among both major religious groups in India, there does not appear to be any serious concern about handling such an eventuality through pre-emptive political action.[35] In Kashmir the low intensity conflicts have caused serious internal security repercussions and the situation can be visualised from the following figures of 1991 :-

1.	No of civilians killed	1028
2.	No of security forces killed	318
3.	Militants killed	1378
4.	Militants arrested	4323
5.	Militants surrendered	585
6.	Militants released	17

Every riot and every communal conflict between communities is an open invitation for criminals and anti-social elements to join in and share the booty. The recent Bombay riots between Dec. 1992 and January 1993 were results of combined anti-social activities of criminals, communalists and the partisan police who were in the forefront of all the looting, killing and destruction.[36] An estimated 784 people lost their lives in Bombay riots. In their long term recommendations the Bombay riot report has urged that the police force be revamped and reoriented and special courts be set up to try riot-related offences. A decade back between October 31 and November 4, 1984 an incredible 2,733 Sikhs were killed in Delhi. Almost 10 years after the Delhi riots despite one commission and two committees, the subject is still not closed and even in several instances the FIRs had not been written. The Committee has recommended severe action against 298 policemen and also urged complete overhauling and re-organisation of the police force. Policemen all over the Country need better training and better understanding of our problems. The Home Minister told Rajya Sabha that a total of 2132 persons were killed in 13 states in connection with 1149 cases of communal riots between June 1, 1991 and July 31, 1993. 14

persons were rendered handicapped, 22 homeless and 15838 arrested during the period.[37] 142 persons were arrested in connection with the chain of bomb blasts in Bombay. Conflicts in a plural society like India have resulted in demands for separate states of Jharkhand in Bihar hill state of Uttarkhand in U.P., and Gorkha land demand. It is a testimony to the resilience of plural society of India that it has been able to withstand the violent social conflicts like communal riots, terrorism, insurgency, caste wars etc during the last 45 years and has been able to maintain its democratic, secular and plural characteristics. Police, administrators and the entire criminal justice system require restructuring and radical reforms to cater for the needs of the plural society which has the difficult task of managing various communal, religious, ethnic and social conflicts.

Low-intensity conflicts and insiduous subversion by foreign powers

Low intensity conflicts involve irregular forces-querrilla armies, national liberation movements, terrorist groups, private militia and narcotic traffickers arranged either individually or in various combinations, against state military and police forces in an unconventional warfare through mostly non-state actors abetted by foreign countries enemical to the nation-state. India today finds itself embroiled in combating an effective low-intensity conflict predicament in Punjab and Kashmir, conflict fomented by Pakistan.[38] Low-Intensity conflicts can be described as confrontation short of full scale war, generally waged in peace-time, in a hostile neighbouring country with the aim of encouraging secession by creating disorder, subversion terrorism and religious struggles. Since independence, India has faced a number of low-intensity conflicts that have revolved around perceived concepts of secession in north eastern states of Nagaland, Mizoram & Tripura and during the last decade in Kashmir and Punjab, abetted and aided by Pakistan. Pakistan has played a master stroke by initiating an effective, well-coordinated and volatile LIC against India in Punjab and Kashmir.[39]

Overhand of intelligence net work, conduct of psychological operations, effective border management, coordination of media, effective civic action programmes are some of the suggested recommendations for combating LIC. Strong political will, effective use of army and Border security force and effective large scale operations against LIC are needed. Since low-intensity conflicts are complex in nature, the battlefield must be shared by soldiers, statesmen, economists, politicians, social reformers and the people of the area and a long range national policy has to be worked out. A recent analysis has revealed that Bangladesh has emerged as the new sanctuary for all the insurgents after the loss of Kachin camps to the Myanmar Army.[40] A considerable number of ULFA activists were still hiding in Bangladesh.

Two aspects of proxy war waged by Pakistan through low-intensity operations in Kashmir need attention. Firstly we do not seem to realise the implications of the fact that Pakistan is increasingly pushing in Afghans, Sudanese and nationals of other countries. It should be clear that infiltration of nations from other countries is designed to internationalise the issue. Secondly experience of the proxy war for three and a half years should make it quite clear that it would be far more cost-effective to squarely confront Pakistan at the border itself and to prevent its intervention rather than dealing with the infiltrators in the cities and towns in the interiors".[41]

Conflicts in Indian Society and their impact on Internal Security

In Bihar, Maoist Communist Centre (MCC), an underground organisation, inflicts crude brutal punishments to those it views as offenders. MCC is in full control of Gaya, Aurangabad, Chatra and Palaman and has strong influence in Gehanabad, Nawadah, Patna (rural), Hazaribagh and Giridh. The MCC activists are reportedly committed Massacre of the people in the past as can be seen in the table:-

Table showing MCC Massacres in Bihar

Year & month	District	Massacred by MCC	
1986 (Sept)	Aurangabad	11	Rajputs.
1987 (May)	Aurangabad	42	Rajputs
1981 (Jan)	Gaya	2	Policemen
1991 (March)	Gaya	5	Muslims.
1991 (May)	Gaya	1	BJP MP
1991 (Dec)	Gaya	3	Bhumihars
1992 (Feb)	Gaya	37	Bhumihars
1992 (Sept)	Chatra	1	Policemam
1992 (Sept)	Gaya	5	MCC Rebels
1993 (Jan)	Gaya	3	Yadavs.

(Source: India Today August 31, 1993. P/71 - FA-RZAND AHMED - Bihar. Crime as punishment)

MCC claims to fight oppression by the upper castes and has taken deep and dangerous roots in the impoverished stretch of Central Bihar. The MCC, according to a social researcher, has been responsible for massacres of ciffer caste exploiters including 37 Bhumihars killed in Bara village in 1992. 68,734 cases of atrocities were committed on Scheduled castes in Uttar Pradesh and Madhya Pradesh and 14157 cases on S.T. in Madhya Pradesh during May 1993, 21 cases of atrocities were committed on SCs in the capital during June 1993.[42] 299 Rape cases were reported during 1992 against Tribal women in the Country with the highest of 21 being from Madhya Pradesh.[43] There seems to be no end of ethnic conflicts in Assam and North Eastern States upto Dec 1992. 3206 ULFA activists had surrendered with 141 assorted weapons and 2648 rounds of ammunition giving hope that peace will come to Assam but about 500 hard core activists are still at large and they are determined to carry on their struggle. The National Socialist Council of Nagaland (NSCN) and Hmar Peoples Convention (HPC) militants have turned the inaccessible jungles of North Cachar hills district into their hide out. India as a plural society finds itself in a bind in the search for a solution to the prolonged social conflicts which constantly effect the internal security of the Country.

In a plural society it is necessary to share power and plural society take to proportional representation with all parties offered seats in all decision-making bodies, including the cabinet itself.[44] There are strong arguments for proportional representation and parliamentary system of democracy in plural societies. The four characteristics of consociational democracy are (1) Government by a grand coalition of the political leaders of all significant segments of the plural society, (2) the mutual veto which serves as an additional protection of vital minority interests, (3) proportionality as principal standard of political representation and (4) a high degree of autonomy for each segment to run its own internal affairs. Such a system can be suitable to consociational government and federalism. Lyphart message to the political leaders of plural societies is to encourage them to engage in a form of political engineering, if they wish to establish or strengthen democratic institutions in their countries, they must become consociational engineers.[45] Jaun J. Linz holds that plural societies should have parliamentary democracies because they provide a greater flexibility in the process of transition to a consolidation of democracy.[46] In a plural society many groups represent various interests and pluralism can be expressed by conflict or agreement among groups. Finally in a pluralistic society, one group is quite, aware of what other groups are doing.[47] Conflicts arising out of the sufferings of the millions due to poverty, discriminations hatred, vested interests and large scale industrialisation need greater attention.

Ethnic conflicts in Manipur, Nagaland and Tripura continue unabated. In Manipur since 1984 the NSCN is reported to have killed 3 officers and 32 personnel of the security forces in 10 different ambushes, looted over 204 crores in 11 incidents of land robberies and killed about 112 people on suspicion till December 1987.[48] In Nagaland NSCN made its presence felt when within a space of five days in Dec

1991, 14 CRP personnel were gunned down and in middle March 1992 six SSB personnel were killed in an ambush. Ethnic conflicts between various ethnic groups of Manipur and Nagaland continue causing violence on large scale. In order to effectively deal with various types of conflicts, police and Central Police Organisations must get regular two months refresher training, latest weapons and equipment and clear cut directions of the Government.

Police Response to Conflicts

The official commissions of Enquiry in India, the Dayal Report of the Ranchi riots (1967), the Madan report of the Bhiwandi riots (1970) and the Reddy report of the Ahmedabad riots (1969) and press reports about police response to riots of December 1992 after destruction of Babri Masjid Ramjanam Bhumi disputed structure all over the Country have inidcated deep bias in the police force of the Country. It is obvious that in the lower and subordinate rungs of the police and probably the army, there is anti-minority prejudice. It is unfortunate that the citizen's approach to the police officers for protection, which is the duty of the police officers to give and not the obligation of the citizens to seek, is considered pestering.[49] In order to develop impartial attitude towards minorities, police training courses ought to evolve better techniques perhaps psycho-analytic in orientation, to make officers introspective about their attitudes to outgroups such as the minorities and the scheduled castes/scheduled tribes and sensitive to the implications of a pluralist state system. A well structure police training course should be able to recognise the realities of the conflicts of a plural society and particularly the psychological barriers to adequate role performance and devise orientation courses to break them down. Sensitivity to the implications of a pluralist state system can only come through the self conscious cultivation of attitudes which foster cordial relationships between communities.[50]

Conflicts of Plural Society and its Policy Perspectives

The basic issues which emerge from the analysis of conflicts are as under:-

(1) What kind of policies should the government implement to minimise the ill effects of conflicts?

(2) How can plural society bring pluralistic adjustments and harmony and build up a strong united nation?

(3) What lessons can we draw in this regard from the experiences of the past?

It has been realized in India that an over-represented minority creates a commensurate anti-minority front.[51] Similarly pampering or overdone protection can create anti-minority backlash in a plural society as can be seen from the aftermath of Ayodhya December 1992 incidents. The time lag in the modernisation process of ethnic groups and the minorities is mainly due to their representation in those sectors of the economy which are the vanguards of technical change and economic development. Sponsored development of one community vis-a-vis another runs into several different kinds of constraints and problems. One of the crucial problems is the limited spread-effect of the community-based economic development measures because the masses of the community are unable to make the leap forward. A government wedded to the free-market economy, inevitably confronts problems of irreconcilable class/community interests which further assumes sharper edges in the context of under-development, delayed industrialisation and uneven regional development.[52] Intra-Community elite conflicts expose from time to time the nature and dimensions of the community-based relative deprivations which inevitably nurse communal and ethnic unrest in plural societies.

Plural societies have to carry out the difficult task of compromising and coalsce many different and conflicting group interests within its broad national-interest perspective. Integrative solution to conflicts are not merely compromises but should provide increasing benefits and fair play to all the parties concerned. The education system of plural societies must have sufficient grasp and appreciation of the plurality of culture which constitute modern nations so that diverse ethnic, religious, racial and social groups may automatically participate in and develop their own culture and special interests, within the limits of the laws of a common civilization of a nation. In a plural society administrators and police personnel should be acutely conscious of their creative role in the healthy development of the pluralist state system. "The consolidation of the pluralists state-system in modern time necessitates a more complex theoretical frame of reference for the understanding of the ethnocentric process than what is available in the social science today....deeper understanding of the social reality of ethnocentrisum would dictate policies" which are more relevant and in conformity with the pluralist state ideology.[53] Legacy of exploiting issues for short-term political gains must be put aside for a politics of consensus to re-establish a dialogue between different groups in a plural society. Management of conflicts need a very scientific and pragmatic approach by the state and the central government.

Prof. Amartya Sen said it was the practice of this pluralism that had been deeply threatened by some recent political developments, particularly by sequence oi violent events at Ayodhya in December 1992.[54] More than 150 places of worships were razed and 90 people killed in Assam violence following Ayodhya developments. Meanwhile Bangladesh immigrants added a new dimension to the infiltration problem. The agitation for Bodoland has resulted in violence in Assam. According to figures released by the Rajya Sabha in April 1989, the Bodos had succeeded in killing 62 people in terrorist attacks with hundred of others dying in related violence. Since 1986 at least 600 people have died in Bodo-related violence.[55] The evolution of ULFA is rooted in the failure of the government to address ethnic conflicts in Assam adequately and ultimately operation Bajrang and operation RHINO were carried out by the Army and Central Police Organisations. Results of operations are given below:-.[56]

Categories	*Operation Bajarang Nov 1990*	*OPS RHINO Sept 91*
ULFA Activists killed	15	—
ULFA Activists held	2867	4212
Weapons seized	1208	850
Cash recovered	Rs. 5 Crores	Rs. 64 Lakhs
Ammunition recovered	—	9946 rounds

The extremist violence in Tripura has been presenting a serious challenge and the All Tripura Tribal Force (ATTE) has been responsible for killing of 22 persons, looting market and banks and extorting money from transporters since April 1993.[57] The victims of the ATTF 's killing squads-altogether 137 in the last four years have been seriously threatening the internal security of the State. A proper solution to ethnic conflicts has to be found through political process and balanced economic growth of the Country.

The spreading rot in the Indian socio-political system is finding cross display in the increasing conflicts of our plural society. The functioning of the various organs of the state including the instruments of law and order as well as criminal justice system, is such that they have lost their credibility. The security situation within the country continues to deteriorate but no comprehensive strategic policies seem to emerge. The entrenched vested interests at different levels and points in the social order, economic structure, political alignments and administrative set are visibly weakening, indeed undermining, the plural democratic system of India." "The present government decided to set up a security council to deal with the increasing security problems but nothing of the sort has happened so far".[58]

Experience the world over demonstrates that for effective management of conflicts of plural societies, a clear policy line helps. "If your policy changes from incidents to incident then you have already lost". "In India unfortunately, the government is doing exactly that. It vacillates between softness and sternness having in the process the words of both".[59] Communal, ethnic and social conflicts have been with us for last four and half decades but inspite of these experiences, lessons have been learnt and no comprehensive strategy evolved to prevent or combat conflicts. Except for empty rhetoric, nothing is being done to permanently cure the diseased base of our politico-social order. On the other hand politics is becoming more and more exploitative, criminalised and unaccountable to the people and economy more and more lop-sided, imbalanced and distorted. The increasing momentum of negative and nihilistic forces is rendering the country incapable of solving, within reasonable time and at resonable cost, any serious problems of conflicts. It is time that we evolve a comprehensive strategy to eliminate the root causes of various conflicts from the plural society and meet the challenges thrown by various types of conflicts by adopting a well structured politico-social strategy having short term and long term action plans as their essential components. The short term measures should include: putting strong and sustained pressure on the leaders of the various conflict groups and their collaborators, denying them extra supply of oxygen through psychological operations, and removing subverting elements. from the government and semi-government organisation; prosecuting speedily through the designated courts and providing the honourable time of retreat to all those willing to side with the Government, launching an educational blitz through media and ultimately exhibiting a firm united national will to resolve the conflicts in a democratic spirit. The long term measures should include fundamental reforms of Indian polity and socio-economic system, having a culture of constructivity creativity and compassion.[60]

The Accommodation of Conflicts by Political, Economic and Social Reforms

W. Arthur Hevis has been one of the first thinkers to pay attention to the crucial role of political institutions in plural societies. In his book politics in West Africa (1965) he argued that in a plural society it is necessary to share power and it can be done by suitable political institutions. The plural society goes back to the primary meaning of democracy and though proportional representation all parties can be offered seats in all decision making bodies including the Cabinet itself. [61] Arend Lyphert has referred to several plural societies in Europe which have achieved stable democracy by consociational methods. The four characteristics of consociational democracy are:-

1. Government by a grand coalition of the political parties of all significant segments of the plural society.

2. The mutual veto which serves as an additional protection of vital interests of minorities and other groups,

3. Proportionality as principal standard of political representation, and

4. A high degree of autonomy for each segment to run its own internal affairs.[62]

To ameliorate ethnic conflicts must be preceded by an understanding of the sources and pattern of that conflict. According to him democratic approaches entail measures to contain, limit, channel and manage ethnic conflict rather than to eradicate it and this needs careful political engineering followed by a good dosage of balanced economic development of the area concerned. The Anglo American plurality electoral system is not well suited to plural societies because it produces discrimination against small groups. A well structured federal system with balanced economic growth and healthy spirit of consociational democracy can alone accommodate all conflicts of plural societies. Federalism can be used as a consociational method when plural societies want to live together by having political engineering to mitigate political ethnic or economic conflicts. Some social scientists believe that the use of consociational methods can mitigate conflicts in many third world countries which have plural societies.[63] Radical political, economic and social reforms with a spirit of the accommodation of conflict hold the key in plural societies. Donald L. Horowitz stresses that asserts that the parliamentary system of government is better suited to plural societies because it makes possible to share the use of executive power among several groups. The success or failure of a plural society is principally related to the way in which all economic, intellectual and other power resources are distributed among competing groups in a fair and just manner. In India, the political institutions established by 1950 Constitution have been sufficiently suitable to maintain a federal, democratic and plural society although not without serious conflicts but it seems that they have also caused malfunctioning over the years which could be corrected or mitigated by progressive institutional reforms in political economic and social system. Democratic sharing of power on more or less equitable and just basis would strengthen the Indian Socio-political system and mitigate various emerging ethnic, religious and social conflicts. The Centre State relations and the nature of Indian federalism need fresh look in this context so that aspirations of all segments of the society are fulfilled.

Concluding Remarks

Where nations can flounder through internal or external conflicts, they can also grow in strength and stature when there is suitable resolution of conflicts. Half the battle is won if one were to foresee an approaching conflict situation and plan in advance to forestall it and be adequately prepared to resolve and sublimate the conflict situation.[64] Intelligence agencies and policy planners have an important role in combating conflicts. Unity in diversity and principle of co-existence along with open discussions for conflict resolutions are essential for a plural society which is wedded to the ideals of democracy, secularism, social justice and federalism. What is needed today is sound political leadership, combined with a strong vision of a secular, democratic and progressive nation, if India is to come in terms with the Caste, ethnic, communal and religious conflicts which at times appear to tear the very fabric of our plural society apart by the frightening intensity of their outbreaks. The challenge in the years ahead will be to mould a frame of participative democracy that will accommodate the various interests of a multi-ethnic, multi-lingual and multi-religious plural society and allow federalism to develop in favour of devolution of power to the states and decentralisation of political authority to the Panchayat Raj institutions.[65] This should be a matter of concern to every Indian: how can we protect our plural society from endemic conflicts and ensure social justice to all citizens.

REFERENCES

1. Lewis A. Coser—"The functions of Social conflict"-1956, P. 151-156.

2. *Ibid*.

3. Talcott Parson —Social system. Routledge & Kegan Paul Ltd-London 1956- P. 27-28.

4. See for further details Stuart chase-Roads to Agreement London; Ross Stagner (ed). The Dimensions of Human conflicts Ditroit 1967; Harold Lasswell, Psychology and Politics, Chicago 1930; T.W Adorno The Authoritarian Personality New York 1956; Kenneth Boulding,Conflict and Defence, New York 1962; Abram Kardiner and Lionel oversey, The Mark of oppression New York 1951.

5. For further details see George Sunimel conflict Illusions 1955; A.W. Small, General Sociology, Chicago 1905; Lewis A. Coser, Functions of conflict, London 1956; Ralf Dharendorf, Class and Class conflict in Industrial society; London 1959.

6. Karl Marx: The Poverty of Philosophy in Mar-Engels-Selected works Vol.4, Moscow 1976.

7. Karl Marx, Perface to a contribution to the critique of Political Economy in Mar-Engels-Selected works Vol.I Moscow 1951.

8. Lewis a Coser in, Social Aspects of Conflict in International Encyclopedia of the social science Vol 3 & 4 complete and unabridged-Edited by Davis L. Sills- London 1972, P. 232.

9. J.S. Furnivall, Netherlands India Cambridge University Press, Cambridge 1967.

10. M.G. Smith—The Plural Society in the British West Indies, University of California Press, Berkley and Los Angeles 1965.

11. John Rex—Aspects of Modern Sociology- Social conflict- A conceptual and theoretical analysis- Longman London 1981, P. 85.

12. Ralf Daharendorf—Class and Class conflicts in industrial societies, Routbedge & Kegan Paul London 1959.

13. Rabushka and Shepsle—1972,P. 62-92.

14. Rabushka and Shepsle—Politics in Plural societies-A theory of Democratic Instability- 1972,P. 20-21,62)

15. The Hindustan Times 3 July 1993- p.4, New Delhi.
16. Sen's lecture on "Indian Pluralism", The Hindustan Times 3 July 1993, New Delhi.
17. Rajni Kothari—Pluralism and Secularism, Lessons of Ayodhya. Economic and Political Weekly Dec 19-26, 1992, P. 2696.
18. Sen's Lecture on "Indian Pluralism" . The Hindustan Times, 3 July 1993- New Delhi, P. 4.
19. Yogendra Singh—(1959) Group States of Faction in Rural Community. Journal of Social Sciences-Vol, I P. 61.
20. Baljit Singh (1961) Next step in village India-A Study of land Reforms and group dynamics, Bombay 1961-P. 108-120.
21. B.K. Roy Burman— Federalism in Perspectives-Problems and Prospects for North-East India-Mainstream, Vol XXXI No.39 Aug 7, 1993, P.8.
22. Dr. B. Varma-Insurgency and Counter Insurgency, Uppal Publishing House, New Delhi-1988 P. 31.
23. Gould, Harold A. Time Dimension and structural change in an Indian Kinship system- A problem of conceptual Refinement in Milton Singer and Bernard Cohn (ed) Structure and change in Indian society.
24. Yogendra Singh— Social stratification and change in India. 1980 P. 48.
25. Dipankar Gupta—Hierarchy and Difference- An Introduction in Social stratification edited by Dipankar Gupta, 1992, P. 18.
26. B.K. Roy Burman— Indigenous Peoples and Their Quest for Justice. Social Action 39, Jan-March (1988).
27. B.R. Roy Burman—Issues in Land Reforms in N.E. Tribal Areas- Mainstream Aug. 1 and 8 (1987).
28. Indian Express 20 August 1993. Lok Sabha Questions.
29. Tatu Vanhamen—"Politics of Ethnic Nepotism- India as an Example".
30. For Similar views see Lt. Genl V.K. Nayar- Threat from within - India's Internal Security Environment- Lancer 1992, P. 250.

31. Source —Times of India (Ahmedabad Edition), January 24, April 13 1981. Quoted by Pradip Kumar Bose- Social mobility and caste violence-A study of the Gujrat Riots -in Caste, Caste conflict and Reservation 1985. Centre for special Studies Surat P.144.

32. Tatu Vanhamen—Politics of Ethnic Nepotism- India as an Example. Sterling Publishers Pvt.Ltd. New Delhi- 1991, P.127.

33. Raj Chengappa and Ramesh Menon. The New Battle Fields. India Today Jan 31, 1993.

34. See Dr. Krishna Mohan Mathur, Police, Laws and Internal Security. Gian Publishing House 1993 & Also Rajya Sabha Questions.

35. Arvind N.Das—Maths of the Aftermath - Monday Dec 21, 1992, The Times of India. New Delhi.

36. See Kalpana Sharma—A story of two riots—The Hindu 20 August 1993. Also Indian People's Human Rights Commission Report on Bombay riots by Justice Suresh and Dand.

37. The Hindu, Delhi 19 August, 1993.

38. V.K.Sood—Low Intensity Conflict: The Source of the Third World Instability Studies in Conflict and Terrorism Vol 15-No. 4 Oct-Dec 1992 Crane Russak- London, P. 233.

39. V.D.Chopra—Genesis of Indo-Pakistan Conflict in Kashmir, New Delhi 1989,Chapter-2.

40. No Solution yet of ethnic unrest. Hindustan Times 31 December 1992.

41. Padam Rosha—Kashmir Policy-An Appraisal- Hindustan Times 28 August 1993 P.13.

42. Questions in Rajya Sabha—Mr Sitaram Kesri told R.S. Hindustan Times,22 August 1993.

43. The Hindu-Delhi 19 August, 1993.

44. See W. Arthur Lewis—Politics in West Africa (1965),P.55-74.

45. Arend Lyphart—Democracy in Plural Societies; a comparative exploration 1980/1977.

46. Linz, Jian J. (1984) Democracy Presidential or Parliamentary; Does it make a difference? Paper for the workship on Political parties in Southern Cone, Washington.

47. Harold Koontz, Cyrial O.Donnel and Heinz, Weihrich-Management-M.C. Grain Hill Instructional Book Company Eighth Edition 1984-86,P.75.

48. The Hindu 21 January 1988. Insurgency in North East.

49. Justice Reddy Report into the communal disturbances at Ahmedabad and other places 1969. Govt of Gujrat 1970,P. 215-16.

50. Ratna Naidu—The Communal Edge to Plural socities- India and Malaysia- Vikas Publishing House, Ghaziabad 1980- P.123.

51. For a detailed analysis—See J.A. Laponce-The Protection of Minorities by the Electoral system- in Western Political Quarterly 10 (2) June 1957, P.318 - 39.

52. Ratna Naidu—The Communal Edge to Plural Society, 1980- P.131.

53. Ratna Naidu—The Communal Edge to Plural Societies- India and Malaysia - 1980, P.147-148.

54. Sen's Lecture on Indian Pluralism. The Hindustan Times 3 July 1993. New Delhi.

55. India Today 30 April, 1989, P.58.

56. India Today 15 January, 1992.

57. Indian Express—Violence in Tripura-Editorial 30 July, 1993.

58. A disturbing Security Scenario-Rajendra Nath. The Tribune 26 August, 1993,P. 8.

59. JAGMOHAN—Terrorism- Causes and Cure. Hindustan Times 25 November, 1992.

60. For similar views see Jagmohan Terrorism—Causes and Cure. Hindustan Times 25 November, 1992.

61. Lewis, W.Arthur (1965) Politics in West Africa London—George Allen and Unwin, P.57-74.

62. Arend Lyphart-1980/1977—Democracy in Plural Societies. A comparative Exploration- London,P.1-60

63. For similar views see Donald L. Horowitz- 1985. Ethnic groups in conflict Berkely pp 568-576; Nohuen Dietor 1984- Electoral Systems between Science and Fiction.

64. J.N. Nanda—Conflict and Co-existence in India. Concepts, New Delhi, 1991,P. 139.

65. For similar views see Alexandra George—Social Ferment in India. Orient Longman 1986,P.324.

5

Management of Disasters and Crisis Situations

World Health Organisation has defined disaster as "any occurrence that causes damage, economic disruption, loss of human life and deterioration in health and the health services on a scale sufficient to warrant an extra-ordinary response from outside the affected community or area." Disaster management aims at reducing the adverse impact of disasters on human health, through preparedness and by bringing the right technology to bear in a timely, coordinated and effective manner, for each phase of operation, i.e. rescue & relief, rehabilitation and reconstruction. On 7 April 1991 all over the Country, World Health Day was celebrated with the slogan: "Should disaster strike, Be prepared". All disasters need very careful management for all phases of operations by various agencies in a most coordinated manner. Crisis refers to the decisive moment or turning point and is synonymous with natural or man made calamities like floods, cyclones, earthquakes, hurricanes, giant storms, landslides, droughts, wars, major air crashes, rail or road accidents or any critical situation which brings in its wake death, destruction and misery. Crisis can also mean a widespread law and order situation, a nation-wide strike, bandh or political agitation, disrupting normal life of the community. Management of crisis situation demand well-prepared contingency plans and effective implementation of these contingency plans at all levels in an effective and well co-ordinated manner. Police Organisations are usually so busy administering current business that they give little thought to the planning of police procedure for times of disaster or catastrophe such as earthquakes, fires floods or tornados or for times of acute social disturbance including demonstrations, mob situations, riots, strikes and political unrest.[1] United Nations has declared 1990- 2000 as International Decade for Natural Disaster Reduction (IDNDR) and has asked states/Nations/ International Organisations response to avert and minimise losses and carry out relief operations in a systematic manner.

Types of Emergencies/Disasters/Crisis Situations

If we trace the history of various disasters in the World in 1988 alone there were 74 major floods, 5 cyclones, 11 hurricanes, 34 giant storms, 17 landslides, 17 earthquakes, 18 droughts and 162 major accidents, of a magnitude exceeding local and national capacities to cope. The earthquake in the Islamic Republic of Iran in June 1990 took an estimated 40,000 lives and left half a million homeless. In the Chinese province of Human floods followed by violent storms affected some 20 million people. Chemical and nuclear catastrophes, oil-spills and new ecological dimensions to the definition of disaster. According to United States data, between 1900 and 1988, some 47 million people worldwide became homeless due to natural disasters. It is unfortunate that natural disasters, cyclones, floods, landslides, storms surge, earthquakes, volcanic eruptions, droughts, forest-fires continue to strike in some part or the other of the World. Major earthquakes recorded in India during the last fifty years are as under:-

Date		Affected State		Richter scale
1. Aug 15, 1950	-	Assam	-	8.5
2. Jan 27, 1966	-	North of Indo-Nepal border	-	6.1
3. Dec 10, 1967	-	Maharashtra	-	6.5
4. April 13, 1969	-	Bhadrachalam (A.P.)	-	6.5

5.	Jan 19, 1975	- Kinnaur/Lahaul/Spiti	-	7.5
6.	Oct 20, 1991	- Uttar Kashi (U.P.)	-	NA
7.	Aug 9, 1990	- North India	-	6.0
8.	Aug 28, 1993	- Maharashtra	-	5.1
9.	Sept 4, 1993	- West Maharashtra/Goa	-	4.7
10.	Sept 4, 1993	- Srinagar (J & K)	-	6.0
11.	Sept 1, 1993	- Jammu and Kashmir	-	5.8

In India four cyclones in quick succession lashed Andhra Pradesh during October and November 1976 to November 1977. The death toll was 9733 persons in the two districts of Krishna and Guntur. In November 1977 Cyclone and tidal wave disaster in all 71 lakh persons in 2302 villages lost their properties and standing crops. The earthquake in Koynanagar area of Satara district in December 1967 has the intensity of 7.5 on the Richer scale. About 200 persons died, 2000 persons were injured and 60,000 houses were damaged due to the earthquake. Recent earthquakes in Uttar Kashi areas of Uttar Pradesh and Lattur areas of Maharashtra State were also serious disasters causing immense loss of lives and property. According to one estimate, approximately 1500 people perished in Uttar Kashi earthquake of October 1991. Broadly speaking there can be following crisis-situations/ diasters which need immediate response:-

1. Earthquakes.
2. Floods.
3. Famines and droughts.
4. Cyclones and Hurricanes.
5. Volcano eruptions.
6. Assassination of Prime Minister/Death of President.
7. Land slides.
8. Bomb-explosion/explosion in mines.
9. National/State level bandhs and strikes.
10. Riots/Terrorist violence.
11. Air crash/air accidents.
12. War
13. Serious railway/bus accidents.

14. Bhopal Gas leak tragedy/environmental tragedies.
15. Resignation of P.M.
16. Miscellaneous situations.

Predict most of Disasters

Lt. Gen. Y. N. Sharma, has observed that an efficient organisation of high standard would be able to predict most of the man-made disasters and could thus either prevent their occurrences or mitigate their effects by early mobilization of resources.[2] It is quite obvious that response to a natural disaster must be based on existing local infra-structure and resources at the initial stages although resources from outside can be mobilised gradually at later stages. The task of disaster management can be broadly summarised as under:-

1. Predictions.
2. Planning.
3. Preparation.
4. Prompt response and public relations activities.
5. Rescue/Evacuation.
6. Relief and first aid.
7. Rehabilitation.
8. Restoration of law and order and normal life.

It can be briefly summned as Four 'P' & Four 'R'. During management of disasters sufficient attention has to be paid to public relations activities and establishment of Centres for giving information to anxious relatives and that correct and timely information could scotch rumours. First aid assistance to the injured need to be given on utmost priority. Coordination of tasks & works between various agencies like civil defence, home guards, medical services, army & other voluntary agencies is one of the most important part of management of disasters.

Serious steps needed for Management of Disasters

1. Planning

For each disaster a contingency plan needs to be worked out well in advance as a part of preparedness. At Central, State and district levels, cirsis management committee must work out various contingency plans and should keep them uptodate. Like Internal Security schemes these contingency plans should contain maps, names of officials & their telephone numbers, various steps required to be taken for each disasters & how information centre cum control rooms will be manned round the clock. Critical areas for rescue and relief operations are to be identified and operational plans have to be worked out in great details. Generally disasters follow a definte time sequence-the threat, the warning the impact and the response.[3] The threat and the warning are virtually absent in the case of all earthquakes. The warning phase is usually much shorter, varying from seconds to hours and the impact phase is the crisis itself. The response involves taking stock of the total loss of life & the response to the disaster in the shortest possible time. Floods cause a greater loss to life and property throughout the world than any other type of disasters.[4] Disaster planning must always be done in advance because there is no time to plan when the disaster strikes. Planning for contingency schemes for disaster-management need to be drawn at the national, state and district levels for each type of crisis situation/disaster. It should broadly contain the following:-

1. Map of area, topographic and administrative set up.

2. Previous history of all disasters/serious crisis situations—An effective warning and Alarm system for disasters.

3. Man Power planning:
   (a) Requisitioning of army and Central Police Org., Home guards, voluntary organisations.
   (b) Available police force.

4. Material Planning:

   (a) Equipment.

   (b) Transport.

   (c) Medical equipment.

   (d) Consumable commodities.

   (e) Other equipments for rescue and relief.

5. Control Room functioning.

6. Alert plans and warning system:-

   (a) move of raising alarms-use of Radio/TV/Public ad dress system.

   (b) Familiarisation of public with warning system.

7. Evacuation/Relief Plan. Establishment of relief camp, salvage operations.

8. Operative Plan-Supply of food & essential necessities.

9. Follow up Stage-Preparation of list of dead, missing and injured persons.

10. Transport arrangement.

11. Hospital/Medical support.

12 Maintenance of Law & Order.

13. Plan for conducting VIP visits.

14. Administrative Coordination.

15. Lessons learnt and issue of appreciation letters to Organisations and individuals-Estimation of loss of lives & property.

16 Miscellaneous details:
   (a) List of vital installations.
   (b) Important Telephone numbers.
   (c) Location of hospitals/Police camps & Army Camps.

For each contingency, a separtae contingency plan for each district and state is to be worked out and it should incorporate all possible matters related to equipment, staffing, procedures and mobilization of assistance from other Organisations/Departments. Red alert is required when a major disaster threatens the safety of the community necessitating total mobilization of manpower and other resources & request for major assistance from all other Organisations.

2. Organising the Management of a Disaster

On occurrence of a disaster, the senior district level officers must report to the state & Central Govts. all known facts relating to disaster and mobilize control room for minute to minute communication. The report should include (1) type of disaster, (2) time it occurred, (3) affected area, (4) estimates of number of dead and injured and homes destroyed or damaged, (5) type of assistance needed, and (6) action taken regarding rescue, relief and rehabilitation at local level within available limited resources. Mobilisation of all local resources has to be done at the earliest possible time. Local officers must take all possible actions for immediate first aid & rescue of persons. Contingency plans should be implemented as far as possible with local available resources and demands for manpower, resources and equipment should be projected to higher formations. Organising a disaster relief would include providing of first aid, rescue of affected personnel, distribution of relief material and succour and coordination with other organisations and voluntary agencies.

3. Staffing the Contingency Plan

For effective implementation of disaster management plan, trained and experienced officers should be utilised at the spot and even at control room level. Services of local army units and home guards and other voluntary agencies should be immediately sought to supplement the available manpower resources. For quick and timely response, immediate mobilization of all resources including army and local Central Police Organisation should be done. In all calamities, the first 24 hours are the most crucial requiring tremendous efforts on the part of the various agencies engaged in relief and rescue operations. Prisoners can help in rescue & relief operations in certain ways.

4. Directing the Implementation of Contingency Operational Plan

It is imperative for effective implementation of disaster management plan that senior officers should immediately rush to the place of disaster to take over all command and direct various rescue & relief operations at the affected location. Army can be requested to establish a Tactical headquarter & control room at the place near the affected site to direct the relief and rescue operations.

5. Co-ordination

Administrative and operational coordination in the rescue and relief operations is an essential requirement for the effective implementation of any disaster management plan. Disaster Management Coordination Committee at Central, state & district level need to be formed for bringing needed coordination. Management of disaster needs integration of multifarious agencies involved in the task to obtain optimum results.

6. Communication, Control Room and Information Centre

During disaster management, control room works as the nerve centre for collection and dissemination of information. Control Room should contradict rumours and exaggerated versions of the disasters. It can give warning to the people in advance, details of precautions to be taken, official plan of rescue, relief and rehabilitation and seek people's cooperation in required areas. There should be joint control rooms at the district headquarters and state headquarters consisting of the representatives of the various organisations involved with disaster management plans. Control Rooms at the State Headquarters should involve head of all concerned departments and should provide policy guidelines. Briefing to the press and electronic media from control room is regularly needed so that people are properly informed about the various efforts being carried out to manage the disaster control room should have all possible information and public should be able to obtain required information from the Control Room/Information Centre.

7. Motivation and Role of Citizens

It is necessary to motivate local citizens and voluntary agencies to provide assistance in coping with disaster situations. Following areas for cooperation and assistance of citizens have been identified and all able bodied young boys & girls/citizens should be encouraged to come forward:

"1. Take the wounded immediately to the nearest health institution for medical care;

2. Do not necessarily crowd around the place of catastrophe;

3 Learn first aid so that your services can be utilised in times of emergency;

4. Donate blood and save a precious life;

5. Ensure proper storage of poisonous gases to avoid leakages;

6. Help save nature's bounties like air water and land from pollution. Conserve Forests as these help in prevailing floods;

7. In times of drought, floods and earthquakes, give top priority to save human life;

8. Help in containing industrial pollution;

9. Wars, riots, bomb-blasts are acts against humanity. Adopt peaceful ways to fight for your cause;

10. Avoid use of private scooters, motor cycles and cars as much as possible to reduce pollution level. Encourage walking, cycling and use of public transport system".[5]

8. Decision-Making

For effective man power planning, requisitioning of equipment and actual disaster relief operations, a number of decisions have to be carried out from time to time. Effective decision making regarding various rescue, relief and rehabilitation matters have to be done keeping into view, available funds, available equipment and available manpower resources. Requisitioning of Army in aid to civil power for rescue and relief work becomes necessary at the initial stages of the disaster, but constant use of army for prolonged duration needs to be avoided. Decision regarding requisitioning of Army has to be timely and prompt for disaster management. Decision regarding use of Home Guards, village volunteer force and Central Police Organisation is also vital.

9. Budgeting and Accounting

For all rescue, relief and rehabilitation programmes, proper accounting and budgeting of all financial resources and donations is of utmost significance. Financial Assistance and grants received from Central Government, state Governments and Non-Government voluntary Organisations in cash and kind must be properly accounted for.

10. Law and Order Maintenance

In all disasters, there are many anti-social elements who try to exploit the situation and commit crimes in affected areas. Therefore maintenance of law and order and prevention of crime in disaster affected areas become an immediate necessity. Protection of relief camps in the affected areas is also an important requirement. A strict surveillance needs to be kept over bad characters and known criminals.

11. Training

Training for disaster management is needed not only for district level and state level officers but also for the grass root level police officers, army jawans and the citizens of the country. Civil Defence Organisations like Home Guards can play a very useful role in rescue and relief operations. Police officers at all levels need disaster management training for effectively facing such situations with confidence. The subject of watermanship, salvage work and first aid should be given due weightage. All police officers, civilian administrators and even citizens have to be given training in management of disasters.

PROBLEM AREAS

1. Corruption and Misutilization of Funds/Resources

It is very unfortunate that during such calamities and disasters, there are "complaints of mis-appropriation against the police".[6] In the seminar held at SVP, NPA Hyderabad in March 1979 it was admitted that there were a few such cases which came to the notice of the authorities. There is a need for proper screening of social service volunteers who offer help to the victims to prevent imposters and corrupt volunteers. During Andhra Cyclone of 1977 a common theme emerged that the state bureaucracy could not be trusted to distribute funds or material. These perceptions were reinforced by reports of suspension of several state govt. officials on charges of corruption and embezzlement.[7]

2. Lack of Coordination

Even though the Union Government controls the early warning system (through radio, T.V. and telegram), precautionary and immediate rescue and relief has to be initiated by local and State officials. Analysing the rescue and relief operations carried out after Killari-Latur Tragedy, a special report observed: "The lack of coordination was abundantly apparent to observers. Tonnes of grain were despatched to Latur but the affected villages had no fuel or firewood. Truck loads of sari and dhoti were distributed but survivors spent days in hospital without a change of underwear".[8] The lack of co-ordination during the earthquake relief operations was cited as the major problem by both local and foreign voluntary agencies that participate in the action.

3. Lack of Clarity of Roles and responsibilities

While exposing the utter bankruptcy of disaster relief planning by the government and non-governmental organisations, the recent earthquake which left 10,000 people dead and some 1.4 lakh displaced, has thrown up important questions regarding the role of defence services, especially the army, in such eventualities.[9] Disposal of death bodies, for example, is not the work of the members of the Armed Forces.[10] After care of the orphan children is an area where voluntary organisations and social welfare departments have an important role to play.

4. Lack of Adequate Training and Preparedness

It is found that many states have only skeleton schemes for fighting natural calamities without adequate details with the result that in times of emergencies many things have to be done afresh and on an adhoc basis at short notice.[11] It is noticed that many states and districts do not formulate a comprehensive anti-disaster plan and no training is given to the police/other organisations regarding their role in anti-disaster operations.

5. Lack of knowledge of role of volunteers and voluntary agencies

Andhra Pradesh cyclone 1977 disaster management review indicate that bureaucracy has no idea how much voluntary organisations can contribute in terms of technical and human inputs. Many voluntary groups failed to get guidance and direction from the bureaucracy concerning their own programmes and information about Govt's programmes including the items of work, location, work schedules etc. The bureaucracy at times has been found to be most unhelpful and sometimes even non-cooperative including their failure to make payment of the matching contribution promised by the Government.[12] There are at times occasions particularly during the first 48 hours when voluntary agencies are not available. It is suggested that the services of school teachers, lecturers and college students should be mustered to carry out evacuation and relief operations. Persons belonging to Home Guards and Civil Defence Organisations should also be utilized for various evacuation and relief work. A deep sense of distrust and dislike grew between many private relief workers and the administrators because adhoc relief groups were prone to dump the relief material during Andhra Cyclone of 1977 in the more accessible villages and were driven by purego-building.

6. Slow and halting responses

During the November 1977 cyclone in Andhra Pradesh there were allegations that police "searched the spot very late, there being a time lag of utmost seventy two hours".[13] Actually at times publicity was given to distorted facts for certain unfortunate political considerations. Quick and immediate response to disasters particularly earthquakes is essential to save lives of people. There is widespread belief that the Govt. of Andhra Pradesh failed to apply available bureaucratic and technical means to prevent or ameliorate the worst effects of the cyclone of 1977.

During management of disasters, many professionals get concern over the "spoon-feeding" of the survivors and the dominant assumptions of their philosophical frame are:

"(a) Prolonged care of a victim develops a dependency relationship that destroys human dignity and self-reliance;

(b) Concentration of the voluntary effort on rapid delivery of relief items on an enormous scale would side-track the long-term issues of rehabilitation, and

(c) Over emphasis on "doles" and "hand-outs" would also prolong the psychological recovery of the victim."[15]

There has been slow and halting response to disasters at times due to development of such philosophical frame. Several voluntary groups complain of red tape and excessive visits to the concerned State officers (even for getting sales tax exemptions for materials they had procured) and thus slow and halting response of bureaucracy to disaster management.

7. Epidemic and Health Problems

During all natural calamities prevention of epidemics is the responsibility of the public health department and the medical services.

8. Disposal of dead bodies and animal carcases

In order to prevent epidemic and other health problems, disposal of dead bodies and animal carcases becomes a big problem in the absence of firewood. Help of local voluntary agencies should be sought in performing this task since armed forces are not supposed to do this job. In Andhra Pradesh Cyclone of 1977, people were stunned by the near total refusal of suviving villagers to help clear corpses and car-cases because of the gruesome, tiring and repulsive nature of the corpse/car-cases removal process. In most of the villages, the survivors refused to remove the corpses or car-cases, even those in front of their houses.

9. Providing Security and Maintenance of Law and Order

Victims of various disaster suffer psychological trauma and in such a critical situation providing them security and maintenance of law and order becomes an urgent necessity. Day and night patrolling of disaster affected areas to prevent crime becomes a problem during such occasions.

10. Lack of Centralised Ambulance, Accident and Trauma (CAT) Services

It has been realised that there is acute shortage of Centralised Ambulance, Accident and Trauma Services in India and there is need for dedicated personnel to carry out such humanitarian services. Temporary morgues have to be opened where the dead bodies could be transported and kept until they are identified and handed over to the relatives after proper verification. At times unidentified dead bodies have to be cremated/disposed off to avoid spread of epidemics. Generally such dead bodies should be transported in covered vehicles.

11. Visit of VVIP/Politicians

Visit of VVIPs/VIPs to the areas where a natural calamity has occurred, are inevitable in a democratic state. Basic minimum security arrangements for such VVIPs/VIPs should be provided by the district administration/local police but it should not divert attention from rescue and relief operations.

12. We refuse to learn from our calamities

The Country suffers as a perverse relief policy starves disaster areas of funds and adhoc responses compound the tragedy.[17] With funds so scarce, rehabilitation is normally dictated by the politics of convenience while unfortunately most rehabilitation projects have been tainted with corruption in the past. We simply refuse to learn from our calamities.

Case Study—Management of Andhra Cyclone of 1977

On the evening of Saturday 19 November 1977, a devastating cyclone struck coastal Andhra Pradesh, killing approximately 8000 people within a few minutes and rendering several thousands homeless and destitute. Eight coastal districts of Andhra Pradesh are prone to cyclones. In 1977 Andhra cycle the districts of Krishna and Guntur bore the brunt of the cyclone although parts of the adjoining districts of Prakasham, West Godavari and East Godavari were also seriously affected. The magnitude of destruction and death was unprecedented in living memory. It is widely held that no relief came the next day (nor were any aircraft over-head) and it was not until the 21st November that relief teams began to filter into the area. There is widespread belief that the Govt. of Andhra Pradesh failed to apply available bureaucratic and technical resources to prevent or ameliorate the worst effects of the cyclone. The whole nation rose to the occasion and there was an extraordinary involvement of many international, national and state voluntary agencies in rescue, relief and rehabilitation efforts. Relief centres were made, and tonnes of rice, loaves of bread, processed food packets and other necessities of life were supplied to the survivors. Millions of pieces of clothing were distributed to the survivors. International, national, state and local service organisations sent their volunteers with all possible assistance. Disposal of the dead, clearance of the debris, restoration of communications; supply of drinking water, medical care and first aid to the survivors were tasks of enormous magnitude and all of them were to be undertaken simultaneously. The surviving villagers refused to help clear corpses and carcases and prisoners sent from jails for voluntary help did this commendable job. Hundred of citizen groups accompanied their relief materials to the rescue and distributed them on the spot personally because state bureaucracy could not be trusted to distribute funds or cash. The bureaucracy is not reaching the most needy and the most distant villages, were assertions made by the voluntary agencies where relief campaigns were underway. Mushrooming of voluntary organisations had been a major source of confusion and disorderliness in relief operations.

In any disaster, even though the union government controls the early warning system, precautionary measures and evacuation, rescue and relief operations have to be carried out by the state authorities and district officers. In 1969 a distinguished Cyclone Distress Mitigation Committee (CDMC) was appointed and it had made a comprehensive report suggesting model plans for guidance and instructions of the field officers. The Committee had suggested an elaborate community preparedness programme. Unfortunately the CDMC report had been literally gathering dust in various Central and State Offices. Two collectors at least turned to the Model Plan for guidance and instructions and did excellent work in their districts. It was felt that personnel within the military organisations did not have the training or expertise to undertake disaster relief activities at many levels. The financial cost of the Andhra cyclone was staggering. Nearly 7 million persons in 2302 villages were affected by the loss of crop, property and other damages. More than 250,000 cattle and 750,000 other animals (sheep, pigs, poultry etc) were destroyed. Approximately 9921 was the death roll of human life. While both the State and Central Governments were eager to blame the other for failure, neither were willing to provide funds and other resources in time to carry out effective management of the disaster. The disaster became intensely politician. Many politicians insisted upon a grand tour of the stricken area. Mrs. Gandhi visited the area with a motor cade of 100 cars. Corruption charges about the utilization of cyclone funds were made at many quarters.

The Andhra Cyclone of 1977 raised many controversial issues namely the role of private groups in the relief process, effectiveness of early warning system, the issue of resources and finances, the role of bureaucracy in rushing relief and the pervasive role of short term political calculations in management of disasters. The meteorological department's predictions became a subject of controversy in the Andhra Cyclone of 1977. According to one estimate approximately 10% of the dead were alive after the cyclone and storm-wave hit and died before relief and rescue team could reach. The Indian Airforce helicopters evacuated and rescued many persons on 22 November and 23 November and Army personnel did praise-worthy work at many places. Police Officers rose to the occasion at many places and supervised rescue and relief operations with utmost devotion. Doctors and medical staff carried out their mission with great zeal and enthusiasm to fight deaths caused by epidemics and unhygienic conditions. The mental status examination of the survivors revealed acute anxiety and depression, characterized by hopelessness and suicidal thoughts. Orphans of the cyclone were adopted and rehabilitated by voluntary organisations. 303 children were brought under the protective wings of the government. Simgarim colliery workers, prisoners, state employees, and employees of state owned enterprises were mobilized for rescue and relief work. Police did "a quiet and efficient job" in most of the places. There was certain confusion at places about the role of police, district authorities, army and voluntary organisations. Early in December Appropriate Reconstruction-Training and Information Centre (ARTIC) financed mainly by OXFAM was set up to train personnel provide guidance and information clearance. Pucca housing scheme for rehabilitation was "an expensive mistake". One of the most gratifying consequences of the Andhra Cyclone was the outpourings of citizens interest in relief and rehabilitation and the complete involvement of many international, national, state and local agencies. The overall individual and institutional responses to the Andhra Pradesh Cyclone of 1977 remained matter of individual perception and opinions. The key to rehabilitation and disaster management lies in ensuring that money and assistance reach those who need it most.

Lessons from Maharashtra Earthquake

Disasters arrive with little warning and inflict heavy losses in terms of loss of life and property. Advance planning enables the management to anticipate emergencies and determine the best methods to tackle them.[18] Procedures for all kinds of emergencies should be laid down in chronological order to avoid confusion and panic during disaster and for effectively managing disasters with minimum response time. There was no help for 30 hours after quake in Maharashtra.[19] The first batch of army jawans arrived, but having got used to working with modern equipment, they could do little in the insurmountable task of removing the dead. The sheer enormity of Maharashtra's tragedy has set bureaucrats pondering over fail-safe, if far-fetched, solutions to the disasters that keep striking all around them. Lt. Gen D. Banerjee of the Institute of Defence Studies and Analysis says; "The armed forces have learnt about mass rescue through sheer practice. They aren't really trained for it. There is a need for an independent disaster management authority that can identify vulnerable areas and ensure that steps are taken to minimize the damage. Relief vans and largesse have already begun to pour into Latur area of Maharashtra but too much kindness can kill far more cruelly than the worst quake. An entire population can become a slave to excess relief and compensation. India must improve its alarm and warning systems as a part of disaster management strategy. Lot of international assistance in terms of services of doctors, material assistance and financial aid has come from all over the world.

Some Concluding Remarks

Disaster Management plans are required to be drawn up for each district, taking into account its topography, and terrain, climate and population, history of previous disasters and lessons drawn from previous experiences in disaster management operations. It is essential to create public awareness about disaster management plans and to seek their help in mutigating disaster by timely assistance. Citizens can help in the following ways:-

"1. Keep shovel, axe, hammer, saw, crowbar to move debris under which someone is trapped.

2. Keep handy match box, candle, flash lights and lamps to meet emergency.

3. Provide first aid to injured and transport them to nearby hospital.

4. Human blood has no substitute. Every drop is precious. Donate blood to save precious life.

5. Water is life but it must be clean. Use water properly. Do not waste it.

6. Use sanitary latrine to prevent flies which may cause cholera, typhoid and dysentry.

7. Do not throw harmful chemicals into drainage.

8. Keep floors free from dust and dirt which may cause proliferation of insects and microbes.

9. Help the poor, needy and disaster-distressed people".[20]

There is need for proper study and research to prepare model contingency plans for each state and district which are prone to natural disasters. It has been found during the study that in the states prone to natural calamities, there is no arrangement for reviewing, analysing and improving the role of police in natural calamities.[21] At state and district levels stock-taking and review of the whole gamut of operations, performance, strong and weak points, should be carried out with a view to learn lessons for future. There is need for speedy recognition of good work done by various agencies and individuals.

In case of disasters like earthquakes international agencies and the friendly nation-states also come forward for help in terms of resources, services and even trained manpower. External assistance should normally supplement local and national efforts in rehabilitation and reconstruction work. Advanced technology and modern scientific equipments should be liberally used to locate and rescue survivors in good time.

Practical experiences of the field conditions have revealed that after any serious natural disaster or crisis, there is almost an initial period of confused information and muddled response. There is need for prompt response in a well planned manner at the initial stage. However the ultimate yardstick to measure the success of a rescue and relief operation is whether the affected community has been able to recover atleast to pre-disaster conditions in the smallest number of days. Another aspect of management of disasters is the long term rehabilitation and reconstruction of the affected area.

Normally assessment reports of disasters are required to be sent from district headquarters and the following points are to be covered in the report:-

1. Time and date of disaster and the area/villages affected.

2. Loss of human lives and injuries.

3. Loss of cattle.

4. Damage to crop and property.

5. Number of houses destroyed or damaged.

6. Particulars of initial rescue relief and rehabilitation services rendered.

7. Epidemics in human and cattle.

8. Assistance required from State/Centre and location of relief camp.

9. Special equipment if any needed for relief work.

10. Establishment of control room cum information centre and its telephone numbers.

Management of disasters, ideally speaking should be a co-operative activity in which four different categories of participants namely survivors, bureaucracy, politicians and voluntary organisations including foreign organisation should work together with a common goal of serving the humanity.

What India needs to do for management of disasters can be briefly summarised as under:-

1. Preventive:
   (a) Authority should identify vulnerable pockets.
   (b) Funds for calamity control infrastructure.
   (c) Develop good alarm system.

2. Rescue:
   (a) Codify a drill for disaster management.
   (b) Provide SOS facilities to vulnerable areas.
   (c) Give specialised training to village officers and citizens particularly youth.

3. Rehabilitation:
   (a) Ensure funds are not misused.
   (b) Shortlist NGOs to supervise rehabilitation.
   (c) Select appropriate strategies and technology.

4. Public Awareness and support programmes:

(a) Education institutions should include disaster management in curriculam at various levels.

(b) Build up people's spirit for service to humanity at the time of disasters.

(c) Neutralize "chest-beating mentality" of the victims of disasters.

(d) Mass media should bring awareness about required public responses to various disasters.

(e) International assistance and help from all quarters should be accepted to minimise sufferings to the victims.

Comprehensive National disaster Management system should be evolved on a national basis and should include (1) Planning period of emergency management to include policies and programme to mitigate the impact of any kind of disaster (2) Preparedness which involves training the organisational response and the positioning of adequate resources and their inventories for emergency use (3) Prompt response to the disaster to include situation assessment, critical resources allocation, command, control and coordination of individual and organisational responses. (4) Post crisis response and longterm recovery and rehabilitation plan. c*[21] It is necessary that a very senior officer should be earmarked as Disaster Management authority for each area/district with specific authority and tasks.

REFERENCES

1. Leonard V.A. Police Pre-Disaster Preparation, Illinois, Charlis-C. Thomas. 1973-P.3.

2. Disaster Management Meet-Hindustan Time, New Delhi. 14 March 1994.

3. Garb, Solomon and Engg., Evelyn: Disaster Hand Book, New York, Springer Publications 1969 P.12.

4. Healy, Richard J. Emergency and Disaster Planning, New York Jolun Wiley and Sons P.167.

5. World Health DAY April 7, 1991. "Should Disaster strike, be prepared". Issued by Health & Family Welfare Department Punjab.

6. Proceedings of the Seminar on crisis management-Background papers and proceedings 23rd and 24th March 1979.

7. Andhra Patrike (T) 11, 13 Dec. 1978.

8. Times of India THE SUNDAY TIMES Special Report Monday 11 October 1993 P.16.

9. Lt. Gen V.K.Sood (Retd)- DISASTER relief- The Army's Role-Hindustan Times 12 Nov. 1993.

10. Proceedings of the Seminar on crisis management held at SVP NPA Hyderabad - Background papers and proceedings 23rd and 24th March 1979.

11. S.V.P. National Police Academy Hyderabad-A syndicate study on "The Role of Police in Natural Calamities". TRANSACTIONS Vol.XXII April 1976 P.103.

12. The Hindustan Times 16 May 1978. Also Mrs. Tigger Stack interview in Vijaywada on 10 Feb. 1978. Also Mark Windas (ARTS IC Consultant) in a talk at Andhra University, Waltair 4 Feb 1978.

13. K.P. Bhowmik-Cuttack Orissa in a Seminar on Crisis Management - SVP, NAP Hyderabad- P.46.

14. Cohen, Stephen P & Raghavalue C.V. The Andhra Cycle of 1977-Vikas Publishing House, New Delhi-1979 P.42.

15. Fredrick Cuny - Interview- The Hindu 26 Dec. 1977. Also ARTIC Minutes and Phillip Knightly - The other side of Charity- SUNDAY 23 April 1978.

16. Cohen, Stephen P & Raghavalu, C.V. The Andhra Cyclone of 1977, New Delhi, Vikas Publishing House, P.26.

17. Rahul Pathak- Can India Cope- Earthquakes- India Today October 11, 1993. P.66.

18. Dey S.C and Kaushal S.C. Industrial Security Management, New Delhi-1987 P.187.

19. Harry David-Times of India News Service-Times of India Oct, 5, 1993.

20. World Health DAY 7, April 1991- Theme-should Disaster strike, Be prepared-Published by State Health Education Bureau, Directorate General of Health Services, Haryana. Chadigarh.

21. For similar views see William A Wallace and Frank De Belogh-"Decision Support System for Disaster Management", Police Administrative Review Vol.45, January 1985 (Spl Issue) P.135.

6

Internal Security Operations and their Impact on Human Rights

The Internal Security operations in a democratic political system assume new dimensions and magnitude in the context of our national commitments to the ideals of socialism, secularism, social justice, liberty, equality and economic development. Internal Security threats in India mainly "consist of insurgency, secessionism, terrorism, sectarian violence (called communal violence) large scale smuggling, drug trafficking and accompanying gangster violence, an undue centralization of authority and the consequent inability to exercise power constructively and effectively, decay of political institutions and so on." Internal Security represents the inner strength and health potential of the nation-state to preserve its international personality by its capacity to secure: (1) its sovereign power, (2) government, (3) defined territory and (4) permanent population, from all internal threats . At a critical time when Pakistan is waging a low intensity war by proxy in Kashmir, India cannot afford to neglect the internal security challenges and has to deploy all available para-military forces and even army to safeguard its existence. The threats to the India polity from the plethora of underground groups like National Socialist Council of Nagaland (NSCN), United National Federal Front (UNLF), Peoples' Liberation Army (PLA), Peoples' Revolutionary Party Kangleipak (PREPAK),

Mizo national Army (MNA), United Liberation Front of Assam % (ULFA) and others operating in North Eastern States have acquired a new dimension in recent years. The concept of internal security has to be re-defined and broadened in the context of present day international power politics. Narco-terrorism and smuggling of gold and silver are threats to the internal security of the state. The nexus between drug traffickers and terrorists must be broken if terrorist activities in India are to be checked and contained. Any attempt to create discord or disturb the harmony among people on grounds of race, religion or region has to be viewed as a threat to the internal security of the country. Communalism, regionalism, sectionalism and linguistic separatism must be viewed as threats to the internal security of the country. Over-population itself has created problems of internal security and therefore, further rise in population is to be considered as threat to India's internal security. Insurgency of North-eastern states is a threat to the internal security since the object of insurgency is to rise in an open rebellion against an established government. Naxalite type of extremism, and regional movements adopting militant postures against the government are all serious threats to internal security. ULFA movement in Assam and Naxalite movement of Andhra Pradesh come under these categories. At present India seems to be on-the top of the list of countries which are targets of destabilisers. The separatist movements and communal agitations are being financed and encouraged by outside foreign agencies through liberal inflow of arms, ammunition and funds. The menacing clouds of terrorism and mindless violence, the aggravation of troubles in Jammu and Kashmir, the continuing insurgency in the North-East, the growing discontent in the vast tribal belt which encompasses parts of Madhya Pradesh, Bihar, Orissa and West Bengal, the increasing fury of the caste conflicts in the countryside and the rising wave of communal tension and rioting in the urban areas, and above all, the general breakdown of the law and order have put the very existence of our nation in jeopardy.

All the terrorists, insurgents and other criminal offenders are violating human rights of ordinary citizens. Therefore the human rights movement has genuinely become world wide. In India the constitution itself safeguards human rights. The permanence of the core of human rights has been ensured in India by our Supreme Court which held in Kasavanand V.State of Kerala (AIR 1973 Sc 1461) that Parliament, in exercise of the power to amend the Constitution, can not destroy or alter its basic structure. The fundamental rights are the heart of our constitution and are custodians of human rights of the Indian Citizens. Protection of human rights requires the eternal vigilance. De Tocqueville made very profound observation that liberty cannot stand alone must be paired with a compassion virtue; liberty and morality; liberty and law; liberty and justice; liberty and the common good; liberty and civic responsibility. It is therefore necessary to study the problems of internal security with a view to analyse their impact on internal security.

Terrorists in Kashmir and Punjab have been violating human rights. Tables B to L given at the end of this chapter will show how terrorists isolated human rights in Kashmir and Punjab in their aimless violence and killings, kidnappings and destruction of property. Incidents of looting done by terrorists in Punjab are given in table 'L'. Recovery of weapons made by the security forces from terrorists in Kashmir is shown in Table 'F'

Human Rights and Ancient Indian Scriptures

It is a matter of great national pride for all Indians that human rights concept prevailed in its highest form in our Indian scriptures and religious books. The Rigveda makes clear reference to the three civil liberties of "Tana" (body), "Skridlu" (dwelling house) and jabbasi (life) and urges all humanity to uphold these civil liberties of others. In Shanti Parva of Mahabharata Bhism Pitamah has clearly enunciated the duties of king that "the best king is one whose subjects live in freedom and happiness as they do in their own father's house" He further emphasises that the very core of a king's duty is the protection of his subjects and their happiness.[1] In Kautilya Arthashastra, it gave an elaborated affirmation not only to the civil and legal rights originally formulated by Manu but also affirmed a number of economic rights.[2] Human Rights have been given due consideration even from the very inception of our ancient civilization. Administration of criminal justice in ancient India under the Hindu legal system was based on socio-religious concepts emanating from vedic revelation, srutis, smritis, puranas and other holy scriptures prescribed and enunciated by ancient sages and human rights in rudimentary forms can be traced at many places. The accused right to counsel and presumption of the innocence of the accused appear to have been well recognised. Thus the ancient Hindu Legal system and the broad concept of "universal family" ("Vasudeva Kutumbkam") recognised the human rights of the individuals. The concept of the kinship of the whole world has been aptly embodied in the following Sanskrit sloka:-

न त्वह कामये राज्यं
न स्वर्ग न पुनर्भवम् ।
कामये दुःख तप्तानां
प्राणिनांड आत नाशम् ।।

(I seek no kingdom nor heavenly pleasures nor personal salvation since to relieve humanity from its manifold paints and distresses is the supreme objective of mankind).

In Atharva Veda it is pronounced that "Man lives, works and dies for society possessed of certain inalienable rights".

Human Rights have been concern of our ancient sages, Indian philosophers and epics from times immemorial. The concept of human rights has been verbalized by the Vedic Rishis in Atharva Ved (3:3) thus:-

"Sa bridayam samnasya avidwesham
krinomi wah
Ma bhara bhrataram divishna ma
swasutswasa
Sanyayanch swarta bhuta wach am
Wadat bhadraya
Samam prya sab woauna bhagah
Samani Yoktre sah wo Yunigui

(Atharva Ved 3.3)

(I shall make you one at heart and free from animosity, Brothers and brothers, sisters and sisters, should not hate each other. All go in together to achieve any object. This I tell you in a friendly manner. Your food and enjoyment be equal. I unite you in a commonly accepted bond). Indian sruti boldly teach oneness of all beings and "he who perceives all the human beings same as one self is not deluded". (Ishoupnishad) Another basic principle of human rights is the distinction between combatants and non-combatants which was profounded, in our ancient Manusmriti. Manu's Manav dharm shashtra expressly prohibits "the killing of the one who is without arm or is sleeping or is naked (unprepared) or is an on looker (Non-combatants)".

न च हन्यात्स्थ नारूढं न क्ली बं न कृताजलिम् ।
न मुक्त केशंना सीनं न तबास्मीति वादिनम् ।।
91: 7 मानव धर्मशास्त्र
न सुप्तं न विसन्नांह नग्नं न निरायुधाम।
ना युध्यमानं पश्यन्तं न परेण समागतम्।।

The prohibition was absolute, irrespective of whether the war fought was just or unjust (Dharmayudh or not). In ancient scripture like Mahabharat and Balmiki Ramayan there are references for the protection of human rights of civilians not involved in war. In Mahabharat Arjun observing the laws of war refrained from using Pashupatastra, a hyper-destructive weapon because when the fight was restricted to ordinary conventional weapons the use of unconventional types of weapons was not even morale, let alone in conformity with the recognised human rights during the warfare:

यत्तदंधोरं पशुपतिः प्रादादस्त्रं महन्मम।
कैराते द्वन्द्वयुद्धे तु तदिदं भयिवर्तते।।
12: 194 उपयोग महाभारत।।

In Ramayan, Lord Ram advised Lakshman not to use a weapon of war which could destroy the entire humanity including those who did not bear arms because such destruction enmass was forbidden in ancient laws of war:

तमुवाच ततो रामो लक्ष्मण शुभलक्ष्मण्।
नैकस्रू हे तो रक्षाति पृत्व्धिांहन्य महर्सि।।
37: 80 युद्धकाण्ड (बाल्मीकि)

One vedic sloka enunciating tenets of human rights is as under:

सर्वे भवन्तु सुखिनः
सर्वे शन्तु निरामय ।
सर्वे भद्राणि पश्यन्तु
मां कश्चिद् दुःख भाग्भवेत् ।

In Markandeya Purana it is sad: "I pray for the well being of all beings, May there be free from fear and afflictions and rejoice in the friendship of all, be it an ally or alien. May he, who loves me now, share the blessedness of human life and he that chooses to hate me here, may he also find the path of goodness."

The Buddhist doctrine of non-violence in deed and through (अहिंसा परमो धर्म) is the humanitarian doctrine par excellence, dating back to the Third Century B.C.

The Human Rights and the Humanitarian Laws

The Universal Declaration of Human Rights was approved by the General Assembly on December 10, 1948 and now forms the most widely accepted document on human rights. (For text of the declaration see appendix- A). Indian constitution has incorporated most of these human rights as fundamental rights. (For comparative study see appendix B). The Criminal Procedure Code 1973 also contains various provisions to safeguard various human rights. (For details see appendix- C). The convention against torture and other inhuman, degrading treatment or punishment 1984, is given in appendix 'D'. Article 21 of the constitution guarantees right to life and personal liberty. Statutory Laws including the Indian Penal Code and the Criminal Procedure Code also ensure the personal liberty of a person against assault and injury. The body of various international humanitarian laws are those principles and rules which limit the use of violence in times of armed conflict. Article 3 of the Geneva Conventions on humanitarian law of 1949 provides that in times of armed conflicts, persons protected by the four Geneva conventions should "in all circumstances be treated humanly, without any adverse distinction founded on race, colour, religion or faith, sex, birth or wealth or any other similar criteria". The International conference on human rights in Tehran in 1968 declared that humanitarian principles must prevail during periods of armed conflicts. In 1965 at Vienna the general Assembly affirmed a resolution which laid down three principles of action in armed conflict and declared as un-acceptable the idea of waging war against the entire population in a attempt to force the adversary to give up. Crime against humanity includes murder, extermination, enslavement, deportation and other inhuman acts done against any civilian population. India is a signatory to the International coernat on civil and political rights (ICCPR)- a treaty which formally binds member of states to respect and ensure the full achievement of a wide range of human rights. Very broadly the concept of human rights has two basic connotations. The first refers to the inalienable and inherent rights due to man simply by virtue of being a human being having his own dignity. The second sense is that of legal rights established through law-creating processes of national and international authorities. Human rights issues become murky and complicated when it becomes difficult to distinguish situations of regular war with politically motivated and foreign inspired terrorist activities.

The apparent silence of many human right activities and groups on the abuses and the excesses of armed political terrorists has led to the popular perception that human right bodies are partisan, unfair and sympathisers of the armed political groups. It is incorrect to brush away the excesses and violation of the human rights by the terrorist/insurgent groups in the name of class violence or revolution.

During the last 5 years total no.of victims of terrorism in J & K and Punjab have as under:-

Year	*J & K*	*Punjab*
1988	31	1949
1989	92	1168
1990	1177	2467
1991	1393	2586
1992	1909	1461

In Jammu and Kashmir alone there have been 14542 nos. of incident of terrorist violence causing serious heavy casualties.

Internal armed conflicts are covered by article 3 common to the four Geneva Conventions and by the entire Protocol Additional to the Geneva Convention of 12 August 1949 and relating to the protection of victims of Non-international Armed Conflicts (Protocol II). Protocol II augments the protection afforded to the victims of internal wars and to some extent intra-state armed conflict. The human rights which are in force during internal armed conflicts raise a number of legal psychological and practical problems because of the unique circumstances of a conflict in which one of the parties is not a government but a group of rebels.

Human Rights and Armed Internal Conflicts

It is common practice to refer to the Geneva Conventions and protocols as international humanitarian laws.

(a) In 1949, four Geneva Conventions, which are still in force today, were adopted, each of them dealing with the protection of a specific category of persons in time of international armed conflicts:

First Convention:	Sick and wounded members of armed forces in the field.
Second Convention:	Sick, wounded and shipwrecked members of armed forces at sea.
Third Convention:	Prisoners of war.
Fourth Convention:	Civilians.

Moreover, article 3 common to the four Conventions gave basic protection to all persons not taking an active part in the hostilities in case of armed conflict not of an international character.

(b) The raison d'etre of humanitarian laws is the regulation of methods and means of warfare as well as the nature or quantum of use of force in armed conflicts, whether internal of international.

(c) The indiscriminate destruction of civilian population or attacks on non-combatants such as infants, pregnant women, aged and infirm, sick or wounded, is prohibited.

(d) There are numerous international conventions and accepted customary principles which constitute the humanitarian laws of war enshrining human rights.

(e) International Humanitarian Law Applicable in Armed Conflicts.

(i) List of Treaties and Declarations on Humanitarian laws:

1856 Declaration of Paris
1868 Declaration of St. Petersburg
1899 Hauge Convention II on Land Warfare
1899 Hauge Declaration on Asphyxiating Gases
1899 Hauge Declaration on Expanding Bullets
1906 Geneva Convention (Wounded and Sick)
1907 Hauge Convention III(opening of Hostilities)
1907 Hauge Convention IV (Land Warfare)
1907 Hauge Convention VI (Enemy Merchant Ships)
1907 Hauge Convention VII (Contract Mines)
1907 Hauge Convention IX (Naval Bombardment)
1907 Hauge Convention XI (Right of Capture)
1907 Hauge Convention XIV (Projectiles from Balloons)
1922 Washington Naval Treaty
1923 Hauge Rules of Air Warfare (unratified)
1925 Geneva Gas Protocol
1928 Pact of Paris (Kellogg Briand Pact)
1929 Geneva Convention on Prisoners of War.

(ii) List of Geneva Convention on Humanitarian Laws:

(1) Geneva Convention for the Amelioration of the Condition of the Wounded and Sick in Armed Forces in the field, of 12 August 1949.

(2) Geneva Convention for the Amelioration of the Condition of Wounded, Sick and Shipwrecked Members of Armed Forces at Sea, of 12 August 1949.

(3) Geneva Convention relative to the Treatment of Prisoners of War, of 12 August 1949.

(4) Geneva Convention relative to the Protection of Civilian Persons in Time of War, of 12 August 1949. Adopted by the Diplomatic Conference on the Re-affirmation and Develoment of International Humanitarian Law Applicable in Armed Conflicts, on 10 June 1977.

(5) Protocol Additional to the Geneva Conventions of 12 August 1949, and relating to the protection of victims of International Armed Conflicts (Protocol 1 of 10 June 1977)

(6) Protocol Additional to the Geneva Conventions of 12 August 1949, and relating to the Protection of Victims of Non-International Armed Conflicts (Protocol II of 10 June 1977).

(7) 1977 Protocols I and II to the Geneva Convention, 1949.

(8) 1981 Convention prohibiting the use of cruel, inhumans and indiscriminate conventional weapons.

(f) Refugee problems arise both in peace and in the aftermath of wars and some of the important international instruments which relate to refugee can be stated below:

(1) General Assembly Resolution 42 8V of 14 December 1950.

(2) Statute of the Office of UN High Commission for Refugees 1950.

(3) The Convention relating to the Status of Refugees 1951. Entered into force April 1954.

(4) Protocol Relating to the Status of Refugees 28 July 1951 and 4 October 1967.

(g) At the 1974-1977 Conference, when those States were able to express their views, thereby promoting the universality of international humanitarian law, they obtained results, *e.g.*:

— The whole of internal humanitarian law may now be applied in wars of national liberations;

— Guerrilleros who are captured are entitled, subject to less restrictive conditions than formerly, to be recognized as combatants to be treated as prisoners of war;

— Mercenaries do not have the right to be treated as prisoners of war.

(h) Protection of victims of non-international armed conflicts.

Protocol II supplements article 3 common to the Geneva Conventions of 1949, by introducing more deatailed rules. It applies to armed conflicts not covered by Protocol I, which take place in the territory of High Contracting Party between its armed groups which, under responsible command, exercise such control over a part of its territory as to enable them to carry out sustained and concerted military operations and to implement this protocol".

The most significant advances introduced by protocol II are the following:

— Fundamental guarantees are granted to all persons who do not take a direct part in hostilities, and special provisions have been introduced in respect of persons whose liberty has been restricted and with regard to penal prosecutions.

— Detailed rules have been introduced to protect the wounded, sick and shipwrecked, medical and religious personnel and medical units and transport, which may display the distinctive emblem of the red cross or red crescent, while provision is made for the general protection of medicaly duties.

— The civilian population is entitled to general protection against the effect of hostilities: The civilian population as such shall not be the object of attack the starvation of civilians as a method of combat is prohibited; objects indispensable to the survival of the civilian population, works and installations containing dangerous forces and cultural objects and places of worship must be protected; forced movement of civilians is forbidden; and relief actions undertaken in aid of the civilian population must be facilitated.

Genocide has been defined as acts committed "with intent to destroy in whole or in part a national, ethnic, racial or religious group as such". Genocide is a crime under international law. Genocide convention of 1948 regards genocide as a matter of international concern.

Article 3 common to the four Geneva Conventions is the mainsty of ICRC action in non-international armed conflicts. It reads as follows:-

"In the case of armed conflict not of an international character occurring in the territory of one of the High Contracting Parties, each Party to the conflict shall be bound to apply, as a minimum, the following provisions:

(1) Persons taking no active part in the hostilities, including members of armed forces who have laid down their arms and those placed hors de combat by sickness, wounds, detention, or any other cause, shall in all circumstances be treated humanely, without any adverse distinction founded on race, colour, religion or faith, sex, birth or wealth or any other similar criteria.

To this end the following acts are and shall remain prohibited at any time and in any place whatsoever with respect to the above-mentioned persons:

(a) Violence to life and persons, in particular murder of all kinds, mutilation, cruel treatment and torture;

(b) taking of hostages;

(c) outrages upon personal dignity, in particular humiliating and degrading treatment;

(d) the passing of sentences and the carrying out of executions without previous judgement prononuced by a regularly constituted court, affording all the judicial guarantees which are recognised as indispensable by civilized peoples.

(2) The wounded and sick shall be collected and cared for an impartial humanitarin body, such as the International Committee of the Red Cross, may offer its services to the Parties to the conflict.

The Parties top the conflict should further endeavour to bring into force, by means of special agreements, all or part of the other provisions of the present Convention.

The application of the preceding provisions shall not affect the legal status of the parties to the conflict.

The Diplomatic Conference on the Reaffirmation and Development of Internal Humanitarian law applicable in Armed Conflicts (1974-1977) explicitly excluded from the scope of application of the Protocol situations of internal tension and disturbances, which it did not define, but of which it gave examples. These are presented as follows in the Commentary to Protocol II: riots, such as demonstrations without a concerted plan from the outset; isolated and sporadic acts of violence, as opposed to military operations carried out by armed forces or armed groups; other acts of a similar nature, including, in particular,large scale arrests of people for their activities or opinions. Resolution VI of the 24th International Conferences of the Red Cross (Manila, 1981), has made solemn appeal "that the rules of international humanitarian law and the universally recognized humanitarian principles be safeguarded at all times and in all circumstances and that the international

Committee of the Red Cross be granted all the facilities necessary to discharge the humanitarian mandate confided to it by the international community." How in situations of internal disturbances, the rules of international humanitarian law can only be invoked by analogy. On the other hand, States must respect certain universally acknowledged humanitarian principles, and the human rights instruments to which they are party, in particular the rights for which no derogation is permitted, even when the life of the national is threatened by an exceptional public danger.

Dissemination of International Humanitarian Law

Trying to promote knowledge of fundamental humanitarian standards against a background of internal violence poses particular problems. First of all, what standards should be emphasized in a situation of internal disturbances where international humanitarian law is not applicable. The "declaration of minimum humanitarian standards" adopted by a group of experts in Turky in 1990 and the "code of conduct" drawn up by Mr. Hans-Peter Gasser for situations which at the time were qualified as internal disturbances and tension are useful reference texts. Nervertheless, instruction for the armed forces when they are called upon to repress disturbances or urban uprising is more complex than that dispensed within the framework of a non-international armed conflict. In this case, the teaching of international humanitarian law is more or less the same as for international armed conflicts, where the distinction between civilians and combatants is clearly established. How should the humanitarian message be brought home to those involved in the violence associated with internal disturbances? Emphasis must be laid on dissemination among young, even the very young, whether or not they attend school, for these age-groups often take part in disturbances and are the first to suffer. They must be reached in schools in slum areas as well as in universities, by way of radio, television, comic strips and plays. In short, apart from the content of the message, which must be simplified, it is the means of communication which must be developed in an imaginative and understanding way.

International humanitarian laws bestow rights not only on human beings as such but also (and chiefly) on states. Broadly speaking human rights in armed conflict can be divided into two categories: (i) rights granted to lawful or privileged combatants i.e. combatants respecting the laws of war and meeting the conditions which that body of law established; (ii) rights accorded to civilians. The significant provisions of four Geneva Conventions of August 12, 1949 can be summarised as under: they outlaw violence to life and person; cruel treatment and torture protect personal dignity; provide for treatment of wounded and sick persons during hostilities and such other measures and prohibit adverse distinctions founded on race, colour, religion, sex, birth, nationality or any other similar criteria.

Violations of Human Rights in the context of Internal Disturbance and Violence caused by Terrorists in Punjab & Kashmir

The key problem that arises concerning human rights relates to their proper enforcement which differs today from state to state for variety of different reasons. Under international human rights law, an individual must not be killed except in closely defined circumstances while under the international law of armed conflicts, it is lawful to kill enemy combatants. Armed conflicts can no longer be seen as necessarily a denial of human rights but it is certainly the case that respect for human rights is most threatened during such conflicts. No sovereign nation can allow people to violate the human rights of its citizens by a group of terrorists or insurgents when the state itself is feeling threatened by its basic existence as a political and social system by armed internal disturbances. In reality the states whose police/security forces/ armed forces have been responsiblc for violations of human rights include USA, USSR, France and Algeria and the U.K. in Northern Ireland. The breaches of the international law of armed conflicts know no barriers of culture, level of development or technological sophistication. During the last forty five years developments in technology of war and subversions, changes in the nature of irregular and unconventional warfare and the characteristics of combatants have undergone vast changes. Terrorism, Insurgency, guerrilla warfare, subversive law intensity operations have confused every one about the operative effects of international laws and application of humanitarian laws. Many foreign countries have double standards as far as respect for human rights are concerned. Racial discrimination and religious bigotry represent a unique and frightening phenomena of human rights violations in USA. In the majority of European Countries racialist or Xenophobic sentiments are shared by an increasingly large percentage of populations and in a number of European countries, immigrants and ethnic minorities are faced with discrimination in access to housing. It is quite clear that west can not teach India regarding human rights. It is not an irony that the worst perpetrators of ethnic clean sing, Bojnian Serbs leaders who are guilty of slaughtering and raping of helpless Bosnian Muslims so ruthlessly, are being wooed by international leaders. What purpose will the setting up of an internal crime tribunal serve. It will only come into play against those who are vanquished, poor or belonging to the third world the victors with all their crime of ethnic cleansing, will be openly welcomed by the western world. USA can not have one standard of itself and another for India. In USA the power of the internal revenue service to extract taxes, the authority of the state to bust trusts and monopolies, the regulation of stock exchanges and security markets and the overall internalisation of the ethnics of capitalism in the civil society is not questioned. Then how the situation can be otherwise for India. The Anmesty International has described as "shameful" the way in wich death penalty is applied in the United States with "ingrained racism" in which 40 percent of the death row prisoners are black, compared to just 12 percent of the population and an astonishing 84 percent of prisoners executed since 1977 were convicted of murdering white victims.

In India it is for the Indian government and the Indian people themselves who care most about human rights, to evaluate and protect the human rights of its citizens and to uphold its international commitments regarding human rights. One of the issues of civilians being caught in cross-fire between militants and armed forces personnel, Major David Stockwell, U.N. Spokesman in Somalia, said that women and children who participated in activity against the UN troops were "part of the enemy". The use of U.S.helicopter gunships which resulted in 100 persons being killed was justified both by the U.S.administration and the U.N.spokesman. In India there has not been a single incident where helicopter gunships have been used. It is an irony of the situation that if you kill some persons in a face to face encounter and in the process, some innocent persons are killed in cross-firing, you are blamed for killing innocent people. Even when you kill a real hard core terrorist in an encounter, who has been identified, you are blamed for having caught and killed him in cold blood. It is an irony of fate that police and para-military forces are condemned for both action or inaction.

In India we face a discomfortable and explosive situation that over whelming evidence of human rights violations does not ipso facto add to the credibility of the human right activists. The entire situation seems so fragile, so insecurity ridden, so full of dark portents about the future that disclosures— be they on Kashmir, Punjab, Assam or Andhra instead of rousing people against the perfidies being committed on them only generate comments about the human activists as dangerous meddlesome, naive, if not fifth-columnists and anti-national.

Main Allegations Against Police/Para Military Forces regarding Violations of Human Rights

There has been growing criticism both nationally and internationally of wide-spread violations of human rights in India by police and para-military forces. Some of the main allegations are as under:-

(i) Arbitrary and unlawful arrests (Art-22 of Constitution of India, Sec 41,55,151 of Cr.P.C.).

(ii) Arbitrary and unlawful searches.

(iii) Arbitrary and illegal detention. (Art. 22 of Constitution of India; Sec. 51,57,58,76 of Cr.P.C.).

(iv) Denying the Rights to be informed, the grounds of his arrest (Art.22 of Constitution of India Sec. 50,55,57 of Cr.P.C.).

(v) Denying the rights of the arrested persons not to be subjected to unnecessary restraints (S/49 of Cr. P.C.).

(vi) Denying right to consult a lawyer of his own choice (Art. 22 (i) of Constitution of India, Sc 303 of Cr.P.C.

(vii) Denying right to be produced before a Magistrate within 24 hrs (Art. 22(1) of Constitution of India Sec. 57 & 76 of Cr. P.C.).

(viii) Denying right not to be witnessed against himself (Art. 20(3) of Constitution of India).

(ix) Denying right to get himself medically examined for evidence (Sec. 45 of Cr.PC).

(x) Denying right to fair and speedy trial and investigation (Sec. 309 of Cr.P.C.).

(xi) Denying right not to be imprisoned upon conviction in certain cases (Sec. 306 of Cr.P.C. & Sec.6 of Probation of offenders Act).

(xii) Denying right of Privacy (Art. 31 of Constitution of India.).

(xiii) Third degree methods of interrogation.

(xiv) Custodial death and "the mystery of disappearing man."

(xv) Custodial rape.

(xvi) Use of third degree methods in interrogation.

In non-international armed conflicts and in internal conflicts, torture is expressly forbidden in the common article 3 of the four Geneva Conventions, as well as in article 4 of Protocol II. The Covenant on civil and political rights sets out various rights to be protected like"the right to life", freedom from torture and inhuman treatment, right detained person to be treated with humanity. But these rights are not absolute. Article 4 provides that in times of public emergency which threatens the life of the nation and the existence of which is officialy proclaimed, states may take measures derogating from their obligations under this covenant. These are provided by law only to protect national security, public order, public health or morals or the rights and freedoms of others. (Articles 12, 14, 18, 19, 21 and 22 of International covenant on civil and political rights 1966).

Factors Responsible for Human Rights Violations by Indian Police

Shri Dharam Vira Chairman of National Police Commission has observed :" we may modify our laws to safeguard human dignity or talk loudly about such dignity or rights but so long as the police behaviour in our country remains as it is today, all such provisions and declarations would prove to be only on paper and not in reality." There is a general feeling of immunity that persists among police officers in India, particularly in the civil police, that they are above law and the system will provide them protection. Modern scientific methods of interrogation like lie detectors are not available at grass root levels in police and there is constant pressure from superior Police Officers and politicans to deliver quick results. There are numerous causes and factors responsible for various violations of human rights by the Indian Police. Inadequate police training, inadequate supervision by superior officers and corruption in police are some of the main causes of violations of human rights. Lack of adequate recongnition of human rights by the police and the police sub culture of violence also contributes for the violations of human rights by the police. "Clearly the rot in top echelon is responsible for the mess down below. A senior Police Officer commented that only extra constitutional methods could restore law and order in Punjab."[10] When Police Officers violating human rights and even indicated by high courts for violations of human rights are awarded medals the message goes round that police could get away with such aberrations. The apathy of the public and insensitivity of the government have emboldened the guardians of law to go ahead with more daring forms of violations of human rights. A retired police chief says all cases of custodial deaths and police misdemeanor are quietly buried after the initial furore is over. The cases are investigated and charges framed in loopholes for the guilty to escape. The political masters are led to believe by the top police leaders that if police are taken to task it would demoralise them and consequently they would not be able to perform their arduous tasks effectively. The police violations of human rights in India have increased over the last five years because of an ineffective criminal justice system. According to Shri N.S.Saksena the dishonest IPS Officer who can not control his station house officers lets this evil degenerate to a point where policemen beat any one who annoys them.[11] Violations of human rights in terms of police excesses in torture and brutality are committed with great frequency and extensively in India where police officers are with sadistic temperament and there is lack of effective supervision by the senior officers. When there is undue delay in bringing the offenders to justice and there is reluctance on the part of the public to come forward as witnesses police start resorting to rough and ready short cut methods to justice. In several states of India the police have emerged into a powerful autonomous body with the senior officers having hardly any effective control over the police men who have close links with politicians and caste lords. "Encounters" and "disappearances" are often reported by human right organisations. Chief Minister Shri Jyoti Basu admitted on the floor of the Assembly on June 4, 1992 that 78 prisoners died in police custody between April 1987 and June 1992 in West Bengal. Since independence a large number of commissions of inquiry to probe into the complaints of torture and death in police custody brutalities committed during police operations have made various recommendations but because of the reluctance on the part of the government to implement their recommendations, all reports are gathering dust. Justice V.V.Chandra Chud, Former Chief Justice of India in 1985 has observed: "Police officers alone and none else can give evidence regarding the circumstances in which a person in their custody comes to receive injuries. Bound by the ties of a kind of brotherhood, they often prefer to remain silent to such situations and when they choose to speak they put their own gloss upon facts and pervert the truth". It is very well established that Indian society tacitly expects and approves the use of violence on suspects to the principle of "an eye for an eye". Many unscrupulous police officers tend to play psychological factors freely in obtaining confessions and work out cases successfully. Over work and pressure of work also tend to cause violations of human rights in a society where professionalism is at a discount and where politicians want quick results ignoring means. Legal hurdles like inability to keep a suspect for longer duration are also responsible partly for violations of human rights by the police. Very often policemen find themselves caught in a dilemma when they find that criminals apprehended after great difficulty and risk is released by courts on bail. Police brutality and violations of human rights are symptoms of a sick society where criminal justice administration has almost collapsed and political masters demand control of crime and violence. However violations of human rights by the police are on the increase, of late because the senior officers and inquiring officers are reluctant and slow to investigate cases of police excess because of the illusion that to do so will sap public confidence in the police generally and will demoralise the policemen. Human Rights violations by police and security forces in disturbed areas are at times due to over-reaction to the most trying and hazardous situations where there is hair-breath distance between life and death for them. Insurgents and terrorist at times attack on security forces in market places and crowded localities and when police/ security forces return fire in self defence, civilian get killed in cross-fire.

Role of Central Police Organisations in Internal Security Duties and Application of Human Rights and Humanitarian Laws

Application of human rights becomes very difficult in the context of armed internal disturbances and low intensity operations which are abetted and supported by foreign countries and various constraints under which Central Police Organisations are performing their difficult role in maintaining law and order as an aid to civil authority. Although maintenance of law and order is a state subject and civil police of the states is responsible for it, Central Police Organisations like CRPF, BSF, NSG, SSB and others are required to assist and supplement the civil police.

Due to various organisational and operational limitations, civil police is unable to cope up with the problems of insurgency, terrorism, left wing extremism etc. Central Police Organisations, being the armed forces of the Union and having specialised training and orientation, are called upon to tackle these problems with the marginal support from the civil police. The Indian political system is quasi-federal. The subjects of public order, come within the perview of the state list whereas subjects like civil and criminal law, administration of justice are in the concurrent list. Central Police Organisations are governed by the legal provisions and rules of the states including special laws like Disturbed Area Act, Terrorist and Disruptive Activities Act, Armed Forces special Powers Act etc. Humanitarian rights can not be effectively protected unless it is consciously and seriously accepted by the personnel of civil police and central police organisations who have been entrusted with the task of policing the people. Malignant diseases call for drastic remedies and deployments of Central Police Organisations are required when terrorism, insurgency and violence disturb the law and order situations of the country. Nation has to enact special laws giving adequate powers to the police/para-military forces for dealing effectively with disruptive activities of terrorists, insurgents and other anti-national elements. Following special laws have been enacted for dealing with anti-national groups of people and foreign mercenaries.

1. Armed Forces (Emergency Duties) Act, 1947.

2. National Security Act, 1983 (Act No.43 of 1988).

3. Unlawful Activities (Prevention) Act, 1967.

4. Assam Maintenance of Public Order (Autonomous District) Act 1953.

5. Nagaland Security Regulations Act, 1962.

6. Assam Disturbed Area Act, 1953.

7. The Armed Forces (Assam Manipur) Special Powers Act, 1958.

8. Punjab Disturbed Area Act, 1983.

9. Armed Forces (Punjab and Chandigarh) Special Power Act, 1983.

10. Chandigarh Disturbed Area Act, 1983.

11. Terrorist affected Area (Spl.Court) Act, 1984.

12. Terrorist and Disruptive Activities (Prevention) Act, 1989 as amended (Act No. 16 of 1989).

13. Indian Arms Act 1959 with special reference to Arms (Amendment) Act 1983 and Act, 42 of 1988.

14. The Disturbed Area (Spl.Courts) Act, 1976.

15. Prevention of Damage to Public Property Act, 1984.

16. Anti-Hijacking Act, 1982.

17. Suppression of unlawful act against safety of Civil Aviation Act, 1982.

18. Religious Institutions (Prevention of Misuse) Act, 1988 (Act 41 of 1988).

19. The Indian Explosives Act, 1984.

20. The West Bengal Maintenance of Public Order Act, 1972.

Enactment of these special laws has conferred a very heavy responsibility on the police/para-military organisations to ensure that while enforcing above laws the human rights have to be protected at all costs and in all circumstances. Supreme Court (AIR 1973 S C 207) has held that Rights of the society as a whole is from its very nature of much greater importance than that of an individual. Allged violations of human rights reported by the Amnesty Internal and facts related to them are shown in Table 'A' given at the end of this chapter.

Human Rights Violations by Police and Security Forces-Problems and Dilemma

In a historic battle against foreign trained terrorist, police and security forces in Punjab and Kashmir are fighting terrorism with rare determination, dedication and highest level of national commitment for the security of the country. Since security forces and police are performing a very difficult and challenging job, certain individual aberrations or over-reactions have to be overlooked. Criminal Justice System in India definitely needs a close look and police need to use scientific methods of investigation and interrogation. There is a lot of scope and need to bring about wholesale changes in the thinking and attitude of police officers of all ranks particularly of investigating officers. It is difficult to understand the reluctance of the successive governments, both at the Centre and at the State level, to introduce reforms which would make the law-enforcing machinery effective and accountable. Amnesty (International) has alleged that torture of detainees continues to be reported from India, resulting in some cases in death. Amnesty International in 1992 listed 415 cases of death in police custody in India between 1 January 1985 to November 1991. It alleged that torture was pervasive and routine in every one of India's 25 states, irrespective of whether the arrests were made by the police, the paramilitary forces or the army and irrespective of the political party in power. The pattern and practice of torture, including rape and deaths in custody have been described in detail in the report "India: Torture, Rape and Deaths in custody". In September 1992 Asia watch produced a report titled Police killings and Rural violance in Andhra Pradesh in which it had not only recorded cases of torture, rape and murder of peasants and tribal villagers by police and security forces in the state. But also it accused the police of intimidating and even killing local journalists and human right activists. On the pretext of operations against the Naxalites. During the last two decades Independent civil liberties Organisations have played a critical role in monitoring and publishing cases of human rights violations. Such Human Rights Organisations include The Andhra Pradesh Civil Liberties Committee (APCLC). The Association for the Protection of Democratic Rights (APDR), The Civil Liberties and Human Rights Organisations (CLAHRO) in Manipur, Citizen for Democracy (CFD) Delhi, The Committee for the Protection of Democratic Rights (CPDR), Bombay, The Free Legal Aid Committee (FLAC) in Bihar. The Jammu and Kashmir Peoples Basic Right (Protection) Committee; the Naga People's Movement for Human Rights (NPMHR); the People's Union for Civil Liberties (PUCL) and the People's

Union for Democratic Rights(PUDR). On June 30, 1993 Asia Watch and Psysicians for Human Rights, Denmark (AW-PHR) published a report titled "The Human Rights Crisis in Kashmir A Pattern of Impunity." The report alleges that "Among the worst violations have been the summary executions of hundreds of detainees in the custody of the security forces in Kashmir." Allegations given in Amnesty Internal report are tabulated and given in Table.1** These allegations can be politically motivated and are at times designed to demoralize the security forces by bringing allegations against them. The police and security forces have to perform their duties pertaining to the security of the country and many human right problems arise because modern insurgency, guerilla warfare and terrorist activities do not recognise clear boundaries and the definition of combatants and non-combatants remain unclear to the security forces which are working beyond normal working hours for many days and months under most hostile conditions. During operations against armed insurgents/ terrorists, the security forces feel compelled in treating the entire population in their zone of operations as legitimate when civilian population provides protection and support to such militant groups. The issue related to human right abuses by terrorists/insurgents/political opposition groups are both real and pressing and it is essential that a broader consenses on the issues of political norms and accountability can be built up from both sides in clear terms. Internal security operations are often very challenging and complex because internal security has to be maintained even in disturbed areas in accordance with the laws of the land and "rule of law."

For maintaining discipiline in police and para-military forces to deal with breach of human rights, Army has a system of Court Martial proceedings and BSF Act provides for " Security proceedings. In CRP Commandants and Assistant Commandants (Now Deputy Commandant) have magisterial powers for carrying out judicial trial under section 9 & 10 of the CRPF Act 1949. Judicial trial in CRPF follow procedure laid down in criminal procedure code 1973

(Act. No. 1 of 1974). There are very few counted cases where CRPF personnel went on berserk and assaulted bystanders when their colleagues were killed in cold blood by the militants. In all such cases exemplary punishments were awarded to the defaulters. Whenever there are violations of human rights by the para-military forces, proper inquiries are conducted and defaulters are dealt in accordance with laid down rules and procedures.

The delays and distortions of judicial system need our immediate attention. The agenda of promotion of human rights in the administration of justice looks staggeringly vast and almost unmanageable. A time bound programme for reforms in criminal justice administration is the need of the hour. K.F. Rustam ji has highlighted the failure and decay of justice. "Today the judges believe their first task is to correct the policeman; all the rest pile up as pending cases. The main task of the policeman is to evade judicial scrutiny and to revel in the fact that politician has given him a free run to do what he likes, provided it controls crime". On the whole the police have done a commendable job, performed many deeds of courage, paid a high price in casualties. Wherever they have dealt with terrorism and insurgency-Nagaland, Mizoram, Manipur, Assam, Punjab and Kashmir they have put out the fires with the help of central police Organisations and the Army. The bold and outspoken policemen say that police is compelled to use wrong methods because there is no such thing as judicial appraised or punishment to the criminals in the land due to complete decay of judicial system. Shri KPS Gill said: "we have registered 17,391 cases under TADA since its reinforcement and only 111 of them were convicted with a percentage of conviction being just 0.05 and this is in a state where terrorism was at its peak. The Punjab Police/ Security forces arrested 15000 people under TADA but now only 750 were in jail. Justice V.K. Krishna Iyer agreed that special situations require special laws after he was convinced of terrorism and shown weapons seized from terrorists and photographs of those killed, in a seminar held at Lucknow on 16 January 1994 on Human Rights and TADA. However use of third degree methods of police cannot be condoned. Whatever the protestations of those in authority, the fact that human rights violations do occur in India in a highly malignant form can not be denied."

During the last five years CRPF, BSF and other CPOs have suffered the following Casualities on the line of duty.

Name of Org	*Year*				
	1987-88	*88-89*	*89-90*	*90-91*	*91-92*
CRPF	91	80	121	153	192
BSF	137	149	192	272	250
Other CPOs	69	55	121	50	55
Total	297	284	434	475	497

Besides above casualties, a large number of force personnel have been seriously injured in encounters, bomb-blasts or other incidents.

In India, there is a very strong pro-torture lobby which argues that torture just can not be completely avoided or eleminated from Indian Police Culture. According to them use of third degree is necessary to extract a confession. In the present broken-down and flawed state of the criminal justice systems when political authorities and police leadership pressurise subordinate police officers for quick results, hardened criminals are repeated released on bail (to return to more crime) and cases remian pending in courts for years together. Most of the police stations do not have even a tie detector and a separate interrogation room. In a recent judgement Supreme Court has opined that the inability of the state to protect a citizen's access to Article 21 should entitle a citizen to compensation for violation of his or her fundamental rights (Case of Suman Behera). In Subastian Hongray (AR 1948 Sc 571, 1026) the principle of compensation have been further developed.

The time has come in India for a frank dialogue between civil liberatrians who champion human rights and senior police officers so that each side understands the other's concern.[1] The human right issues need to be analysed in a total national scenario. Advanced countries like Europe and America cannot have the right to preach about the human rights to the third World Countries of Asia when they are themselves violating human rights in their countries. Human rights are universal and violations of these anywhere is universally condemnable.[2] Amnesty International and many other human right groups are clamouring all the time about the human rights of merchants of terror, secession and mayhem and remaining silent about the rights of the innocent victims of the killer gangs.[3] No person or group of people can be allowed to take away human rights of others in a civilized society. It is not the claim of the Govt of India, indeed no country and no Government can make such a claim that no human rights violations ever occur in India. We do however claim that we have as a Country a strong commitment to human rights and that we have in our legal system a remedial framework as well as a strong tradition of punishing human rights violations whereas they are found to occur.[4] The world conference on Human Rights held at Vienna in June 1993 adopted unanimously "the Vienna Declaration" and Programme of Action. This declaration is meant to guide and modulate the important policy formulations by all the governments in the world including India. The Declaration accepts that all human rights are universal, indivisible and inter-related and that democracy, development and respect for human rights and fundamental freedoms are inter-dependent and mutually reinforcing. The Constitution of a Human Rights Commission through an Ordinance on 28th September 1993 reflects the concern of the Government of India for the protection of human rights in the Country. Human Rights are not distinct and different from the fundamental rights guaranteed by the Constitution of India. The fundamental rights recognised in the Constitution of India, in their application to the administration of criminal justice, are sought to be realised through various means including the procedure established by law in India through the Code of Criminal Procedure 1973. It was on 10th December 1948 that the General Assembly of the United Nations Organisation adopted and proclaimed the Universal Declaration of Human Rights (Appendix 'A'). A comparative table of Fundamental Rights incorporated in the Indian Constitution and United Nations Declaration of Human Rights are given in Appendix 'B'. It is however necessary that the human rights of the individuals who are opposed to the democratic political system of India and commit mayhem should be seen in the overall context of the rights of their innocent victims.

Central Reserve Police Force and its Role

Central Reserve Police, from its inception in 1939, has been performing its assigned tasks and responsibilities with great effectiveness and impact. Now it has recently started a new wing called Rapid Action Force (R. A. F.) which is primarily meant to deal with communal riots and other emergencies. The men and women in blue dangarees are members of the elite group of R.A.F within the CRP who are to be deployed in the riot-torn areas to restore confidence and sense of security amongst the masses. Members of the RAF have been selected through a psychological examination to test their secular and patriotic credentials. [5] The Battalions of RAF are to be deployed at sensitive places in different parts of the Country and at each location. Sub-Units are always ready to move at very short notice to meet emergencies. Central Reserve Police Force has a very glorious history of its development and service to the nation. [6] C.R.P. F. is a time-tested and dependable national police force which has continuously contributed to a very large degree in maintaining the integrity, unity, secular, federal and democratic nature of the Indian Republic. C.R.P.F is one of the most mobile armed police force in the World. The splendid performance of CRPF over the last 54 years has earned appreciation from all quarters and this versatile force is fondly looked upon by the state police forces as the citadel of strength in restoring normalcy in disturbed areas. Central Reserve Police also assists local police in rescue and relief operations and even in peace-keeping operations. Central Reserve Police has done excellent work in Punjab and has been to a large extent responsible for restoring normalcy by liquidating terrorists. Achievements of CRP in Punjab for two years are given below:-

Item		*1985*		*1986*
(1) Terrorists caught	-	336	-	991
(2) Terrorists killed	-	1	-	38
(3) Terrorists wounded	-	3	-	31
(4) Weapons seized	-	49	-	296

During 1989 there were approximately 191 Coys of CRP deployed in Punjab while in 1990, there were 194 Coys of CRP deployed on anti-terrorist duties. Deployment of Central Reserve Police Force in various states changes with the changes in the pattern and intensity of internal security problems and their perception by the Centre. There is an increasing demand for C.R.P. from all states to strengthen their law and order machinery but C.R.P. present strength is not able to fulfil all the demands of the States and Union Territories. C.R.P. is a secular force which has representation from people of all religions and regions. It is really a credit to the CRPF that it has been able to adopt itself not only to the multifarious problems but also to the different functional environments. It is perhaps the adaptability and versatility of the force that has made it stand out as one of the elite Central Police Organisations of the nation today. CRPF, in spite of its excellent performance is having a number of internal organisational problems like role contradictions, inadequate family accommodation, long hours of work without adequate compensation, defective career planning for senior ranks and problems of lack of adequate opportunities for refresher and specialised training for all ranks. For the personnel of Central Reserve Police Force (CRPF) carrying out a fight against terrorism in Punjab and Kashmir and anti-insurgency duties in north-eastern states, there is a hair breadth difference between life and death every day. In order to combat terrorism, insurgency and other violence crimes CRP has formed "Quick Reaction Teams" and " Special Task Force" with very quick and bold responses. CRP personnel get "Commando training and special anti-terrorist training."

The Protection of Human Rights in Indian Society

The Human Rights enshrined in the Universal Charter of the United Nations have been incorporated in the Indian Constitution and other major criminal laws of the land. Preamble of the Indian Constitution, Part-III relating to Fundamental Rights (Arts 12 to 35) and part IV Directive Principles of State Policy (Arts. 36 to 51) have covered almost the entire field of the Universal Declaration of Human Rights. Indian Penal Code, Criminal Procedure Code, Protection of Civil Rights Act, 1975, Suppression of Immoral Traffic in Women and Girls Act, 1956, Bonded Labour System (Abolition) Act 1976, Probation of Offenders Act 1958, Citizenship Act 1955, Requisitioning and Acquisition of Immovable Property Act 1952, Hindu Succession Act 1956, Representation of the People Act 1950, and other progressive legislations have provided adequate protection to the human rights. Provisions pertaining to arrest, search, seizure and bail provide adequate safeguards and protection of human rights. In order to implement human rights Bank Nationalisation Act 1969, Coking Coal Mines (Nationalisation) Act 1972, General Insurance Business (Nationalisation) Act 1972, Estate Duty Act 1953, Gift Tax Act 1958 were passed by the Indian Parliament. The Bonded Labour system (Abolition) Act 1976 abolished the exploitation of people as the system of bonded labour holding generations under bondage for the repayment of paltry sums and thus abolished forced lobour. The Urban Land (Ceiling and Regulation) Act 1976 was designed to prevent concentration of urban property in the hands of a few persons ensuring equitable distribution of urban land. Art. 1 of the Declaration of Human Rights is covered under Preamble and Art.51A (e) of the Constitution of India. Art.2 of human rights declaration has been provided for in Arts. 15, 16 and 17 of the Constitution and in Protection of Civil Rights Act, Sec. 416 and 432 to 434 of Criminal Procedure Code cover Art.3 of human rights. Sections 49, 50, 56, 57 of Criminal Procedure

Code and Art. 22 of Constitution of India Provide Protection against arbitrary, arrest, detention or exile. Actually, almost all human rights have been granted to the citizens under various laws of the Country. However, implementation of human rights depends not on law but on its proper enfocement by the Police and law enforcement agencies.

Article 11 of the Universal Declaration of Human Rights envisages right to be presumed innocent unless proved guilty, prohibition of retroactive penal laws and of double jeopardy. Art. 20 of Indian Constitution provides above mentioned human rights to all citizens of India. Justice Gajendra Gadkar has stated the protection under Art. 20(2)as follows "The Constitutional right guaranteed by Art.20(2) against double jeopardy can be successfully involved only where the prior proceedings on which reliance is placed are of a criminal nature instituted or continued before a Court of law or a tribunal in accordance with the procedure prescribed in the statute which creates the offence and regulates the procedure...(Naryan Lal Vs M.P. Minister AIR 1961 SC 29 P/38). In a leading case of State of Bombay Vs Kathi Kalu, Supreme Court bench consisting of eleven judges held: "It is well established that clause (3) of Article 20 is directed against self-incrimination by an accused person, self incrimination must mean conveying information based upon the personal knowledge of the person giving the information and can not include merely the technical process of producing documents in court which may throw a light on any of the points in the controversy, but which do not contain any statement of the accused based on his personal knowledge." (AIR 1961 SC 1808). Supreme Court has held that Domiciliary visit by police in the night to the private house were an invasion on the part of the police of the sanctity of a man's home and an intrusion into his personal liberty of the individual unless authorised by a valid law. (Kharak Singh Vs State of UP AIR 1963 SC 1295). In a recent Supreme Court Judgement it has been held that "(a) Pre-trial release should be granted in appropriate cases on personal bond of accused without surities and without any monetary obligation; (b) Speedy trial is a part of fundamental right to life and liberty; (c) For under trial prisoners detention in jail for periods longer than the term for which they would have been sentenced if convicted is illegal as being violation of Art. 21 of the Constitution". (Justice P.N. Bhagwati and J.A.P. Sen and D.A. Desai AIR 1979 SC 1369 Cr.L.J. 1036).

Code of Criminal Procedure 1973 has provided a number of safeguards and mandates pertaining to human rights. Sections 41, 55 and 51 of Cr.P.C provide protection against arbitrary and unlawful arrests while section 300 provides protection against arbitrary or unlawful searches. Section 243 safeguards right to produce defence witnesses and section 313 guarantees right to have an opportunity for explaining the circumstances appearing in evidence against him at the trial. Sections 235(2) and 248(2) of Cr.P.C guarantee right to be heard about the sentence upon conviction and section 309 provides right to flair and speedy investigation and trial. However, our judicial system denies justice to the poor as it is very expensive and suffers from a number of defects. If human rights and personal liberties of the poor are to be protected our judicial system has to be revamped and reconstructed so that the poorest of the poor may get a fair deal.

Human Rights and Internal Security of the Country

According to Art. 19 of the Universal Declaration of Human Rights, everyone has the right to freedom of opinion and expression; this right includes freedom to hold opinions without interference and to seek, receive and impart information and ideas through any media and regardless of frontiers. According to Art. 20(1) everyone has the right to freedom of peaceful assembly and association. According to Article 21(1) everyone has the right to take part in the Government., of his Country directly or through freely chosen representatives. Indian Constitution has incorporated above mentioned human rights as fundamental rights for the Indian Citizens and these fundamental rights are "the very foundation and corner-stone of democratic way of life ushered in this country by the Constitution".[7] Dr Ambedkar was right in declaring that the fundamental rights are not absolute and we have to accept some limitations and restrictions to fundamental rights in the interest of corresponding rights and freedom of others or in larger collective interests such as national security, public order or sovereignty of the Country. While maintaining fundamental rights to the citizens is an important goal of democratic societies, the health, safety, moral, well being, and security of the community are also of important values which no society can afford to neglect. Striking a proper balance between these competing interests has been one of the most difficult and challenging tasks of law enforcement agencies in modern times. In a pronouncement Mr. Justice Goldberg, speaking for the United States Supreme Court wrote:"The Constitutional guarantee of liberty implies the existence of an organised society maintaining public order, without which liberty itself would be lost in the excesses of anarchy." (Cox V Louisian a 379 US 536 1965). Under a Constitution which guarantees the fullest possible opportunity for free discussion, there will always be a limited number of fanatics and irresponsible people who take advantage of the constitutional privilege to hurl vilifications at others or to work a crowd by inflammatory and provocative speeches. If the speaker is haranguing an audience with intemperate language or intentionally working the crowd upto commit a breach of the peace, the police can break up the assembly as soon as it becomes reasonable to conclude that an out-break is imminent. If the police detachment at the scene of demonstration is over-whelmingly out-numbered by an enraged and uncontrollable crowd, the police officer would be justified in requesting the speaker or group to yield their rights temporarily to the good order of the community and in offering their protection. If their officer is refused, the arrest would then be justified. Wholesale or mass defiance of public law on a political plane is a problem more in the area of politics than in the area of administration of law and order. The politicians tinker with the laws in an arbitrary manner, and political parties of all colours and shades urge upon the people to fight for political ideals of social justice. But the speed with which parliamentary apparatus has moved during the last few decades in formulating laws, indicates that law in India has not only lagged behind but has acted as a brake, and sometimes as a dead weight, on the wheels of politico-socio-economic change. The anatomy of public disorders reveals a deep-seated malady which symptomatically manifests through processions, rallies, strikes, gheraoes, civil disobedience, satyagraha, political fasts and fasts unto death. The administration of law and order traditionally responds to such political agitations and public protests in the following ways:-

(a) Imposing Sec. 144 of Code of Criminal Procedure.

(b) Arrest of miscreants and main rights leaders.

(c) Preventive action u/s 106, 107, 108, 109 and 110 of Cr.P.C.

(d) Unlawful assemblies—action can be taken u/s 142 to 153 of Indian Penal Code.

(e) Under Secs. 13, 14, 15-15-A, 17, 25, 30 & 34 of I.P.A. (Indian Police Act)

(f) Registration of cases against offenders.

(g) Investigation of cases including interrogation of accused/witnesses.

(h) Prosecution of those involved in violent activities.

(j) Reaching some agreed settlememt through negotiations.

(k) Releasing all those arrested in the process and withdrawing of criminal cases from courts.

After every big political agitations, political agitators know that they will not only be exonerated/acquitted but will emerge as more effective leaders for their followers. "Administrative processes are circumvented by political bargaining and when people at large see this kind of governmental connivance at the contempt of law, they ipso facto lose respect for law and its sovereign majesty.[8]

On 25th June, 1975 the President of India issued a proclamation under clause (1) of the Art. 352 of the Indian Constitution declaring that "a grave emergency exists whereby the security of India is threatened by internal disturbances." Shrimati Indira Gandhi, the then Prime Minister of India, justifying the Proclamation of Emergency said in a broadcast on the morning of June 26, 1975: "Duly elected governments have not been allowed to function, and in some cases force has been used to compel members to resign in order to dissolve lawfully elected assemblies. Agitations have surcharged the atmosphere, leading to violent incidents.....certain persons have gone to the length of inciting our armed forces to mutiny and our police to rebel.....The forces of disintergration are in full play and communal passions are being aroused, threatening our unity..... How can any Government., worth the name stand by and allow the country's stability to be imperilled." "During the Emergency, 29,795 persons were detained under the Maintenance of Internal Security Act 1971 by invoking Sec. 16-A of the Act. 59 Detenus died while in custody and 14 died while on parole".[10] According to Amnesty International Report, 1977, "massive imprisonment of Prisoners of conscience in India ended as a result of political developments in early 1977. At least 40,000 and perhaps as many as 100,000 political detainees were released following imprisonment without trial under emergency provisions".[11] During the Emergency, Political prisoners were hung upside down and beaten, lit candles were placed under the sole of their feet and rats were tied inside their trousers. On 10th April, '77 Shri S.N. Singh, General Secretary of CPI (ML) claimed that there were as many as 12,000 Naxalites detained all over India, 6,000 of whom were held under MISA.

Unfortunately, Govt., can always conceal information in the garb of public interest. Om Mehta told the Lok Sabha on August 11, 1976 that "it would not be in the public interest to disclose information regarding the persons detained in the context of emergency.[12] The months passed since the declaration of internal emergency have been a nightmare of fear and humiliation, reminiscent of days foreign domination. There is no doubt that during the interval of Emergency proclaimed in June, 1975 there was wide spread curtailment of freedom and liberty of the individual coupled with the deprivation of the right to move the courts for redressal of grievances in the area of human rights.[13] Justice Chinnappa Reddy in his paper 'The Police, the Public and the Law' held the view that "the restraint and circumspection with which the police of the country invade this freedom is to a large extent a measure of health of the democratic tradition of the country" and concluded that the future of democracy depends on the respect of rule of law and nobody should be allowed to take the law into his own hands even for the purpose of putting down what is unlawful.[14]

Police Including Security Forces and the Human Right Issues

Police are the real custodian of human rights and whenever human rights of individuals are violated, they are supposed to come to police and complaint against such violators. Such violations of human rights have been identified as offences under various provisions of law and the process of law is put into motion by the police. Therefore police as custodians of human rights must know all the articles of the U.N. declaration of human rights. The security forces while operating in Jammu & Kashmir, Punjab and North Eastern States of India have made great sacrifices. Terrorists have killed 1778 security men in Punjab since 1981. These include 1016 policemen, 180 SPOs, 106 BSF personnel 174 CRP personnel and 48 Army men excluding those killed during "the operation Blue Star".[15] No state can remain a mute witness when large sections of its people are terrorised by a microscopic minority. Some violations of human rights might have been committed during exchange of fire against terrorists by the security forces in a bid to restore peace and security.

The Human Rights Commission

Protection of Human Rights Act 1993 (No 10 of 1994) provides for the constitution of a National Human Rights Commission for better protection of human rights and for matters connected therein. Human Rights in India are being protected by the National Human Rights Commission which has received more than 400 complaints so far. The commission is spreading education about human rights in a big way.

Terrorism versus Dilemma of Protection of Human Rights

Terrorism is generally defined as "the illegitimate use of threatened use of coercion, resulting or intended to result in, the death, injury, restraint or intimidation or persons or the destruction or seizure of property.[16] Today all liberal democracies have become targets for campaigns of political violence and terrorism. There are many facets of violence and terrorism-killing individuals, killing a group of people (class enemies by Naxalites), hijacking of planes, buses, etc. kidnapping of diplomats and VIPs, extortion of huge sums as ransom money, arson, sabotage, despatch of letter-bombs, liberation of prisoners and throwing of bombs to scare people. The law enforcement agencies and the police in particular have the duty to protect and prevent the society from these acts of violence and terrorism. The Universal Declaration of Human Rights reminds us that "it is essential, if man is not to be compelled to have resource, as a last resort, to rebellion against tyranny and oppression that human rights should be protected by the rule of law". The resort to acts of violence committed indiscriminately and dis-proportionality by the insurgents, terrorists and other individuals can not be allowed in a liberal state and police have to deal with such individuals family. "Acts commonly referred to as terrorism are often done under the claim that they are intended to uphold human rights, but paradoxically they also usually violate human rights by endangering the personal safety, fundamental freedoms and property of persons uninvolved in the original violation allegedly sought to be redressed".[17] Failure to implement and enforce human rights breeds terror and campaigns of violence are generally attributed to tiny conspiratorial groups of criminal psychio-pathers. "One of the paradoxes of our modern day twentieth century society is "the power of the fanatic few"-that is, as our society becomes more urban industrial, complex and inter-related the greater becomes the power of a fanatical minority, sometime one or two individuals or a small handful, if it so desires, to disrupt, inconvenience, destroy and endanger the rights, lives and property of others".[18] The recent crescendo of bomb threats, sabotage, annihilation, hijackings, and attack on police has posed serious and continuous problems for the law enforcement agencies. Law enforcement is the first line of defence of our democratic society and have to deal with all such violent groups and fanatics within the bounds of criminal law. Dr E1 Angi has rightly held that view that "Human Rights protection in the criminal process will not be effectively implemented unless it is consciously and seriously accepted by the personnel entrusted with the criminal process." The police find themselves in serious predicament when they are required to combat lawlessness and terrorism in a "soft state" with the help of inadequate and ineffective criminal justice system. In this connection William Kornhavser has pertinently observed: "Unless democratic processes can be combined with stable and limited authority, they favour mass movement subversive of liberty and democracy itself".[19] To apply principle of minimum force to armed violence and terrorists inevitably call for superb discipline and professionalism, a studied impartiality and neutrality in matters of political controversy and considerable patience and firm moral courage. Some members of the police and security forces will be tempted to accrite extra-legal powers and to hid behind the shield of superior orders or security interests and ultimately establishing a power-hungry security apparatus which acquires an appetite for extra-judicial reprisals. Alas, Solzhenitsyn was too sanguine in assuming that "the only punitive organ in human history that combined in one set of hands investigation, arrest, interrogation, prosecution, trial and execution of verdict was the Cheka"[20]. But one cannot deny the necessity for effective criminal justice system to deal with political violence and terrorism. Historical experience indicates that democratic states need to react more positively and forcefully to defeat armed revolutionaries, guerrillas and terrorists. "In what is after all, an internal was situation, the forces of the state have to be empowered to take was measures, to go over to the offensive and to use all military means necessary to defect a direct challenge to the survival of the state".[21] Unfortunately, the democratic governments conveniently ignore the facts of life and expect policemen to deal with terrorists and violent insurgents/criminals with the normal laws of the land. The Police-men's predicament voiced by John Edgar Hoover, is even true today when he said: "Nothing discourages and disheartens the law enforcement officers more than the knowledge that efforts in apprehending criminals are too often no more than useless expenditure of time and money useless because unwarranted leniency in the form of suspended sentences, parole or probation so frequently makes a mockery of the good police work. Consideration must be given to protecting society by isolating depraved individuals who have no respect for law and order or the rights of others".[22] For a peaceful and wholesome society it is imperative that the rights of law-abiding citizens be given atleast the same respect and consideration as the rights of law-breakers. Only a stern action in our Courts involving a philosophy of making the punishment fit the crime and realistic administration of rehabilitation measures can force back the criminal plague. To a policeman it does not stand to reason why correctional methods should be applied to a criminal who commits acts of in human violence and terroristic acts for ransacking the society. Certain situations of insurgency and militancy require a different set of laws and criminal justice procedures to deal with violators of laws. Human rights should not be violated even in these special situations but society should be intelligent enough to find answers to deal with those who are out to demolish the system.[23] Human rights violations by police and paramilitary forces need to be seen in proper national perspective and the supremacy of state sovereign authority over terrorists, insurgents and criminals. It is better to perform one's duty even if some mistakes are committed than not to perform the duty at all. Custodial deaths bring out civil police and security forces in a very exposed form. The contributing factors for custodial tortures and deaths include the negative police image, bad working conditions of police, inadequate training and facilities, high degree of political interferences and lack of effective political leadership.[24]

Human Rights and Developing Societies

In the matters of human rights, all the countries of the world are at best at the developing stage and in all countries we can find instances of blatant discrimination between human beings and violation of basic human rights. Growing rate of crime, racial discrimination, women's inequality, unemployment and infringement of civil liberties of individuals are still affecting millions of people all over the world. Human Rights are in fact threatened by:-

(i) Racial discrimination.

(ii) New economic imperialism and restrictive trade policies.

(iii) Overt and covert influence and interference by powerful nations and exploitation of weaker nations by powerful nations.

(iv) Excessive concentration of wealth and means of production and exploitation of working classes.

(v) Mass poverty, inequality and social injustice.

In a resolution submitted to the United Nations Economic and Social Council in July 1976, more than 20 leading international organisations recognised the following three categories of rights:-

(a) The right to be free from government violation of the integrity of the person. Such violations include torture; cruel, inhuman or degrading treatment or punishment, arbitrary arrest or imprisonment, denial of fair public trial and invasion of the home.

(b) The right to be fulfilment of such vital needs as food, shelter, health care and education, and

(c) The right to enjoy civil and political liberties-freedom of thought, of religion, of assembly, of speech of the press; freedom of movement both within and outside one's own country; freedom to take part in Govt.

There is need for protection of aliens and "non-citizens" from discrimination in respect of human rights. It is hoped that the code of human rights will probably be progressively refined in harmony with the policies necessary to conferring on them all human rights. Peter Berger, Rutgers University Sociologist, believes that there is a universally valid standard of morality and human rights now to which one can appeal in making judgements about countries with different traditions. "Making a distinction between notions of human rights that emerge from a western view of the world and those that states that election irregularities, suppression of press and political inequalities differ from genocide, torture, and enslavement which are violations of human rights."(Peter Berger-Are Human Rights Universal? Commentary September 3,1977 p.60-63). According to C.R. Vance "no member of the United Nations can claim that violation of internationally protected human rights is solely its own affair." According to Richard John Neuhaus, the commitment to sustain human rights must depend, not on practice, law or the passing policies of the government but on a promise that bestows dignity upon every person and demands of every person a respect for the dignity of all others. "(Richard John Neuhaus-"What we mean by human rights and why-" Christian Century, December 6, 1978-p.1179). A new movement is arising within science, with strong political and social connotations, heavily valueladen and yet entirely consistent with the metaphysical frame work of science. Ziman believes that "in the last few years the call for the protection of human rights of scientists and others has become a significant factor in world politics." (John ZIMAN-"Human Rights and the Politics of Science"-Bulletin of the Atomic Scientists, October 1978, p.19-23). Although liberty and equality have achieved constitutional status and genuine political visibility, they have remained largely a matter of state responsibility.

Need for Attitudinal Change in Behaviour of Police and Security Forces

According to Amnesty International Report (March 1992) cases of deaths in police custody in different states between 1985-1991 were as under: Andhra Pradesh 31, Assam 32, Bihar 49, Jammu & Kishmir 23, Haryana 4, Karnataka 6, Kerala 12, Madhya Pradesh 20, Maharashtra 21, Mainpur 19, Orissa 6, Punjab 23, Rajasthan 6, Sikkim 1, Tamil Nadu 19, Uttar Pradesh 25, West Bengal 43 and Delhi 37 making a total of 415 custodial deaths in India. A 10 point plan to combat torture has also been suggested in the report unless there is a simultaneous overhauling of the entire criminal justice system-Police, judiciary and jails and unless police chiefs are held responsible for police excesses, it is difficult to stop the present rot. According to available report a magisterial enquiry was conducted in 114 cases. In 37 cases there were prima facie abuse of authority and criminal proceedings had been launched against the police officials. Amnesty Report was found to be baseless in 46 cases and in 15 cases the listed information was too vague to be followed up. However behaviour and conduct of police officers at grass root level needs to be controlled by effective supervision. Police can be made more accountable by adopting following four categories of control:-

(a) Organisational control or intradepartmental control,
(b) Government control,
(c) Political control, and
(d) Societal control.

Humanising the police behaviour is an important need of the hour. Organisational environment has to be conducive for proper attitudinal change in the policemen particularly at lower and middle ranks.[25] According to National Police Commission judicial enquiries should be mandatory and held promptly in all cases of death or grievous hurt caused while in police custody. Intellectual dishonesty, favouritism, use of third degree methods, fake encounters, indulgence in corrupt practices, indecision at crucial matters of decision making, sympathy for wrong doers, alignment within certain political parties, dictatorial style of functioning are some of the negative aspects of leadership found at certain places in the police organisations. [26] These negative aspects of police leadership need to be changed through behavioural modifications.

Training for Human Rights in CRPF

CRPF personnel of all ranks are at present getting regular training in human rights through specialised courses for various ranks. In all basic and in-service CRP courses and training programmes human right issues are being given due importance. A code of conduct for police officers adopted by the General Assembly on December 17, 1979 exists under which substantive norms are prescribed for the effective maintenance of ethical standards for the officials. Article 5 prohibits the law enforcement officials from inflicting, instigating or abetting any act of torture. CRPF jawans and officers are given training in "Code of Conduct" and also given input of protection of human rights issues in various training programmes. Respect for the due process of law and for basic human rights is the hall-mark of CRP culture. As law enforcement agency and an instrument of the state, police are expected to uphold the human rights of the law abiding citizens. The human rights of the law-abiding citizens should get precedence over the rights of the militants, secessionists and criminals. Rights of the accused are given in Appendix 'C' which need to be learnt by all police officers.

Human Rights Panel Bill Re-Introduced

The Home Minister Mr. S.B. Chavan on 9th December 1993 introduced in the Lok Sabha afresh a bill providing for the setting up of a National Human Rights Commission and similar commissions in states and courts for better protection of human rights. The protection of Human Rights Bill 1993 was brought following the promulgation of a presidential ordinance providing for the setting up of human right commission. The Bill seeks to empower the Centre to constitute a state human rights commission in Jammu & Kashmir. The chair person of the nine member National Human Rights Commission will be a former Chief Justice of the Supreme Court. The Commission will have the power to inquire sinomoto or on a petition presented to it by a victim or any person on his behalf regarding violations of human rights or abetment thereof. It could also inquire into negligence in the prevention of such violations by a public servant.

Concluding Remarks

(i) All administrators, police personnel and public servants should be educated regarding the importance and value of "Universal Declaration of Human Rights" and should be urged to observe and provide protection to Human Rights. In all basic training courses and in inservice training courses, syllabus for civil police officers, Universal Declaration of Human Rights and its enforcement should be given due importance and weightage.

(ii) In educational institutions/universities and colleges students should be educated about the human rights because in the ultimate analysis public consent is the only real sanction for human rights. Implementation of human rights depends not on any abstract principles or declarations but upon the will of the community as expressed in acts of parliament which could enlarge, abridge or redistribute the rights and liberties among the people.

(iii) Democratic Society alone can provide fullest protection of human rights and eternal vigilance is the price which each citizen has to pay for nurturing the democratic institutions on healthy lines. Use of third degree methods of interrogation, abuse of police powers, police corruption, police violence and police brutalities are some of the known stigmas of police profession. A concerted effort is needed to eradicate this deep-rooted malady from the police organisations. The policemen, due to their extra-ordinary discretionary powers are the most powerful criminal justice officer and, therefore, should act as guardian and custodian of human rights and civil liberties. "The quality of a nation's civilization can be largely measured by the methods it uses in the enforcement of its criminal law". [26] The entire system of criminal justice should be dedicated for the ideal of protection of human rights and civil liberties. Legislative assemblies, courts, and all other law enforcement agencies and even the public must effectively ensure protection of human rights and civil liberties. Law is necessary but it is not the last word. In words of Judge Learned Hand: "Liberties lie in the hearts of men and women; when it dies there, no Constitution, no law, no court can save it; no constitution, no law, no court can even do much to help it. Where it lies there it needs no constitutions, no law, no court to save. An alarmingly large number of poor men and women including children are behind prisoner bars for years awaiting trial in the courts of law because they are unable to furnish bail securities of heavy amounts. The bail system as it operates today, is a source of great hardship to the poor. The Supreme Court of India has observed: "We are shouting from house tops about the protection and enforcement of human rights. We are talking passionately and eloquently about the maintenance and preservation of basic freedoms. But, are we not denying human rights to these nameless persons who are languishing in jails for years for offences which perhaps they might ultimately be found not to have committed. Are we not withholding basic freedom from these neglected and helpless human beings who have been condemned to a life of imprisonment and degradation for years on end ? Are expeditious trial and freedom from detention not part of human rights and basic freedom ? Many of these unfortunate men and women must not even be remembering when they entered the jail and for what offences? They have over the years ceased to be human beings; they are mere ticket-numbers. It is high time that the public conscience is awakened and the government as well as the judiciary begin to realise that in the dark cells of our prisons there are large number of men and women who are waiting patiently, perhaps, but in vain, for justice— a commodity which is tragically beyond their reach and grasp. Law has become for them an instrument of injustice and they are helpless and despairing victims of the callousness of the legal and judicial system. The time has come when the legal and judicial system has to be revamped and restructured so that such injustice do not occur and disfigure the fair and otherwise luminous face of our nascent democracy. [27]

TABLE A

FACTS REGARDING ALLEGATIONS CONTAINED IN THE AMNESTY INTERNATIONAL REPORT "INDIA:TORTURE, RAPDE AND DEATHS IN CUSTODY"

State	*Prosecutions*		*Convictions*		*Acquittals*		*Departmental Actions (Persons)*	*Sub-judice*		*Under investigations*	*Cases not sustained after Eng.*
	Cases	*Persons*	*Cases*	*Persons*	*Cases*	*Persons*		*Cases*	*Persons*		
@											
Andhra Pradesh	6	19	1	1	2	11	8	3	7	1	8
Assam	2	10	-	-	-	—	-	2	10	-	12
Delhi	6	28	-	-	-	—	2	6	28	2	19
Haryana	2	3	-	-	-	—	2	3	1	2	—
Jammu & Kashmir	1	2	-	-	-	—	-	1	2	-	20
Karnataka	5	22	1	5	-	—	-	4	17	-	—
Kerala	3	18	-	-	2	13	2	1	5	1	8
Madhya Pradesh	6	24	1	7	3	13	9	2	4	2	13
Maharashtra	9	41	-	-	3	6	-	6	35	3	10
Manipur	-	-	-	-	-	-	-	-	-	-	1
Nagaland	-	-	-	-	-	-	-	-	-	-	1
Orissa	3	9	2	3	-	-	2	1	6	1	2
Pondichery	1	1	-	-	1	1	-	-	-	-	—
Punjab	-	-	-	-	-	-	-	-	-	-	21
Rajasthan	5	15	-	-	1	4	-	4	11	-	2
Sikkim	1	2	-	-	-	-	-	1	2	-	—
Tamil Nadu	8	37	1	2	2	4	7	5	31	1	16
Tripura	-	-	-	-	-	-	-	-	-	-	2
Uttar Pradesh	3	@	-	-	-	-	-	3	@	-	1
West Bengal	2	6	-	-	1	5	-	1	1	-	25
Total	65	243	6	18	15	57	32	43	168	12	153

.2 Police personnel were convicted but their convictions were not maintained by Higher Courts.

@ Figures not available.

TABLE B

TERRORIST VIOLENCE IN JAMMU & KASHMIR

Year	*Total incidents*	*Attacks on SF*	*Attacks on others*	*Explosion & Arsons*	*Other Incidents*
1988	390	6	1	142	241
1989	2154	49	73	840	1192
1990	3905	1098	485	1810	512
1991	3122	1999	321	611	191
1992	4971	3413	507	744	307
Total	14542	6565	1387	4147	2443

TABLE C

KILLINGS IN TERRORIST VIOLENCE IN KASHMIR

	1988	*1989*	*1990*	*1991*	*1992*	Total
Total Killed	31	92	1177	1393	1909	4602
SF Personnel	1	13	132	285	177	508
Govt. Officials	1	3	62	57	36	158
Top Political leaders	-	-	1	-	-	1
Politicians	-	3	24	10	4	41
Judiciary	-	3	-	1	-	4
Pressmen	-	-	1	1	1	3
Civilians	28	70	774	525	857	2256
Militants	1	-	183	614	873	1671

TABLE D

KIDNAPPINGS BY TERRORISTS IN KASHMIR

	1989	*1990*	*1991*	*1992*	*Total*
Incidents	2	57	100	124	283
Persons abducted	2	70	159	183	414
Foreigners	-	-	12	-	12
Women	-	8	8	13	29
Politicians	-	33	53	26	112
Govt. Officers	-	21	27	43	91
SF Personnel	-	12	44	30	86
Killed	1	29	29	38	97
Released *	1	32	73	112	218

* In most cases released after extortion, torture, exchange of terrorists, rape (remaining untrated)

TABLE E
DESTRUCTION OF PROPERTY BY TERRORISTS IN KASHMIR

Year	*Total Incidents*	*Govt. Bldgs*	*Educational institutions*	*Private Houses*	*Bridges*
1988	128	4	4	19	1
1989	294	191	172	427	16
1990	646	501	129	1242	172
1991	391	45	24	819	24
1992	564	65	57	2312	28
Total	2023	806	386	4819	241

TABLE F
RECOVERY OF WEAPONS FROM TERRORISTS IN KASHMIR

Weapons/Explosives	*1988-90*	*1991*	*1992*	*Total*
Rocket Launchers	141	140	174	455
Machine Guns	124	176	174	47
AK Series Rifles	1474	2602	3775	7851
Sniper Rifles	1	3	13	17
Pistols/Revolvers	858	946	808	2612
Ammunition (Assorted)	242007	318623	343699	904329
Grenades	2994	2236	2818	8048
Rockets	370	329	267	966
Rocket Boosters	156	203	144	503
Mines	1101	217	307	1625
Guns	30	79	81	190
Explosives (Kg)	1966	588	436	2990
Bombs	708	72	228	1008
WT Sets	22	37	68	127

TABLE G

PROFILE OF VIOLENCE IN PUNJAB

Year	*No. of Persons Killed*	*No. of Policemen Killed*
1981	13	2
1982	13	2
1983	75	20
1984	359	20
1985	63	8
1986	520	42
1987	910	95
1988	1949	110
1989	1168	152
1990	2467	493
1991	2586	493
1992	1461	252
Total	11584	1689

TABLE H

COMMUNITY WISE BREAKUP OF PERSONS KILLED IN PUNJAB

Year	*Hindu*	*Sikhs*	*Others*	*Total*
1981	10	3	-	13
1982	8	5	-	13
1983	35	40	-	75
1984	237	122	-	359
1985	45	17	1	63
1986	324	193	3	520
1987	425	478	7	910
1988	858	1044	47	1949
1989	422	734	12	1168
1990	743	1694	30	2467
1991	719	1836	31	2586
1992	534	913	14	1461
Total	4260	7079	145	11584

TABLE I

INCIDENTS OF MASS VIOLENCE IN PUNJAB

Year	*Total Incident*	*Persons Killed*
1988	7	52
1989	3	47
1990	64	298
1991	38	377
1992	38	303
Total	150	1077

TABLE J

VIOLANCE AGAINST JUDICIARY/MEDIA MEN/SENIOR OFFICIALS

	86	*87*	*88*	*89*	*90*	*91*	*92*	*Total*
1. Judicial officers killed	1	1	-	-	3	2	2	9
2. Senior officials killed	-	-	-	-	9	14	10	33
3. Media Persons killed (Journalist/ Editors/Reporters and other personnel)	-	-	9	21	18	13	1	62
4. Bank officers killed	-	-	3	-	-	6	1	10
5. Teaching staff killed	-	-	-	-	9	9	16	34

TABLE K

PARLIAMENT/LEGISLATURE CANDIDATES KILLED IN PUNJAB

	1988	*89*	*90*	*91*	*92*	*Total*
Cong-I	10	4	12	6	10	42
BJP	3	-	5	5	9	22
CPI	2	3	14	4	5	28
CPM	7	3	1	9	1	21
SAD	6	2	7	10	2	27
HSS	2	-	-	-	-	2
LD	1	-	-	-	-	1
AISSF	-	1	-	-	-	1
DYF	-	1	-	-	-	1
Others	If not available	26	48	75	26	175
Total	31	40	87	109	53	320

TABLE L

INCIDENTS OF LOOTING IN PUNJAB

Year	*Incidents*	*Amount Looted In (Rs.)*
1987	383	7, 32, 55, 593
1988	297	1, 08, 17, 719
1989	200	1, 09, 27, 979
1990	451	3, 49, 23, 429
1991	541	1, 82, 91, 926
1992	48	36, 24, 519
Total	1920	15, 18, 51, 165

REFERENCES

1. Dr. Krishna Mohan Mathur-Indian Police-Role and Challenges-Gyan Publishing House, New Delhi. 1994 P. 97.

2. Rajinder Sachar-Human Rights-West Can't Preach Hindustan Times-8 October 1992.

3. Balraj Puri- Human Rights Key to Kashmir Policy-Times of India-11 February 1992.

4. Singhvi Challenges Amnesty Report-Hindustan Times-17 September 1992.

5. Vinay Pandey-Force to Reckon with- Times of India-27 October 1992.

6. For detail of history and development of CRP see K.M. Mathur-Police in India-Gyan Publishing House, New Delhi.

7. C.J. Gajendragadkar-Sajjan Singh Vs State of Rajasthan AIR 1965, SC 848.

8. Dr. P.D. Sharma-Indian Police-A Developmental Approach-1977 P. 226.

9. Lok Sabha Debate- June 15, 1977-Q.No.47-Figures given by the then Home Minister Sri Charan Singh-Indian Express-February 23, 1977.

10. Lok Sabha Debate- 22, January 1976, Speech of Sri H.M. Patel.

11. Amnesty International Report 1977-Vikas Publishing House-New Delhi, 1978, P.179

12. Lok Sabha Debate on 11 August 1976.

13. Subhash C.Kashyap-Human Rights and Parliament, 1978-P.90.

14. Journal of Constitutional and Parliamentary Studies Vol.VII, No.3 July-September 1973, P.126

15. Times of India Ahmedabad-5 December 1993.

16. Paul Wilkinson-Terrorism and the Liberal State, 1977 P.23.

17. Prof. M.C. Bassiouni-"Final Document-Conclusions and Recommendations"-International Terrorism and Political Crime, 1975-P. XI.

18. John E. Hoover-The Revolutionary Guerrilla Attacks Law Enforcement and Democratic Society: An analysis of the Destructive power of the Fanatic Few, Albany Law Reporter 1971, Vol. 85 No.4.

19. William Kornhauser-The Politics of Mass Society-1960. P.129.

20. A Solzhenitsyn-The Gulag Archipelago, 1918, 1956,Translated by Thomas P. Whitney, 1974, p. 28.

21. Paul Wilkinson-Terrorism and the Liberal State pp. 43-44.

22. John Edger Hoover-FBI Law Enforcement Bulletin, Vol. 30. No.8 August, 1961.

23. K.P.S. Gill in Seminar on Human Rights- Times of India-15 December 1993.

24. Dr. Krishna Mohan Mathur, Police-Law and Internal Security- Gyan Publishing House, New Delhi-1994 p. 21.

25. K.M. Mathur-The Problems of Police in a Democratic Society, RBSA Publishers, Jaipur 1987 p. 29

26. Dr.K.M.Mathur-Police in India Problems and Prospects-Gyan Publishing House, New Delhi 1991 p.188.

27. Walter V. Schaefer-Federalism and the State Criminal Procedure-Harward Law Review 70-November 1956.p. 26.

28. P.N. Bhagavati and D.A.Desai-Hussamara Khatton and other Vs Home Secretary, State of Bihar Supreme Court, AIR 1979, SC 1869 Cr.L.J. 1979 (1036).

APPENDIX-A

Universal Declaration of Human Rights

Preamble

WHEREAS recognition of the inherent dignity and of the equal and inalienable rights of all members of the human family is the foundation of freedom, justice and peace in the world.

WHEREAS disregard and contempt for human rights have resulted in barbarious acts which have outraged the conscience of mankind, and the advent of a world in which human beings shall injoy freedom of speech and belief and freedom from fear and want has been proclaimed as the highest aspiration of the common people.

WHEREAS it is essential, if man is not to be compelled to have recourse, as a last resort, to rebellion against tyranny and oppression, that human rights should be protected by the rule of law.

WHEREAS it is essential to promote the development of friendly relations between nations.

WHEREAS the peoples of the United Nations have in the Charter reaffirmed their faith in fundamental human rights, in the dignity and worth of the human person and in the equal rights of men and women and have determined to promote social progress and better standards of life in larger freedom.

WHEREAS Member States have pledged themselves to achieve, in co-operation with the United Nations, the promotion of universal respect for and observance of human rights and fundamental freedoms.

WHEREAS a common understanding of these rights and freedom is of the greatest importance for the full realisation of this pledge.

Now therefore The General Assembly Proclaims

This Universal Declaration of Human Rights as a common standard of achievement for all peoples and all nations, to the end that every individual and very organ of society, keeping this Declaration constantly in mind, shall strive by teaching and education to promote respect for this rights and freedoms and by progressive measures, national and international, to secure their universal and effective recognition and observance, both among the peoples of Member States themselves and among the people of territories under their jurisdiction.

Article 1. All human beings are born free and equal in dignity and rights. They are endowed with reason and conscience and should act towards one another in a spirit of brotherhood.

Article 2. Everyone is entitled to all the rights and freedoms set forth in this Declaration, without distinction of any kind, such as race, colour, sex, language, religion, political or other opinion, national or social origin, property, birth or other status. Furthermore, no distinction shall be made on the basis of the political, jurisdictional or international status of the country or territory to which a person belongs, whether it be independent, trust, non-self-governing or under any other limitation of sovereignty.

Article 3. Everyone has the right to life, liberty and security of person.

Article 4. No one shall be held in slavery or servitude; slavery and the slave trade shall be prohibited in all their forms.

Article 5. No one shall be subjected to torture or to cruel, inhuman or degrading treatment or punishment.

Article 6. Everyone has the right to recognition everywhere as a person before the law.

Article 7. All are equal before the law and are entitled without any discrimination to equal protection of the law. All are entitled to equal protection against any discrimination in violation of this Declaration and against any incitement to such discrimination.

Article 8. Everyone has the right to an effective remedy by the competent national tribunals for acts violating the fundamental rights granted him by the constitution or by law.

Article 9. No one shall be subjected to arbitrary arrest, detention or exile.

Article 10. Everyone is entitled in full equality to a fair and public hearing by an independent and impartial tribunal, in the determination of his rights and obligations and of any criminal charge against him.

Article 11. (1) Everyone charged with a penal offence has the right to be presumed innocent until proved guilty according to law in a public trial at which he has had all the guarantees necessary for his defence.

(2) No one shall be held guilty of penal offences on account of any act or omission which did not constitute a penal offence, under national or international law, at the time when it was committed. Nor shall a heavier penalty be imposed that the one that was applicable at the time of penal offence was committed.

Article 12. No one shall be subjected to arbitrary interference with his privacy, family, home or correspondence, nor to attacks upon his honour and reputation. Everyone has the rights to the protection of the law against such interference or attacks.

Article 13. (1) Everyone has the right to freedom of movement and residence within the borders of each state.

(2) Everyone has the right to leave any country, including his own, and to return to his country.

Article 14. (1) Everyone has the right to seek and to enjoy in other countries asylum from persecution.

(2) This right may not be invoked in the case of prosecutions genuinely arising from non-political crimes or from acts contrary to the purposes and principles of the United Nations.

Article 15. (1) Everyone has the right to a nationality.

(2) No one shall be arbitrarily deprived of his nationality nor denied the right to change his nationality.

Article 16. (1) Men and women of full age, without any limitation due to race, nationality or religion have the right to marry and to found a family. They are entitled to equal rights as to marriage, during marriage and at its dissolution.

(2) Marriage shall be entered into only with the free and full consent of the intending spouses.

(3) The family is the natural and fundamental group unit of society and is entitled to protection by society and the State.

Article 17. (1) Everyone has the right to own property alone as well in association with others.

(2) No one shall be arbitrarily deprived of his property.

Article 18. Everyone has the right to freedom of thought, conscience and religion; this right includes freedom to change his religion or belief, and freedom, either alone or in community with others and in public or private, to manifest his religion or belief in teaching, practice, worship and observance.

Article 19. Everyone has the right to freedom of opinion and expression; this right includes freedom to hold opinions without interference and to seek, receive and impart information and ideas through any media and regardless of frontiers.

Article 20. (1) Everyone has the right to freedom of peaceful assembly and association.

(2) No one may be compelled to belong to an association.

Article 21. (1) Everyone has the right to take part in the government of his country, direcly or through freely chosen representatives.

(2) Everyone has the right of equal access to public service in his country.

(3) The will of the people shall be the basis of the authority of government; this will shall be expressed in periodic and genuine elections which shall be by universal and equal suffage and shall be held by secret vote or by equivalent free voting procedures.

Article 22. Everyone, as a member of society, has the right to social security and is entitled to realisation through national effort and international co-operation and in accordance with the organisation and resources of each State, of the economic, social and cultural rights indispensable for his dignity and the free development of his personality.

Article 23. (1) Everyone has the right to work, to free choice of employment, to just and favourable conditions of work and to protection against unemployment.

(2) Everyone, without any discrimination, has the right to equal pay for equal work.

(3) Everyone who works has the right to just and favourable

remuneration insuring for himself and his family an existence worthy of human dignity, and supplemented, if necessary, by other means of social protection.

(4) Everyone has the right to form and to join trade unions for the protection of his interests.

Article 24. Everyone has the right to rest and leisure, including reasonable limitation of working hours and periodic holidays with pay.

Article 25. (1) Everyone has the right to a standard of living adequate for the health and well-being of himself and of his family, including food, clothing, housing and medical care and necessary social services, and the right to security in the event of unemployment, sickness, disability, widowhood, old age or other lack of livelihood in circumstances beyond his control.

(2) Motherhood and childhood are entitled to special care and assistance. All children, whether born in or out of wedlock, shall enjoy the same social protection.

Article 26. (1) Everyone has the right to education. Education shall be free, at least in the elementary and fundamental stages. Elementary education shall be compulsory. Technical and professional education shall be made generally available and higher education shall be equally accessible to all on the basis of merit.

(2) Education shall be directed to the full development of the human personality and to the strengthening of respect for human rights and fundamental freedoms. It shall promote understanding, tolerance and friendship among all nations, racial or religious groups, and shall further the activities of the United Nations for the maintenance of peace.

(3) Parents have a prior right to choose the kind of education that shall be given to their children.

Article 27. (1) Everyone has the right freely to participate in the cultural life of the community, to enjoy the arts and to share in scientific advancement and its benefits.

(2) Everyone has the right to the protection of the moral and material interests resulting from any scientific, literary or artistic production of which he is the author.

Article 28. Everyone is entitled to a social and international order in which the rights and freedom set forth in this Declaration can be fully realised.

Article 29. (1) Everyone has duties to the community in which along the free and full development of his personality is possible.

(2) In the exercise of his rights and freedoms, everyone shall be subject only to such limitations as are determined by law solely for the purpose of securing due recognition and respect for the rights and freedoms of others and of meeting the just requirements of morality, public order and the general welfare in a democratic society.

(3) These rights and freedoms may in no case be exercised contrary to the purposes and principles of the United Nations.

Article 30. Nothing in this Declaration may be interpreted as implying for any State, group or person any right to engage in any activity or to perform any act aimed at the destruction of any of the rights and freedoms set forth herein.

APPENDIX-B

United Nations Declaration of Human Rights of 1948 and the Fundamental Rights Incorporated in the Indian Constitution

The Fundamental Rights incorporated in the Indian Constitution have a close similarity with the United Nations Declaration of Human Rights of 1948 in content and in form. The comparative table of Articles is as follows-

Fundamental Rights under the Indian Constitution	*UN Declaration of Human Rights*
1. Article14—The State shall not deny to any person equality before the law of the equal protection of law.	1. Article7—All are equal before the law and are entitled without any discrimination to equal protection of law.
2. Article 15(1)—The State shall not discriminate against any citizen on grounds only of religion race, caste, sex, place of birth or any of them.	2. Article7—All are entitled to equal protection against any discrimination in violation of this declaration and against any incitement to such discrimination.
3. Article 16(1)—There shall be equality of opportunity for all citizens in matters relating to employment.	3. Article 21(2)—Everyone has right to equal access to public service in his country.
4. Article 19(1) (a)—All citizens shall have the right to freedom of speech and expression.	4. Article19—Everyone has the right to freedom of opinion and expression.

5.	Article 19(1)(b)—Right to assemble peacefully without arms.	5.	Article 20(1)—Everyone has the right to freedom of peaceful assembly and association.
6.	Article 19(1) (c)—Right to form unions and association.	6.	Article 20(1) and Article 23(4)—Every one has the right to form and join Trade Unions for the protection of his interests.
7.	Article 19(1) (d)—Right to reside and settle in any part of the territory of India.	7.	Article 13(1)—Everyone has the right to freedom of movement and residence within the borders of each State.
8.	Article 19 (1) (b)—Right to acquire, hold and dispose of property.	8.	Article 17(1)—Everyone has the right to own property alone as well as in association with others.
9.	Article 29(1)—No person shall be convicted of any offence except for violation of law in force at the time of commission of the act charged as an offence.	9.	Article 11(2)—No one shall be held guilty of any penal offence on account of any act or omission which did not constitute penal offence under national or international law.
10.	Article 21—No person shall be deprived of his life and personal liberty except according to the procedure established by law.	10.	Article 9—No one shall be subjected to arbitrary arrest, detention or exile. Article3—Everyone has the right to life, liberty and security of person.

11. Article 23—Traffic in human beings and beggary or other similar forms of forced labour are prohibited.	11. Article 4—No one shall be held in slavery or servitude slavery and the slave trade.
12. Article 25(1)—All persons are equally entitled to freedom of conscience and the right freely to profess, practice and propagate religion.	12. Article 18—Everyone has the right to freedom of thought, conscience and religion.
13. Article 29(1)—Citizens residing in the territory of India having distinct language script or culture of its own shall have the right to conserve the same.	13. Article 22—Everyone has the right to social security and is entitled to realisation of the economic, social and cultural rights indispensable for his dignity and the free development of his personality.
14. Article 30(1)—All minorities whether based on religion or language shall have the right to establish and administer educational institutions of their own choice.	14. Article 26 (3)—Parents have the prior right to choose the kind of education that shall be given to their children.
15. Article 31(1)—No one shall be deprived of his property saved by authority of law.	15. Article 17(2)—No one shall be arbitrarily deprived of his property.
16. Article 32—The right to move Supreme Court by appropriate proceedings for the enfocement of the right conferred by this part is guaranteed.	16. Article 8—Every one has the right to an effective remedy by the competent national tribunal for acts violating the fundamental rights granted by constitution or by law.

APPENDIX-C

Human Rights in Criminal Procedure Code

1. Protection against arbitrary or unlawful arrests (Article 22 of the Constitution and sections 41, 55 and 151 Cr. P.C.).

2. Protection against arbitrary or unlawful searches (Sections 93, 94, 97, 100(4) to (8) and 165 Cr. P.C).

3. Protection against 'Double Jeopardy' (Article 20(2) of the Constitution and section 300 Cr. P.C.).

4. Protection against conviction or enhanced punishment under ex post facto law (Article 20(1) of the Constitution).

5. Protection against arbitrary or illegal detention in custody (Article 22 of the Constitution and sections 56, 57, 58 and 76 Cr.P.C.).

6. Right to be informed of the grounds of his arrest immediately after the arrest (Article 22(1) of the Constitution and section 50 Cr.P.C. See also sections 55 and 75 Cr.P.C.).

7. Right of the arrested person not to be subjected to unnecessary restraint (Section 49 Cr.P.C.).

8. Right to consult a lawyer of his own choice (Article 22(1) of the Constitution and section 303 Cr.P.C.).

9. Right to be produced before a magistrate within 24 hours of his arrest (Article 22(1) of the Constitution and sections 57 and 76 Cr.P.C.)

10. Right to be released on bail, if arrested (Sections 436, 437 and 439 Cr.P.C. Also see sections 50(2) and 167 Cr.P.C.).

11. Right not to be compelled to be a witness against himself (Article 20(3) of the Constitution).

12. Right to get copies of the documents and statements of witnesses on which the prosecution relies (Sections 173(7), 207, 208 and 238 Cr.P.C.).

13. Right to obtain receipt when property is seized (Sections 100(6) and 100(7) Cr.P.C.).

14. Right to have the benefit of the presumption of innocence till the guilt is proved beyond reasonable doubt (Sections 101-104 Evidence Act).

15. Right to insist that evidence be recorded in his presence except in some special circumstances (Section 273 Cr.P.C. See also Section 317 Cr.P.C.).

16. Right to have due notice of the charges (Sections 218, 228(2), 240(2), 246(2) etc. Cr.P.C.).

17. Right to test the evidence for the prosecution by cross-examination (Section 138 Evidence Act.)

18. Right to have an opportunity for explaining the circumstances appearing in evidence against him at the trial (Section 313 Cr.P.C.).

19. Right to have himself medically examined for evidence to disprove the commission of offence by him or establish commission of offence against his body by any other person (Section 54 Cr.P.C.).

20. Right to examine himself as a witness on his own behalf (Section 315 Cr.P.C.).

21. Right against harassment, torture and ill-treatment during investigation (See Sections 330 and 331 I.P.C.).

22. Right against unduly prolonged interrogation.

23. Right to produce defence witnesses (Section 243 Cr.P.C.).

24. Right to be tried by independent, impartial and competent judge (The scheme of separation of Judiciary as envisaged in Cr.P.C. Also see sections 479, 327, 191 etc., Cr.P.C.).

25. Right to submit written arguments at the conclusion of the trial in addition to oral submission (Section 314 Cr.P.C.).

26. Right to the legal aid at the expense of the State in certain cases (Section 304 Cr.P.C.).

27. Right to be heard about the sentence upon conviction (Sections 235(2) and 248(2) Cr.P.C.).

28. Right to fair and speedy investigation and trial (Section 309 Cr.P.C.).

29. Right to appeal in case of conviction (Sections 351, 374, 379, 380 Cr.P.C. and Article 132(1) 134(1) and 136(1) of the Constitution).

30. Right not to be imprisoned upon conviction in certain circumstances (Section 360 Cr.P.C. and section 6 of the Probation of Offenders Act).

31. Right to refrain police from intrusion on his privacy (Article 31 of the Constitution).

32. Right to secrecy of communication.

33. Right of release of a convicted person on bail pending appeal (Section 389 Cr.P.C.).

34. Right to get copy of the judgement when sentenced to imprisonment (Section 363 Cr.P.C.).

APPENDIX D

Inaugural Address of Dr/ Krishna Mohan Mathur by Director Delivered on the Occasion of 38th Internal Security Seminar for DisGP on 2 May 1994 at Mount Abu

Distinguished members of the panel, participants for the DIsGP Seminar and friends.

It is indeed my very great pleasure to extend a hearty welcome to all of you at the Internal Security Academy Mount Abu. The objective of the Seminar is to provide an opportunity to the participants and the faculty members to discuss and analyse various internal security challenges and their impact on human rights. The objective of the Seminar is to create heightened awareness about human rights and to sensitive the participants for protection of human rights of the citizens.

We will be devoting the first three days i.e. 2, 3 and 4th May 1994 for the topic "Internal Security Challenges and their impact on Human Rights". For the next three days i.e. from 5 May to 7 May 1994 we will be discussing on the theme "Improving Police performance through training-Search for thrust areas". I hope this Seminar will be able to achieve its objective with the active co-operation of all the participants. We have organised this Seminar to provide you all with an opportunity to interact frankly and freely and share your vast experience of the field with other delegates.

1. The Concept of Internal Security

It is difficult to define internal security but broadly it connotes the inner strength and health potential of the nation-stable to preserve its international personality by its capacity to secure (1) its sovereign power and authority; (2) government; (3) defined territory and (4) permanent population from all internal threats, subvertive interventions and destabilisation attempts carried out at the behest of the foreign nations. The concept of internal security has to be redefined and broadened in the context of international power politics and global perceptions about human rights.

2. The Main Challenges of Internal Security

The main challenges of internal security of the Country can be enumerated as under:-

1. Terrorism in Kashmir and Punjab.
2. Insurgency in North Eastern States of India.
3. Communal riots and violence.
4. NARCO - Terrorism and Drug addiction.
5. Atrocities on weaker sections of society particularly on women and children.
6. Regionalism and linguistic movements.
7. Naxalite etremism.
8. Ethnic conflicts and urban and rural violence.
9. Agitations, demonstrations and protests.
10. Increasing crime, economic offences and white collar crimes.
11. Law and order problems and frequent violations of rule of law.

3. The Human Rights and Indian Constitution

The Constitution of India, in its preamble, resolves to secure to all its citizens:-

Justice - Social, economic and political.

Equality	-	Of status and of opportunity and to promote among all.
Fraternity	-	Assuring the dignity of the indi vidual and the unity and integrity of the Nation
Liberty	-	of thought, expression, belief faith and workship.

Human Rights as enumerated in the Indian Constitution are as under:-

1. *Right to Equality*

(i) Equality before Law; (Article 14).

(ii) Prohibition of discrimination on grounds of religion, race, caste, sex or place of birth; (Article 15).

(iii) Equality of opportunity in matters of public employment; (Article 14).

(iv) Abolition of untouchability; (Article 17).

(v) Abolition of titles (Article 18).

2. *Right to Freedom*

(i) Freedom of speech etc (Article 19).

(ii) Protection in respect of conviction for offences; (Article 20).

(iii) Protection of life and personal liberty (Article 21).

(iv) Protection against detention in certain cases (Article 22).

3. *Right Against Exploitation*

(i) Prohibition of traffic in human beings and forced labour (Article 23).

(ii) Prohibition of employment of children in factories etc. (Article 24)

4. Right to Freedom of Religion

(i) Freedom of conscience and free pursuit of profession, practice and propagation of religion (Article 25).

(ii) Freedom to manage religious affairs; (Article 16).

(iii) Freedom as to payment of taxes for promotion of any particular religion; (Article 27).

(iv) Freedom as to attendance at religious places or religious worship in certain educational institutions. (Article 28).

5. Cultural and Educational Rights

(i) Protection of interests of minorities; (Article 29).

(ii) Right of minorities to establish and administer educational institutions. (Article 30).

6. Right to Constitutional Remedies

(i) Right to Constitutional remedies. (Article 32).

All public servants including members of the police organisations are duty bound to uphold the Constitution of India. Under Article 51 A, citizens of India have ten fundamental duties and the first duty is "to abide by the Constitution, respect its ideals and Institutions, the National Flag and the National Anthem". The third fundamental duty of the citizens is "to uphold and protect the sovereignty, unity and intergrity of the Country. Human Rights jurisprudence has grown enormously over the last four decades and there is an urgent need to give training to all ranks of the police forces in human rights. Violations of human rights are committed on a large scale by the terrorists, secessionists, fundamentalists, extremists and criminals who have no regards for life and property of the people of the Country. All over the World, democratic societies are threatened by violence which is practiced and exploited by secessionists, terrorists, fundamentalists, smugglers, drug traffickers and criminals. During the last ten years in Punjab, 12000 civilians and 17000 police personnel have been killed by the terrorists. In Kashmir during the last five years 4602 persons have been killed by the terrorists and there have been 14542 terrorists incidents of violence in the Valley. Police has to face the eternal dilemma of Ends Vs Means in tackling various internal security problems. At theoretical level, generally five levels of situations have been adopted by the international human rights organisations in determining a Country's human rights status. The focus is based on the incidence of torture, political murders, brutal political imprisonment and detention with or without trial. These factors are undergirded by the extent of the endemic nature of the occurrences. Most Countries of the World appear to be observing human rights more in their breach.

In ancient Hindu scriptures particularly Vedas and Puranas, the concept of human rights existed. In Markandeya Purana it is said "I pray for the well being of all beings May they be free from fear and applications and rejoice in the friendship of all, be it an ally or an alien. May he, who loves me now, share the blessedness of human life and he that chooses to hate me here, may he also find the path of goodness" The Rig Veda makes clear references to the three civil liberties of "Tana" (body), Skridhu (dwelling house) and jabbasi (life) and urges all humanity to uphold these civil liberties of others.

The Protection of Human Rights Act 1993 (No 10 of 1994) has defined the term as under "Human Rights means the rights relating to life, liberty, equality and dignity of the individual guaranteed by the Constitution or embodied in International Covenants and enfrorceable by Courts in India". According to section 2 (1) (6); International Covenants on civil and political rights and the International

Covenant on Economic, Social and Cultural Rights adopted by the General Assembly of the United Nations on the16th December 1966.

4. The National Human Rights Commission

In less than a year of its inception the National Human Rights Commission of India has not only recorded with grave concern the human rights violations but has also asked the government to act with speed.

The National Human Rights Commission has asked District Collectors all over the Country to report to it any custodial deaths, within twenty four hours. In the Bijbehra case, Commission has recommended "dual proceedings" by way of prosecution of the personnel responsible as well as disciplinary action under the BSF Act. In the Punjab "tattooing case" the Commission has succeeded in adequate compensation for the victims. By and large India's record of protection of human rights is pretty good though certain foreign countries are trying to malign its performance due to international power-politics.

To quote A.G. Noorani - " No one denies that the Constitution embodies fundamental rights and that our record on human rights, on the whole, is the best in the third world. It is also a fact that to large segments of our society justice is denied and not merely because of economic and social reasons. Justice is denied partly because the judicial process is slow. Sluggish, expensive and yet inadequate, and is moreover not completely free from the taints of corruption". The seriousness and swiftness with which the national human rights commission is going about its business of recording and correcting human rights issues in India amply gives the clear impression that the Government of India is committed to the protection of human rights. Everyone has the right in all circumstances to be treated with humanity and with respect for the inherent dignity of the human person. The National Human Rights Commission has the right to enquire suomotto or on the basis of a petition into any complaint of violations of human rights or negligence in the provision of Constitution violation by a public servant. Although the overall record of human rights of India is certainly creditable yet time and again there are allegations about violations of human rights by the Police personnel."

They include:

1. Denying the right to be informed to the grounds of his arrest immediately after the arrest (Article 22 (1) of the Constitution and Section 50 Cr. P.C. and sections 55 and 75 Cr. P.C.).

2. Denying the right of the arrested person not to be subjected to unnecessary restraint (Section 49 Cr. P.C.).

3. Denying right to consult a lawyer of his own choice (Article 22 (1) of the Constitution and Section 303 Cr. P.C.).

4. Denying right to be produced before a magistrate within 24 hours of his arrest (Article 22 (1) of the Constitution and Section 57 and 76 Cr. P.C.).

5. Denying right not to be a witness against himself (Article 20(3) of the Constitution).

6. Denying right to have himself medically examined for evidence to disprove the Commission of offence by him or establish Commission of Offence against his body by any other person (Section 54 Cr. P.C.).

7. Denying right to fair and speedy investigation and trial (Section 309 Cr. P.C.).

8. Right not to be imprisoned upon conviction in certain cases (Section 306 Cr. P.C. and Section 6 of Probation of Offenders Act).

9. Denying right to refrain police from intrusion of his privacy (Article 31 of the Constitution).

10. Custodial Rapes.

11. Custodial Deaths.

12. The Mystery of the disappearing men and fake encounters.

When USA and Pakistan call us to account for human rights violation by our police and security forces, we must remind them of the standards they have proclaimed for their own conduct.

5. Improving Police Performance

The second theme which has been selected for the Seminar is "Improving Police Performance through training search for thrust areas". Police performance can be improved through a well-organised training system provided the police organisation develops and supports "a learning culture". Continuous improvement in police performance requires continuous organisation commitment to cyclical process of learning, unlearning and relearning. In Police organisations regular training evaluation and learning audits should be carried out to measure performance levels and to find out areas where training is needed. Police Organisations must create an organisational culture and environment which can support training and learning. The most basic and fundamental problem regarding the police organisations today is how to make them effective and efficient in performance of their duties under the most hazardous and difficult circumstances, keeping them motivated and guided by the objectives of service to the public at large, upholding the constitutional rights and liberty of the people and at the same time maintaining the internal security of the Country. The police and security forces are often provoked in Kashmir to retaliate by firing at them from behind the shield of innocent and not so innocent crowds, to discredit them as violators of human rights. On occasions, deviations and aberrations in police behaviour do occur under extreme, grave and deliberate provocation. To teach them restraint and self discipline, training is needed. Training is basically a planned organisational function which identifies the current and future performance needs of the employees and provides them the knowledge, attitude, skills, habits and the techniques required to equip the employees for an efficient and effective performance of their present and future jobs. Performance is to be identified both in terms of quality and quantity.

6. Factors Effecting Performance

Effective Performance by the police organisations depends on the following factors :-

"1. Quality and Quantity of police personnel and their time management.

2. Legal framework and social milieu which forms working environment of the police.

3. Recruitment standards and selection process and their basic induction training.

4. Organisational infrastructure, equipment and logistics.

5. People's support in police work and police public relations.

6. Social value system and orientation and their support to police in role performance.

7. Organisational environment and sub-culture.

8. Police leadership at various levels.

9. Level of motivation and value-orientation of policemen.

10. Priorities in law enforcement and role of personal discretions.

11. Level of professionalism and organisational development and level of commitment.

12. Organisational health and discipline".

7. Need for Attitudinal Change and Behavioural Orientation

Aberrations of police behaviour are generally noticed in the following areas:-

(i) Discourteous behaviour with complainants and ordinary citizens.

(ii) Arrogant behaviour with people of low status, poor economic background and the weaker sections.

(iii) Illegal detentions in police custody.

(iv) Custodial violence and rapes.

(v) Burking of crime and padding up of evidence.

(vi) Falsely implicating the innocents and fabrication of evidence.

(vii) Excesses during crowd control and anti-insurgency operations.

(viii) Corruption and nepotism.

(ix) Nexus with criminal and politicians.

(x) Organisational deviance and false encounters.

(xi) Succumbing to political interference.

(xii) Indifference and dereliction in normal duties.

(xiii) Violations of human rights.

8. Focus Areas for Training

Gore-Committee on Police Training has identified the following six areas for training.

1. Loyalty to the Constitution, commitment to the goals of the nation and the concept of an egalitarian society and the need for national integration.

2. Awareness of the problems that arise in the wake of the developmental process including conflicts. Social disorganisation, scarcity and control, regional imbalances etc.

3. A deep social awareness for comprehending and reacting to complex situations.

4. Development of analytical and innovative skills since situations will continue to change and no readymade solutions can be prescribed.

5. A few orientation in dealing with masses, who come from various strata of society.

6. Need for the application of scientific techniques, management concepts and skills and constructive attitude and values in police work.

Some of the other main areas for training are as under:-

7. Sensitisation to human right issues.

8. Behavioural change and more humane approach.

9. Effective management of police organisations and concern for human resources development.

10. Eradicaion of corruption.

11. More effective and healthy police-public.

12. Providing effective motivational techniques and communication skills.

13. Building up of a democratic organisational environment.

14. Improving general discipline and conduct of the police.

15. Professionalism including latest guidelines issued by the Supreme Court for arrest and on human rights.

9. Limitations of Training

The expectation that training can cure all the problems of an organisation is unrealistic as there are many factors that training cannot remedy. Training can not neutralise unwise promotions or ineffective methods of work nor can it replace intelligent supervision, favourable organisational conditions. Individual willingness to accept responsibility. Training alone can not bring and sustain attitudinal change and behavioural modifications unless organisational climate environmental conditions and organisational structure system can further support and nuture such changes. Good and meaningful training supported by organisational culture can go a long way in improving police performance and reducing aberrations in police behaviour.

10. Concluding Remarks

I would like to reiterate what U.N. Secretary General, Brutros Ghali has said : In our efforts to build a culture of human rights, we must not forget the importance of human right workers and non-governmental organisations nor the courage shown by many (police and security forces), who risk their lives and security for the rights of the other".

I have only given some introductory remarks on both the topics which will be discussed in depth during the next six days. Our sincere efforts have been to provide good background reading material for the benefit of the participants. I hope that the Seminar will bring out useful and constructive suggestions which will go a long way in improving overall police performance. Participants have been divided in two groups and on the last day of the Seminar, each group may please present their recommendations on the given subjects.

I am thankful to all of you for having given me very patient hearing. On behalf of the Director ISA who will be joining us shortly and on behalf of all the faculty members I again extend a hearty welcome to all of you and I wish you a very comfortable stay.

Thanking you.

A SELECT BIBLIOGRAPHY

The background studies, specially in respect of criminology, world history and India's political and economic developments, have been spread over a long period out of these, only a select inventory of books which have directly or indirectly contributed to various formulations arrived at, is given below, under a few broad categories.

World History

1. A Study of History by—Arnold J. Toynbee Abridgement of volumes I to VI—by D.C. Somervell.
2. An Unfinished History of the world—by Hugh Thomas.
3. Glimpses of World History—by Jawahar Lal Nehru.
4. The Global Conflict (International Rivalry of the Great Powers, 1880-1970)—by C.J. Bartlett.
5. Modern Europe to 1870—by C.J. Hayes.
6. Europe since Napoleon—by David Thompson.
7. A History of the Far East in Modern Times—by Harold M. Vinacke.
8. A Concise History of China—by Jian Bozan, Shao Xunzheng and Hu Hua.
9. Hellenism: The History of a Civilisation—by Arnold J. Toynbee.
10. Roman Britain—by R.G. Collingwood and J.N.L. Myres.

Political Science and Public Administration

11. Recent Political Thought—by Francis W. Coker.
12. Introduction to Political Analysis—by David E. Apter.
13. A History of Political Theories (Ancient and Mediaeval)—by William Archibald Dunning.
14. Political Behaviour—edited by Heinz Eulav, Samuel J. Eldersveld and Morris Janowitz.

15. Politics and the Social Sciences- —edited by Seymour Martin Lipset.

16. Capitalise, Socialism and Democracy—by Joseph A. Schumpeter.

17. Comparative Politics: A Developmental Approach—by G.A. Almond G.B. Powell.

18. The Modern State—by R.M. MacIver.

19. A History of Political Theory—by George H. Sabine and Thomas L. Thorson.

20. Modern Political Thought:The Great Issues—by William Ebenstein.

21. World Politics since 1945—by Peter Calvocoressi.

22. Constitutional Government and Democracy: Theory and Practice in Europe and America—by Carl Frederich.

23. A Grammar of Politics—by Harold J. Lasky.

24. The Policy Predicament : Making and Implementing of Public Policy— by George C. Edwards III and Ira Sharvansky.

25. Introduction to the Study of Public Administration—by Leonard D. White.

26. Management : Tasks, Responsibilities, Practices—by Peter F. Drucker.

27. Bureaucracy, Organisational Behaviour and Development—by Prayag Mehta.

Criminology, Crime and Police

28. Criminology—by Ruth Shonlecavan.

29. Comparative Criminology—by Hermann Mannheim.

30. Criminology—by Hurwitz.

31. Crime and the Social Structure—by John Barron Mays.

32. Group Problems in Crime and Punishment—by Hermann Mannheim.

33. Facets of Crime in India—by Venu Gopal Rao.

34. Published Papers of Police Science Congress—1961
35. do do —1962
36. do do —1967
37. do do —1970
38. Papers presented at 'All India Seminar on the Role of the Police in A Changing Society in India' Organised by Law Research Institute, Calcutta and Indian Institute of Management, Calcutta, 1985.
39. Papers presented at an International Seminar on "Crime Prevention: National and International Aspects" at the International Centre of Sociological, Penal and Penitentiary Research and Studies, Messina, Italy, 1986.
40. Police Today—by Sankar Sen, 1986.
41. Police in India, 1986.

India's History, Political Thought and Leaders

42. A History of India—by Romila Thapar.
43. Ancient India: An Introductory Outline—by D.N. Jha.
44. The Oxford History of India—by Vincent A. Smith—edited by Percival Spear.
45. The Glory that was India—by A.L. Basham.
46. A New Look on Modern Indian History—by B.L. Grover.
47. The Writings and Speeches of Edmund Burke- Volume V-India-1774-1785—edited by P.J. Marshall.
48. Social Background of Indian Nationalism—by A.R. Desai.
49. India's Struggle for Independence—by Bipan Chandra, Mridula Mukherjee, Aditya Mukherjee, K.N. Panikkar and Sucheta Mahajan.
50. Discovery of India—by J.L. Nehru.
51. Modern Indian Political Thought—by V.P. Varma.
52. Studies in the Social Thought of M.G. Ranade—by P.J. Jagirdar.
53. Contemporary Relevance of Gandhi—edited by M.P. Sinha.
54. Gandhi and the American Scene—bv C. Seshachari.
55. Inside Asia—by John Gunther.

56. Builders of Modern India : Jawahar Lal Nehru—by M. Chalapathi Rao.

57. The Nehru's and the Gandhis : An Indian Dynasty—by Tariq Ali.

58. Nehru : The Making of India—by M.J. Akbar.

59. Nation Building in India : Jay Prakash Narain—edited by Brahmanand.

Post-Independence and Contemporary Political Scenario

60. India : from Curzon to Nehru and After—by Durga Das, 1971.

61. The New Dimensions of Peace—by Chester Bowles, 1955.

62. India's and the West—by Barbara Ward, 1961.

63. India Today—by Frank Moraes, 1960.

64. The Government and Politics of India—by W.H. Morris-Jones, 1964.

65. The Nature of the Non-Western World—by Vera Micheles Dean, 1957.

66. The Crisis of India—by Ronald Seagal.

67. Old Societies and New States : The Quest for Modernity in Asia and Africa—edited by Clifford Geertz Indian Edition, 1971.

68. Politics in India—by Rajni Kothari, 1970.

69. Indo-Pak War 1971—by V.P. Juneja.

70. The Judgement—by Kuldip Nayyar, 1977.

71. All the Prime Minister's Men—by Janardan Thakur, 1978.

72. The Case that Shook India—by Prashant Bhushan, 1978.

73. An Area of Darkness—by V.S. Naipaul, 1964.

74. India : A Wounded Civilisation—by V.S. Naipaul, 1977.

75. Ministers' Misconduct—by A.G. Noorani, 1973.

76. India : The Crowded Decade—by P.N. Mehta, 1980.

77. From Raj to Rajiv : 40 years of Indian Independence—by Mark Tully and Zareer Masani, 1988.

78. India : The Siege Within—by M.J. Akbar, 1985.

79. Terrorism : History and Facets in the World and in India—by N.S. Saxena, 1985.

80. The Republic of Bihar—by Arvind N. Das, 1992.

81. Bihar: 'Rajniti Ka Apradhikaran (Criminalisation of Politics)—by Vikas Kumar Jha, 1992.

82. Economic Development and the Political System—by Sudipto Kaviraj.

83. Indian Polity : A Plea for Reform—by R.A. Gopala Swami, 1970.

84. In Pursuit of Lakshmi—by Rudolf and Rudolf.

85. India : A Million Mutines now—by V.S. Naipaul, 1990.

86. Poverty Alleviation and Rural Development—by J.S. Sodhi, 1990.

87. Rural Employment Programmes in India—by R.K. Tiwari, 1990.

Enquiry Commission Reports

88. Report of Justice T.L. Venkatarama Aiyar Commission of Enquiry into Corruption charges against Bihar Ministers, 1970.

89. Report of Justice Mudholkar Commission of Enquiry against some Ministers of United Front Government of Bihar, 1969.

90. Recommendations of the Committee on Prexention of corruption set up in 1962 under K. Santhanam.

91. Findings of the Commission of Enquiry against Sardar Pratap Singh Kairon-CM of Punjab, set up in 1963.

92. Findings of the Commission of Enquiry against Life Insurance Corporation (involving T.T. Krishnamachari as Finance Minister) under Justice M.C. Chagla, set up in 1958.

93. Findings of the Enquiry Committee against Dr. Jayanti Dharma Teja of Jayanti Shipping Company under Y.N. Sukhtanka, set up in 1966.

94. Findings of the Committee on Prevention of Corruption Government of India, 1964.

Basic Laws and Judicial Verdicts

95. Introduction to the Constitution of India—by Durga Dass Basu.

96. Constitutional Government in India—by M.V. Pylee.

97. Indian Government and Politics—by J.C. Johari.

98. The Representation of the People Act 1951 (amended upto 1992).

99. Prevention of Corruption Act, 1988.

100. The Indian Penal Code.

101. The Code of Criminal Procedure.

102. All India Reporter 1984—Supreme Court : Judgement in Criminal appeal No. 356 of 1983 and transferred cases Nos. 347 and 348 of 1983: R.S. Nayak Appellant versus A.R. Antulay Respondent.

103. All India Reporter 1979 Supreme Court: Judgement in Criminal appeal Nos.270-271 of 1977 : M. Karunanidhi Appellant versus Union of India Respondent.

104. Patna High Court Judgement in Election Petition No.2 1985: Lt. General (Retd.) S.K. Sinha Versus Dr. C.P. Thakur.

105. The Bihar Conduct of Examination Act 1981.

Youth Alienation

106. Youth Unrest: Conflict of Generations—edited by Dr. L.M. Singhvi.

107. Student Unrest: Causes and Cure—by Prof. Humayun Kabir.

108. Student Unrest: Emergency and Post-Emergency Phases—by Durga Nand Sinha.

109. Indian Youth: A Profile—by P.S. Nair, Murlidhar Venuri and Faujdar Ram.

110. Student Activism—editor Alexander Deconde.

111. Youth and Dissent—by Kenneth Keniston.

112. Youth in the 1980's A UNESCO Publication.

113. Street Fighting years: An Autobiography of the Sexties—by Tariq Ali.

The World Perspective

114. The Affluent Society—by J.K. Galbraith.

115. The Achieving Society—by David C. Mcclelland, 1967.

116. The Third Wave—by Alvin Toffler, 1980.

117. Power Shift—by Alvin Toffler, 1990.

118. Beyond Burnout—by L.David Welch Donald C. Medeiros and George A.Tate, 1982.

119. Islamic Threat: Myth or Reality?—by Dr. John Exposito, 1992.

For contemporary, day to day developments in national and international political arena, I have liberally drawn upon national dailies, 'The Times of India' Nav Bharat Times', 'The Hindustan Times' 'The Indian Express' 'The Hindu' in particular, national news magazines 'India Today' and 'Frontline' and 'The Economist' and 'Time' magazine, London.

Articles and papers presented at numerous seminars and symposia personally attended have also been of great help.

Index

Accommodation of conflicts by political, economic and social reforms, 146
Action on withdrawal, 48
Allegations against police/military forces, 197
Amaty, King, 8
Anti-Hijacking Act, 1982, 30
Appraisal of police performance, 71
Area for improving police performance, 87
  Police behavioural modification, 87
Armed forces (Spl. forces) Act. 1958, 30
Arms Act 1959 as amended up- to- date, 30
Arthasashtra, 9
Assam, 6
Atharva ved, 184
Aviation research centre, 19
Aviation security, 39

Banerjee, Lt. Gen. D., 173
Bangladesh, 6
Behavioural orientation, 260
Bombay, 8
Bonded labour system, 113
Break up of, Soviet Union Threat to internal security, 50
Budgeting and accounting, 164

Cabinet secretary, 7
Case studies of successful police performance and areas for improvement, 75
CBI to modernise probe techniques, 33
Central and State levels, 10
Central Intelligence Agency (CIA), 18
Central Reserve Police, 8
Centres for excellence, 91
Ceylon, 6
Chandra chud, Justice, Y.V., 201
Chief Minister, 6
Chief Secretary, 6
Civil Defence Act, 1968, 30
Code of Criminal Procedure 1973, 209
Communication, Control-room and Information Centre, 163
Communist manifesto (1939), 117
Community support needed for internal security, 45
Community-wise break up of persons killed in Punjab, 233
Concept of Internal in ancient Indian Scriptures, 8
Concept of internal security, 251
Concept of plural society, 119
Conflict—a conceptual background, 116
Conflicts as regular political phenomenon democracy, 121
Conflicts in Indian Society, 139
Conflicts in the political system having implications for internal security, 125
Conflicts of plural society, 142
Confrentation action, 48
Constraints and limitation of

training, 86
Control as a management tool, 26
Control of firearms and explosive, 27
Coordination as a management function, 22
Co-ordination, 162
Corruption and misutilization of funds, 165
Crime in Bihar, 13
Crimes in certain Countries in 1980, 68
Criminal procedure code, 30
Crisis of Police leadership, 34
Criteria for Police performance, 64
Critical evaluation of management of internal security, 40
Cyclone distress mitigation committee, 177

Decision-making for internal security, 28
Decision-making, 164
Diploment and planning action, 47
Deputy Inspector General of Police, 4
Deputy Superintendant of Police, 4
Detection of Crime, 69
Destruction of property by terrorist in Kashmir, 232
Directions through law making for internal security, 32
Directors General of Intelligence Bureau, 8
Directorate General of Police, 6, 8
Director Intelligence Bureau, 10
Disposal of dead bodies, 168
Dissemination of international humanitarian, 194
District Magistrates, 4
Drucker, Peter, 63
Dubai—based, 8
Duration, 124

Effective management internal security, 51
Effective training for improving performance, 89
Electronic Technical Section, 19
Environment protection act, 1986, 31
Epidemic and health problem, 168
Essential service maintenance act, 1968, 30
Enternal vigillance and security preparedness, 50

Ethnic conflicts in India, 130
Ethno-religious, 10
Evaluation of police performance, 67

Factors effecting performance, 259
Factors responsible for conflict in India, 129
Fayol, Henri, 6
Focus areas for training, 261
Future training requirements, 84

Gandhi, Indira, 109
Geneva convention, 186
Gill, K.P.S., 28
Grawing lowlessness in Police, 13

Hindu Kings, 9
Hmar peoples convention (HPC), 140
Home minister, 6
Home minister and State Ministers security, 6
Home secretary, 10, 78
Human rights and ancient Indian scripture, 182
Human rights and armed internal conflicts, 188
Human rights and developing societies, 227
Human rights and humanitarian law, 186
Human rights and Indian constitution, 252
Human rights and internal security of the country, 214
Human rights commission, 219
Human rights criminal procedure code, 248
Human rights panel bill re-introduced, 226

Human rights violations by police, 204

Ibrahim, Dawood, 8
Indian Explosive act, 1978, 30
Indian Penal code, 30
Incidents of looting in Punjab, 235
Incident of mass violence in Punjab, 235
Industrial conflicts and disputes, 133
Intensity of caste conflicts in different distts.of Gujarat, 134
Intensity, 124
Internal security, 69
Internal security threat analysis and the security survey, 10

Janapada, 8

Karl Marx, 117
Karnataka Rajya, Raita Sangh, 109
Kautilya, 89
Kharvatika, 9
Kidnappings by terrorits in Kashmir, 231
Kosa, 8
Krishna, Raj, 106

Lack of adequate training and preparedness, 166
Lack of centralised ambulance, accident and trauma (CAT) services, 169
Lack of clarity of roles and responsibilities, 166
Lack of coordination, 166
Lack of knowledge, 167
Land struggle, 100
Law and order maintenance, 165
Limitation of training, 262
Low-intensity conflicts and insiduous, 138

Mahabharat, 9
Maharashtra earthquake, 173
Main challenges of internal security, 252
Maintenance of order, 69
Maintra, 8
Management of Andhra Cyclone, 1977, 170
Management of aviation Security,5
Management of Bangladesh, 6
Management of Intelligence for internal security, 18
Management of Internal Security, 7
Management of I.S., 2
Management of Internal Security, 6
Management of law and order and riot situations, 45
Management of Security, 5
Management of Terrarism, 38
Managerial Approach to Internal Security, 2
Manifestations of violent social conflict, 134
Maoist communits centre, 75
Marginal farmers and Agricultural Labourer Dev. Agency, 113
Matrix for Management of Internal Security, 56
Mazdoor Kissan Sangram Samiti, 110
Media management, 27
Ministry of Home Affairs, 8
Ministry of Internal Security, 8
Mizo National Front, 111
Mizoram, 6
Modernisation of Police, 32
Motivation and role of citizens, 163
Mt. Abu, 4

Narcotic drugs and psychotropic substance acts, 31
National Police Commission, 54
National sample survey 1964-65, 103
National Security act 1980 as amended up-to-date, 30
National Security Council, 42
National Sociolist Council of Nagaland, 140
Natalite movement a manifestation of conflict, 132
Need for a National Security, Council, 42
Need for change in behaviour of Police, 224
Negative to positive behaviour, 87

Organisational development, 85
Organisations for internal security duties, 16
—CRPF, 16
BSF, 16
RPF, 16
Assam Rifles, 16
National Security Guards, 16
—SPG, 17
Costal Guard, 17
CBI, 17
Army, 17
Organising the management of a disaster, 161

Pakistan's I.S.I., 11
Pakistan, 6
Panchayat Raj, 97
Parliament and legislature candidates killed, 235
Plasants movements in India, 97
—initial phase, 97
second phase, 98
post independence phase, 98
Peoples Liberation Army, 180
Peoples Revolutionary Party Kangleipak, 180
Pervasiveness, 124
Pilot, Rajesh, 7
Planning Commission, 106
Planning for Internal Security, 14
Plural Executive, 6, 7
Police act, 1861, 30
Police and human right issues, 218
Police and protection of human rights, 37
Police personnel, (in 0001), 68
Police Response to Conflicts, 142
Politicians, 6
Posdcorb, 2
Preliminary preparations, 46
President, 7
Prevention of Crime, 69
Prevention of Corruption, act, 31
Prevention of seditions meetings act, 1911, 30
Prevention to damage to public property, act, 1984, 30
Prime Minister, 7
Prime Ministers secretariat, 6
Problem areas the challenge of widening chasms, 34
Problems of CRPF and BSF and other CPOS, 36
Profile of Violence in Punjab, 233
Protection of Civil rights act. 1976, 31
Protection of human rights in Indian society, 212
Providing security and maintenance of law and order, 169
Public service executives, 6

Raj, Dr. K.N., 103
Rapid Action Force, 210
Reasons for unsatisfactory police performance, 78
Recent Internal Security challenges, 9
Recovery of weapons from terrorists in Kashmir, 232
Research and Analysis Wing (RAW), 18
Responsible for human rights violations by Indian Police, 199
Restoring normaley, 49
Richer scale, 157
Rights, 253
—equality, 253
freedom, 253
against exploitation, 253
freedom of religion, 254
cultural and educational, 254
constitutional remedies, 254
Role of Central Police Organisations, 202
Role of Electronic and Mass Media, 45
Role of CRPF, 210
Rural scone in India, 102
Rural Violence rises with expectations, 102
Rustamji, K.F., 6, 36
Saheli U. Commissioner of Police, 26
Saxena, S.N., 7

Sangrahana, 9
Saxena, N.S., 26
Security at Indian missions abroad, 40
Security Involves, 10
Sen. Dr. Sunil K., 99
Sen, Prof., Ayodhya, 144
Serious steps needed for management of disasters, 159
Shah, Justice, J.C., 19
Shanti Parva, 9
Sharma Lt. Gen. Y.N.,158
Singh, J.P., 71
Singh, Yogindra, 121
Slow and halting responses, 167
Small Farmers Development Agency, 113
Sociological approach to conflicts, 129
Some dimensions of management of internal security, 4
Special Security Force, 38
Special Service Bureau, 19
Special Task Force, 211
Shrinivas, M.N., 107
Staffing and Personal Policies for Internal Security Organisations, 19
Staffing the contingency plan, 162
State Police Organisations, 4
State Police to look after VVIP security, 38
Steps in management of internal security, 57
Sthaniya, 9
Sukra, 8
Suppression of Unlawful act against safety of civil aviation act. 1982, 30
Terrorism V. Clilemma of protection of human rights, 219
Terrorist affected area (Spl. counts) act 1984, 30
Terrorist and Disruptive activities (Prevention) act 1987 as amended up-to-date, 30
Terrorist Violence in J & K, 230
Theory of Collective behaviour, 123
Thrust areas for police training, 83
Timing of intervention confrontation and intervention, 47
Traffic Control, 69
Training, 66, 165
Training and motivation for management of internal security, 24
Training as a concept, 79
Training for human rights in CRPF, 225
Training for improving performance, 77
Tripura, 6
Twenty-four more RR Battalions to be raised, 41
Types of emergencies, disasters and cris situations, 156

United National Federal Front, 180
United Nations declaration of human rights 1948, 245
United States National Security Act 1947, 42
Universal declaration of human rights, 238
Unlawful activities (Pervention) Act 1967, 30

Vedic Samhitas, 8
Violations of human rights, 195
Violence against Judiciary, 234
Visit of VVIP/Politicians, 169
Vohra, N.N., 15

Woman police stations for each district in Tamil Nadu, 21

G